Scotland, the UK and Brexit

Scotland, the UK and Brexit

A Guide to the Future

Edited by

GERRY HASSAN and RUSSELL GUNSON

Luath Press Limited

EDINBURGH

www.luath.co.uk

First published 2017

Reprinted 2018

Reprinted 2019

ISBN: 978-1-912147-18-2

The authors' right to be identified as author of this book

under the Copyright, Designs and Patents Act 1988 has been asserted.

The paper used in this book is recyclable. It is made from low chlorine pulps

produced in a low energy, low emission manner from renewable forests.

Printed and bound by Bell & Bain Ltd., Glasgow.

Typeset in 11 point Sabon by Lapiz

Contents

Acknowledgements

A book like this is a product of many different hands. It has gained from much support, advice and the enthusiasm and skills of many people. It is impossible to individually thank each person who assisted and made this possible, but to everyone who played a part, we gratefully thank you.

First and foremost, we would like to thank every single contributor who gave their time, expertise and knowledge to make this happen. We gave people difficult remits, asking them to address a whole host of issues, many of which will evolve and change dramatically in the next few years, and asked them to bring calm heads and clear analysis. We could not have wished for a more impressive list of contributors to whom we are enormously grateful.

We would also like to thank colleagues in the Institute for Public Policy Research and in particular, Rachael Thomas in IPPR Scotland's offices. Many thanks are also due to numerous people who gave their advice in the shaping of this book and its contents and contributors: Kirsty Hughes, Michael Keating, Nigel Smith, Douglas Fraser, Jeremy Cliffe of *The Economist*, and Stephen Booth of Open Europe.

Significant thanks are also due to the national treasures that are Luath Press - Gavin MacDougall and all his staff - who have been exemplary champions of this book from the outset, and who have, from the beginning to the end of this, made us confident that the entire project was safe in their formidable hands.

Finally, a project such as this has many eyes and supports, and this book would not have been possible without the insights and checking of Rosie Ilett and Ash Burnel who assisted in the latter stages of production.

The enclosed contents do not represent the collective opinions of IPPR or IPPR Scotland, but are an offering and contribution to inform this important and historic debate. We hope that readers will find the enclosed of interest, illuminating and stimulating, and a worthy contribution and guide to the next few years of developments in Scotland and the UK in relation to Brexit.

A final word over timing. In these bewildering and often fast-changing times, this book was written before the UK 2017 election was called by Theresa May, lost by her and the Tories, and won by no one. The entire book has been reviewed in light of this, and revised in several, but not all places. The general thesis of the challenges and ambiguities of Brexit for Scotland and the UK, and the absences of serious preparatory work and strategy by the UK Government remains as a factor which will define much of future events.

Gerry Hassan   Russell Gunson

gerry@gerryhassan.com   r.gunson@ippr.org

Scotland, the UK and Brexit: an introduction

Gerry Hassan and Russell Gunson

Introduction

WE LIVE IN dramatic and unpredictable times. On 23 June 2016 UK voters were asked 'Should the United Kingdom remain a member of the European Union or leave the European Union?' and responded:

- *Remain*   *16,141,241*   *(48.11%)*
- *Leave*   *17,410,742*   *(51.89%)*

Thus began the 'post-Brexit Britain' political environment – with a majority of 1,269,501 voting to leave the EU; a decision that has understandably dominated and overshadowed British politics since. It was not, of course, a united UK that made that decision. Scotland voted (62:38) to remain, Northern Ireland (56:44), so too did significant parts of England, such as London (60:40).

The challenge this poses to the UK and its component parts is immense – as this IPPR Scotland book explores. Specifically, it addresses the consequences that flow from Brexit for Scotland, while also examining UK and international implications. It analyses the terrain, the major issues and possible developments, the context in which this takes place and how some of the major actors including the Scottish and UK governments, and the EU itself, may act.

The Scottish dimension

All of this poses numerous challenges for Scotland. One major factor is that in 2014 Scotland voted by 55 per cent to 45 per cent to remain in the UK. Yet less than two years later, in June 2016, by the margin of 62 per cent to 38 per cent, Scots voted to remain in the EU. This has brought to the fore one of the central tensions in Scottish politics – of two competing and contradictory mandates. People in Scotland are, in essence, told in no uncertain terms by the UK government, and by a significant proportion of Scottish parliament politicians, that they cannot have a political settlement that respects both.

There are problems for everyone politically. Much of pro-union opinion has come to state that Scotland voted to remain in the UK, and then voted as part of a UK that decided to come out of the EU. This is a literal interpretation of the events of the last two years which, while factual, does not really address issues of political legitimacy and perception. This is particularly the case, given the prominence of the EU in the first independence referendum campaigns.

The Scottish government, on the other hand, decided to set out its position post-Brexit in a White Paper, *Scotland's Future in Europe*, which was seen by many as considered and thoughtful and a search for a middle ground (Scottish Government, 2016). The commentator Hugo Rifkind, normally no friend of the SNP, called it 'a well-judged approach, because it cuts right to the heart of the current Scottish political crisis' (Rifkind, 2016).

However, the case made by the Scottish government has significant political and constitutional consequences. First, there are the practical issues of how Scotland could sit in the single market and Customs Union while the rest of the UK (rUK) does not. How this would work economically and practically – as Tobias Lock addresses in his contribution – is filled with complications.

Second, and more important in exploring the possibilities of such arrangements, is the presence of political will (and goodwill) to see them a reality. This seems to be lacking from one part of the equation, the UK government, rather paradoxically in that the UK's political elites have often celebrated their adaptability in governmental and constitutional manners. The UK government has so far, post-Brexit, shown no interest in pursuing a flexible and hybrid approach – a constitutional response so regularly championed within the UK – through a serious consideration of what a geographically differentiated Brexit would like within the UK, as opposed to sector-by-sector deals.

The next two years of Brexit Britain

The next two years, and more, will be full of drama, tension and high-wire negotiations as the UK, following the triggering of Article 50 in March 2017, tries to agree a deal and the details of withdrawal with the EU: the context and choices of which are laid out by Kirsty Hughes in her contribution. This will not be smooth or easy, as we enter uncharted waters with no member state having previously withdrawn. There have been three previous departures – Algeria in 1962 (it not officially being a French colony, but in a union with France, and hence part of the original six), Greenland in 1985 and Saint Barthélemy in the Caribbean in 2012. Similarly, there have been other examples of EU flexibility relevant to Scotland and Northern Ireland, such as the fast-tracking of East Germany into the EU in 1990 and the divided island of Cyprus becoming a member in 2004.

None of the examples of EU withdrawal were those of a member state, and there were none of the complexities and intricacies that will be associated with UK withdrawal. The attitudes that frame the UK-EU discussions take everyone into unknown territory – with very different expectations on both sides.

Two main deals need to be negotiated: an exit deal, which will cover the Brexit bill the UK will pay and a transition agreement to cover the period between UK withdrawal and a new trade agreement; secondly, a comprehensive UK-EU trade deal, alongside other cooperation agreements on judicial, foreign policy and security matters (Hughes, 2017).

With Article 50 triggered, negotiations begin between UK government ministers and the EU Commission, but one big question concerns who the UK is actually negotiating with. Formally it is the Commission and its chief negotiator Michel Barnier (acting on behalf of the European Council of Ministers and following their guidelines), but equally important are the individual EU27 states, bilateral relations with each member state, and in particular, Germany and France. At the same time, the UK government is, at least informally, in a process of negotiations with the devolved administrations of Scotland, Wales and Northern Ireland, which will have an impact on the UK-EU discussions, and attitude of the EU27.

One of the first substantive issues will be that of the 3.3 million EU citizens living in the UK – and the 1.2 million UK citizens living in the EU. This has proven enormously contentious with the UK government, who before triggering Article 50, refused to offer any guarantees to EU citizens in the UK and are being accused of using them as bargaining chips.

After this, the even more serious and complicated discussions begin. This will start with the exit deal, with huge tensions between the UK government and EU already evident about whether to start by talking about monies and the UK's Brexit bill. There will also be issues between the exit and trade deals – and to what extent they run in tandem.

Then there are the specific details of how the UK secures, or does not secure, tariff-free access to the free market, alongside factors such as how the City of London's special status as the financial capital of the EU (where 70 per cent of the euro denominated interest rate derivatives market takes place) is protected (*Economist*, 2016). All of this will keep the UK government busy, before it thinks about Scotland, Northern Ireland, Gibraltar and other sticky areas. A UK-EU deal has to be agreed by the British government and EU Commission, approved by the British and European parliament (with the prospect of one or both rejecting any deal) whilst some, such as the Lib Dems, are calling for a second referendum on any deal. And of course, there is even the prospect of no UK-EU deal.

The UK government and, even more, pro-Brexit opinion, seems to be based on an optimistic, somewhat rosy, version of the UK economy and its prospects post-withdrawal. It buys into hype about 'the British jobs miracle' in right-wing opinion, and has stressed the positive performance of the economy since the 23 June vote. What this willfully ignores are the long-term structural inadequacies of the British economy. These include poor productivity; low research and development; the highest Balance of Payments deficit in UK history; household, financial and corporate debt; 'the lost decade' of living standards which is now predicted to last at least fifteen years (2007-2022) and the over-dominance of London and the South East (which make up 40 per cent of the UK economy). None of these will be addressed or aided by Brexit, and indeed many could become more accentuated. These trends have been considered by IPPR through http://www.ippr.org/publications/out-of-shape and will be considered, among others, over the coming years through IPPR's Commission on Economic Justice.

The United Kingdom, power and devolution

What does this situation say about the United Kingdom in terms of who has and does not have power? Firstly, the Supreme Court Article 50 process and decision in January 2017 underlined what has long been known: that the UK parliament is seen as 'sovereign' (Bowcott et al, 2017). The Scottish parliament, along with the Welsh and Northern Irish Assemblies, are not viewed as such but as creations of Westminster, with no right to a veto or substantive say in the Brexit process. Despite this, legal challenges by the devolved administrations may continue throughout the many stages of Brexit.

The Joint Ministerial Council (JMC), that brings together the UK government and the devolved administrations, could have become one of the key forums in which a UK-wide position was discussed and formulated in relation to Brexit. But it has not. Instead, the UK government has seemingly not used it to shape its negotiation positions, but instead to present its own Brexit position as a fait accompli, much to the loud and public dissatisfaction of the Scottish government (*BBC News*, 2017a).

The Brexit vote has exposed that the UK constitution and state has not adequately responded to the devolution of power to the nations of the UK. It has not developed many of the constitutional safety valves and safeguards at the

UK level that would reflect the more dispersed nature of constitutional arrangements. This inaction has weakened the UK's ability to respond to the multiple mandates offered by the Brexit vote. Many of these UK-wide constitutional responses, that have been lacking in their response to devolution, as exhibited in many other more federal countries, could have helped the UK to plot a path through the conflicting geographical mandates within the UK stemming from the Brexit vote.

Devolution, since 1999, should have been about the political centre of the UK reforming and democratising, changing its own character and the nature of its relationships with the devolved nations. This is missed by many accounts that describe the semi-federal, or emerging federalism, of the UK (for example, Blick and Jones, 2010). Federalism cannot come about by unilateral actions of Scotland, Wales and Northern Ireland. It requires the political will and action of Westminster, and a popular shift in English public sentiment that, for the foreseeable future, seems to be completely lacking.

Secondly, is what this says about the UK as an idea, and existentially, what does it say about the nature of the union, about the UK as a partnership of four nations, supposedly based on mutual understanding and respect? The UK is a multi-national, multi-cultural state and a union of four nations. The territorial dimensions of the UK are underpinned by political traditions and practices that reflect this patchwork, organic, even haphazard nature that has evolved over centuries, rather than by some grand design. However, little consideration has been given to which of the decisions faced by the UK should be taken by each of the nations with an equal 25 per cent say and for which should be based on population share; consideration that would have been very useful prior to the EU referendum.

At its heart the UK is meant to be what is called a union state: a state made up of a number of unions that retains some of the pre-union arrangements and characteristics of its constituent parts. An example of this is the institutional autonomy of Scotland that was specified in the Acts of Union of 1706–7, preserving the distinctiveness of the Kirk, law and education.

The union-state perspective used to be heretical as it challenged the British unitary state tradition, but slowly over the devolution years it became the conventional position, certainly amongst academics and British constitutional matters (see Mitchell, 2014; Bogdanor, 2009). Yet the experience of Brexit, coupled with the growing lack of understanding of the UK by its political elites, has shown that the earlier revisionism was overstated. Thus, while the UK has many characteristics of a union state, its political classes increasingly inhabit a unitary state idea of Britain, with devolution and Brexit aiding a return to this bunker. This is more than an arcane set of distinctions, for what it illuminates is how the

British political establishment see the UK, where power lies, and the unfinished business of devolution, which to them was not, it seems, about changing the UK's basic character.

Brexit challenges for the British and Scottish governments

Over the next two years the British government will have to conduct a series of fraught, multi-front debates with the EU, filled with tensions and potential conflicts and, now it seems, with Scotland and Northern Ireland. It needs to maintain, as much as is practically possible, a UK-wide united front – or at the very minimum, give the appearance of one – over the period of formal EU negotiations.

The Brexit vote brings with it the fundamental question of what kind of country the UK is, what it aspires to be and how it sees its role in the world. The right-wing Eurosceptic view of Brexit is one that the vast majority of the Scottish public would baulk at, as indeed would a majority of the public in the UK. But it has become increasingly influential, aided by the blank canvas of what Brexit is, and by the absence of coherent UK opposition to the UK government in the House of Commons; the House of Lords being a different proposition.

Brexit will test the UK government in how it can best do statecraft, diplomacy and the politics of deal making. Given the UK has long been considered 'an awkward partner' in the EU, this will be a severe test. The Scottish government on the other hand has little direct experience of diplomacy, but post 23 June has engaged in a politics of paradiplomacy, emphasising soft power, that could affect future Scottish positioning and influence leading into any EU negotiations – an arena that John Edward's contribution considers.

The Scottish government is not an official player in the forthcoming EU-UK talks, by dint of the UK being the member state. It is not recognised by any of the EU member states or by the EU. Scotland does, on the other hand, have a lot of friends and sympathy in Europe. This does not translate into hard political power, but there are dynamics of timing, waiting and choosing the right moment to move, with huge awareness in EU elites and the EU27 of Scotland's predicament.

The big Scottish question: a second independence referendum

With no Scottish-tailored solution looking likely to be offered from the UK government as a result of Brexit, the prospect of a second independence referendum has become real. Nicola Sturgeon has stated that in her dealings with the UK government post-Brexit she has 'been met with a brick wall of intransigence' which has not seen any compromise to Scotland. She called for the Scottish parliament to pass a Section 30 request to the UK parliament giving them the power to decide to hold another independence referendum (Sturgeon, 2017); and Holyrood voted on 22 March 2017, split down constitutional divides, for such a motion.

There are, in spring 2017, many variables: of timing, content and context. A critical factor for both the UK and Scottish governments is when any second independence referendum would take place in relation to Brexit: the UK government wanting any vote, if it happens at all, to take place after the culmination of the Brexit deal and process, and the Scottish government ideally wanting one before the UK, and thus Scotland, leaves the EU. This could, if both parties were prepared to compromise, and a second independence referendum were to be agreed, allow the ground to be identified for any vote from late 2019 onward – after the UK has just left the EU – into early 2020. But this supposes that the UK and EU negotiations keep to a two-year timetable. It is also based on assumptions prior to Theresa May calling a surprise UK general election for 8 June 2017 which resulted in her losing her majority and governing as a minority government, and in the SNP being reduced from 56 to 35 Westminster seats, which threw into doubt the calling and timing of any independence referendum before the next Scottish Parliament elections.

Nicola Sturgeon and the SNP's thinking has initially pointed towards a preference for a vote before Brexit talks concluded, while seeing merits in a vote immediately after Brexit. Not surprisingly there is a degree of anxiety and nervousness in the party. This is because none of the above scenarios and dates are ideal, and each carry huge risks not only of losing, but of what could follow afterwards, and the economic and social dislocation associated with Brexit for Scotland.

A second independence referendum would clearly and obviously entail huge political questions. A major one is how a reformed independence offer would be put together in light of Brexit, particularly as Brexit negotiations are likely to be fluid and non-linear. If that were not enough in terms of hurdles to jump there are also significant challenges, not just in terms of the electoral terrain as described by John Curtice in this volume, but in the legality of a referendum investigated by Matthew Qvortrup.

In any complex standoff and dance between the Scottish and UK governments on holding a second independence referendum, a critical question will be the Westminster procedures to allow for a legal vote. This is because Section

Five of the Scotland Act 1998 identifies 'the constitution' as 'a reserved matter' meaning reserved to Westminster. The 2014 referendum took place in the context of David Cameron passing a Section 30 order that gave the Scottish government temporary responsibility to hold an independence vote. This was part of the Edinburgh Agreement between the two governments in October 2012 that laid out the framework for the 2014 vote.

This time round the UK government has not indicated whether it will or will not facilitate such a Section 30 order, as it is clearly calculating the cost of any action north of the border and how any such referendum could unfold. A high cost approach would be to completely rule out a Section 30 which would risk giving the Scottish government the moral high ground and, importantly, potentially the democratic argument. It is also less likely that the UK government would give the Scottish government a Section 30 in the same form as last time in the terms the SNP want. So far the UK government has been playing for time, not acceding to the SNP's requests or timetable, with Theresa May declaring, in response to Nicola Sturgeon stating she wished a 2018 or 2019 vote, that 'now is not the time': a holding statement which demands greater clarity down the line (BBC News, 2017b).

If a second independence referendum takes place at all, it is more probable that the UK government will offer what it will portray as a middle position, saying to the Scottish government that it cannot have a Section 30 order until the processes of Brexit UK-EU negotiations are completed and agreed in March 2019. Therefore, under this scenario, it would offer a Section 30 with both a sunrise and a sunset clause, which allows the Scottish government to call a vote post-Brexit. This would mean that the UK, including Scotland, would have left the EU by the time any second independence referendum took place: thereby leaving Scottish voters faced with Brexit as a fait accompli and thus, after one disruption, depicting independence as a second and unnecessary disruption.

Scotland isn't the only constitutional problem facing the UK government. There is also Northern Ireland. Not only did it vote against Brexit, but the March 2017 Northern Irish Assembly elections provided another complication with, for the first time, the unionist community losing its majority in votes and Assembly seats. Such an event cannot be underestimated – it changed the nature of the dynamic between unionists and nationalists and dealt a severe blow to the psyche and confidence of the unionist political community.

Brexit brings big headaches to Northern Ireland around the sustainability of the peace process, the longevity of Stormont power-sharing, the nature of all-Ireland cooperation, and, in particular, the issue of what has been called 'the borderless border' (Meagher, 2016). With the UK outside the EU, the Irish-Northern Irish border becomes one between an EU member state and non-EU member state. This brings concerns about how to maintain the soft border that exists today. If that were not enough, any UK flexibility about the maintenance of a soft Irish border has implications for Scotland: either in any differentiated deal offered in the union (or why what is offered to Northern Ireland isn't on offer to Scotland), or in a post-independence settlement.

Whatever happened to progressive Britain?

This brings us to the feasibility of a progressive Brexit. This was always one possible outcome of Brexit, given the blank canvas upon which people voted. However, this possibility is narrowing by the day, driven by politics, and the dynamic of the hard-Brexit agenda of influential sections of the Conservative Party and right-wing opinion.

Adding to this state of affairs is the, at times, incoherence of the Labour Party – Her Majesty's Official Opposition – when it comes to Brexit. This has inevitable consequences for all British politics, democracy and thus Brexit, potentially splitting Labour's traditional coalition in England, between the cities (more pro-remain) and the post-industrial areas of England (more pro-leave).

Fundamentally, without a differentiated Brexit deal, the feasibility of a progressive Brexit has to be underpinned by a progressive Britain. That is still there, but struggling to find a coherent voice and influence. It is not an accident that the main opposition to Brexit in the Commons has come from the pro-European SNP and Lib Dems. Or that former UK Prime Ministers Tony Blair and John Major, in their high profile February 2017 interventions, created impact (Blair, 2017; Major, 2017). Blair's brought with it all the resultant baggage he comes with post-office: his opinion poll rating is well below Jeremy Corbyn's at 14 per cent satisfaction (compared to Corbyn's 24 per cent in February 2017). While Tory Brexiteers dismissed Major's intervention as 'bitter', it was a calm, considered and rigorously argued case against Brexit. All of these interventions underline the deep vacuum at the heart of British politics that has life-changing consequences.

The present impasse should be seen as influenced and shaped by a series of multiple crises of the UK and its political traditions. This runs from unionism, to Toryism and Labourism: the tension points of the latter two explored by Jim Bullitt and Stephen Bush in their chapters on Tory and Labour Britain.

It was illuminating, in terms of the idea of Britain and unionism, that a recent Conservative Home blog survey of Tory members showed that the party of traditional unionism was at grass-roots-level seeing its commitment ebb away (Goodwin, 2017). Only 33 per cent of Tory members thought Scottish independence would cause 'serious damage' to the 'remaining parts of the UK'.

Another 22 per cent said independence would not be in the interests of rUK but any damage could be contained; 15 per cent thought independence a 'shame', but of 'no real significance'; the remainder welcomed the prospect of ending 'the unreasonable demands on England to provide ever-greater financial and political concessions to Scotland.' An emphatic 93 per cent of English Tory respondents said devolution 'has been harmful to England'.

A guide for non-Scottish readers

This brings us to a few key observations for English, Welsh and Northern Irish readers, as well as those in Europe, about what is happening and why, and where Brexit might take Scotland. First, the argument of some in UK and Scottish politics that the Nationalists should just drop any idea of a second independence referendum and concentrate on governing, while understandable as a political argument, is a misreading of the situation.

For a start, the trigger for the process of a second independence referendum in Scotland was the UK government calling and losing of the EU referendum. UK Prime Minister Theresa May's criticisms of the SNP on their 'constitutional obsessions' and 'tunnel vision nationalism', could be seen as disingenuous (May, 2017), tapping into how majority nationalisms (British) the world over fail to see or understand themselves as nationalism.

Second, whether, or when, Scotland has a second independence referendum is one thing, but the threat of holding a vote is a powerful political weapon in the hands of the Scottish government. Why would they, in this taut and difficult period, want to unilaterally renounce its possible use?

Third is the democratic case contained in this. To only invoke the mandate of the UK vote is to miss the much more nuanced mandate when seen across the UK. Fourth, just as Scotland's first independence referendum did not come from nowhere, this is also true of the 2016 EU vote. Instead, it was part of a forty-year, ongoing debate about whether the UK was a European country, in relation to the EU membership and project. That has now been decided, but carries with it consequences for the UK, Scotland and Northern Ireland which cannot be wished away.

An additional point is that Scotland is an increasingly self-governing nation, already quasi-independent in relation to many aspects of domestic policy.

Scotland, as a nation and a polity, voted by a significant majority to remain in the EU but is not having its wishes heard and respected. Consequences flow from such a situation and the perceptions associated with it. If the vote had been in favour of leave, it is interesting to consider what reforms and action would have taken place to respond to the significant and strong leave votes in many parts of the UK.

A helpful tool for understanding the UK, and specifically Scotland's, predicaments is Albert O. Hirschman's influential 'Exit, Voice and Loyalty' (Hirschman, 1970). In this analysis, voice is the act of dissent, agitation and lobbying, loyalty is the power of the group, collective action and solidarity, and exit concerns removing yourself from the situation or relationship. Hirschman took loyalty to be the traditional approach of the left, and exit of the right, while the greatest power was the often underused force of 'voice'.

The UK's relationship with the EU over the past 40 plus years has not shown much loyalty or attachment to the European project. Successive UK governments consistently portrayed EU membership on pragmatic, transactional terms. The UK, instead, expressed over these four decades, the politics of voice, of dissenting, complaining and advocacy for its own national interests. And over the period, this gave the UK what could be called the best of both worlds – membership of the EU, acting as an influencer and shaper in EU corridors, while being semi-detached and having rebates and opt-outs from the areas it did not like, such as the euro and euro bailout fund. This truly has been the power and potential of voice on display. But despite this, the UK has now decided to embark on the ultimate politics of exit and withdrawal from the EU.

Similarly, Scotland's relationship within the UK union has historically been defined by both loyalty and voice. This was at its height a union with a deep, emotional and committed bond; that was much more than instrumental or merely transactional. Scotland has traditionally, through the years of loyalty, displayed a twin-track approach by also utilising voice. Pushing, agitating and lobbying for Scotland's special interests, greater public spending and contracts, and that, over the three centuries, has paid impressive dividends (for example: the Scottish Office pre-devolution; Barnett and before Barnett, the Goschen formula).

This brings us to the politics of exit in both the UK and, separately, Scotland. The nature of the deal, and the price the UK is willing to pay to leave the EU, will be influenced by whether it is a complete or clean break, and whether, beyond transitional arrangements, the UK and EU continue to co-operate deeply. And the form of this exit will influence how the politics of exit take shape in relation to Scottish independence. In both cases, the psychologies of exit, and the crosscutting influence of Brexit and Scotland on each other, will be a major factor.

A Scotland with more powers and what that does to Scottish politics

An important dimension in Scotland's debate will concern the powers that come to the Scottish parliament as a result of Brexit. This could include farming, fishing, food safety and numerous other areas such as VAT or immigration, and as important to how this pans out are the processes and consultations that the UK and Scottish governments enter into. EU powers will be repatriated to the UK parliament, with agreement then reached on powers devolved to Scotland and to elsewhere in the UK.

In this scenario there is room for the UK government to be bold and ambitious and to make real its commitment to a different kind of union, but there is also potential for major disagreements, in substance and process. If the UK government holds on to all-UK frameworks in farming and fishing for example, there is an opportunity for the Scottish government to claim it is acting in bad faith.

Moreover, a bigger set of dynamics are at work in the above, noting that new powers have come to the Scottish parliament in the Scotland Acts of 2012 and 2016. These dynamics are two-fold. Firstly, there is how the Scottish government chooses to use these powers on taxation and welfare. Opponents of the SNP government will perceive even not using them as a political act. Second there is how this environment affects the character of the SNP and Scottish nationalism (the two are not synonymous).

The successive devolution of powers northwards brings dilemmas for the Nationalists. Do they embrace the new Brexit-derived powers as part of a more autonomous and powerful Scottish parliament? Or while welcoming them, do they see them in a wider frame of Westminster belittling and diminishing the Scottish parliament?

A negative attitude will gain plaudits from the SNP base, and many independence supporters, but will not win over many new friends and converts. Opponents of the Nationalists portray their approach as 'the politics of grievance'. While this is a caricature, the SNP have to speak with a voice that is measured and responsible, both as the Scottish government and as a party aspiring to speak for all of Scotland, not just to win a second referendum, but as good political practice.

This touches the wider terrain of political change and disruption within which Brexit, and any independence referendum, is located and how it is discussed and debated. Laura Cram's chapter explores how Scottish nationalism has contributed to debates, and the importance of empathy, respect and understanding in how people interpret the world and make decisions. Madeleine Bunting takes us into the meanings of borders and borderlands, and how despite the 'island history' of the UK, this has also been a powerful thread in British history: the subtext being the prospective changing nature of borders, with the EU, Scotland and rUK, and on the island of Ireland.

The fraught natures of too many post-Brexit debates in the UK pose a responsibility to conduct political and public exchanges in a manner that reflects our mutual humanity. The language of portraying remainers, who want to contest the result as 'remoaners', or caricaturing all Brexit supporters as anti-immigration, racist little Englanders, does no one any favours and harms the wider body politic. Social media the world over hasn't helped in this – from Brexit to Scottish independence and US politics in the age of Trump – with one Harvard University Professor, Cass Sunstein, calling for 'an architecture of serendipity' to counter the personalised echo chambers of social media, which masquerade as greater choice (Sunstein, 2017).

Finally, the entire Brexit debate has to be understood geo-politically. The United Kingdom is on the move in where it sees itself internationally, in trade, in diplomacy and in how it makes friends and allies. As Andrew Gamble points out in the concluding chapter, the UK could not be embarking on this at a more unpredictable time; Donald Trump's inauguration as US President in January 2017 has to be seen not as the origin of disruption, but instead as a manifestation of the confused times we live in.

Brexit cannot be seen in isolation, instead it must be viewed as part of the picture of voter dissatisfaction across the West and disillusion with the EU as a project and set of institutions. This has direct impact on the Scottish debate and choices, with SNP policy since 1988 towards the EU under the auspices of 'independence in Europe' framed on the assumption of a stable, progressive EU that benignly looked after the smaller members of the club.

This position was already looking more in doubt prior to the Brexit vote, with mounting disquiet about how the eurozone worked, the huge financial and social costs inflicted on a host of 'ClubMed' countries, and in particular, the extreme example of how the EU handled the Greek crisis. Brexit, and the ruling out of any differentiated Brexit by the UK government for Scotland, makes it more likely that an independent Scotland would find itself outside the EU for at least a period. This has caused some senior SNP politicians to consider other options to the party's traditional position of the last three decades, such as membership of the European Free Trade Union (EFTA) and through it, the single market via the European Economic Area (EEA).

This could allow independence to be reframed – sidestepping Spain, Schengen and the spectre of the eurozone – and even lead to the re-invoking of Alex Salmond's vision of an 'arc of prosperity' of northern European countries – involving Norway and Iceland but minus Ireland (Dunt, 2017). However, it would require tactical dexterity by the SNP alongside public support of such a proposition when Europe is no longer, both in terms of the EU and as an idea, clearly associated with the positive or progressive qualities that it once was.

This collection does not claim to offer all of the answers. What it does is bring together an impressive range of experts and authorities from different backgrounds and perspectives to offer an informed guide to Brexit and to future developments over the next few years. We have done so in an open-minded and ecumenical way, commissioning across numerous areas of life – from Marco Biagi from the SNP, Adam Tomkins from the Conservatives, and Douglas Alexander from Labour, as well as perspectives from Spain by Ana Romero Galán, from Germany by Michael Wohlgemuth and from many other diverse perspectives.

The next few years will not be easy for Scotland or the wider UK, or indeed the EU. We can expect the unexpected to happen and can say with absolute certainty that nothing will ever be the same again. Brexit will affect nearly every single aspect of our lives, and be a profoundly disruptive act, whatever Scotland's constitutional future. The UK is changing politically, diplomatically and geo-politically. So is Scotland. In both, we can already mark out the direction of travel, but not yet the final destination. Yet, Europe itself is also in flux and the European project itself is in crisis and facing questions of legitimacy and popular consent.

The UK Brexit and Scottish debates touch some of the most fundamental questions about what democracy means, who has power and voice, and how it lives and breathes in everyday life. In the next few years, we have to aspire to a level of debate and exchange of ideas that reflects this importance, and demand that our politics, politicians and governments live up to this. But it is about something even more profound: what kind of society do the citizens of Scotland aspire to live in, and what political and social union is the best way to nurture this? That is something that rightly concerns, and is the responsibility of, all of us.

The context of Brexit and this book does not need to over-emphasise the seriousness of the issues we are dealing with. In the course of the production of the book, Theresa May called the 2017 UK general election, lost her majority, and was returned with a minority government. At the same election, the SNP experienced a major setback, falling from 56 to 35 seats, while remaining by far the leading party in Scotland.

This has major implications for how the UK Government addresses Brexit: its lack of a clear mandate, status reduced, deep divisions in the governing party, and clear absence of preparatory work in the year after the Brexit vote. Similarly, the retreat of the SNP necessitates that the party think anew not just about an independence referendum, but also the multiple layers of Brexit, as well as wider politics. What is clear is that the next two years and beyond aren't going to be simple and involve a clear cut divorce between the UK and EU, and that we are instead in for a bumpy, unpredictable ride: one with profound consequences for the people of Scotland and the UK.

References

BBC *News* (2017a), 'Devolved administrations hold 'difficult' Brexit talks', 19 January.
http://www.bbc.co.uk/news/uk-scotland-scotland-politics-38670128

BBC *News* (2017b), 'Scottish independence: Referendum demand 'will be rejected'', 17 March.
http://www.bbc.co.uk/news/uk-scotland-39293513

Blair, T. (2017), 'Open Europe Speech', 17 February.
http://www.open-britain.co.uk/full_tony_blair_speech_17th_february_2017

Blick, A. and Jones, G. (2010), *A Federal Future for the UK: The Options*, London: The Federal Trust.

Bogdanor, V. (2009), *The New British Constitution*, Oxford: Hart Publishing.

Bowcott, O., Mason, R. and Asthana, A. (2017), 'Supreme Court rules Parliament must have vote to trigger Article 50', *The Guardian*, 24 January.
https://www.theguardian.com/politics/2017/jan/24/supreme-court-brexit-ruling-parliament-vote-article-50

Dunt, I. (2017), 'May just handed Nicola Sturgeon the greatest gift she could ever ask for', *politics.co.uk*, 16 March.
http://www.politics.co.uk/blogs/2017/03/16/may-just-handed-nicola-sturgeon-the-greatest-gift

Goodwin, P. (2017), 'Scotland, independence – and our survey finding. Are Conservative Party members Just about Unionist?', *Conservative Home*, 2 March.
http://www.conservativehome.com/thetorydiary/2017/03/scotland-independence-and-our-survey-finding-are-conservative-party-members-just-about-unionist.html

Economist (2016), 'International banking in a London outside the European Union', 24 June.
http://www.economist.com/news/business-and-finance/21701334-after-post-vote-turmoil-international-banks-will-have-think-about-their

Harris, J. (2017), 'Hard Brexit makes the case for Scottish independence', *The Guardian*, 4 March.
https://www.theguardian.com/commentisfree/2017/mar/04/hard-brexit-case-scottish-independence-second-referendum

Hassan G. and Barrow, S. (eds) (2017), *A Nation Changed? The SNP and Scotland Ten Years On*, Edinburgh: Luath Press.

Hirschman, A.O. (1970), *Exit, Voice and Loyalty: responses to Decline in Firms, Organisations and States*, Massachusetts: Harvard University Press.

Hughes, K. (2017), 'Brexit Talks: What will we know in autumn 2018?',
    European Futures, 9 March.
http://www.europeanfutures.ed.ac.uk/article-4693
Macwhirter, I. (2017), *Twitter*, 3 March.
https://twitter.com/search?q=iainmacwhirter%20devolution&src=typd
Major, J. (2017), 'Speech on the Realities of Brexit for Britain and Europe',
    Chatham House, 28 February.
https://www.chathamhouse.org/file/john-major-realities-brexit-britain-and-
    europe
May, T. (2017), 'Speech to Conservative Party annual conference', 3 March.
http://www.scottishconservatives.com/2017/03/
    theresa-may-speech-to-scottish-conservative-conference/
Meagher, K. (2016), *United Ireland: Why Unification is Inevitable and How It
    Will Come About*, London: Biteback Publishing.
Mitchell, J. (2014), *The Scottish Question*, Oxford: Oxford University Press.
Rifkind, H. (2016), 'Canny Sturgeon can make fairytale come true', *The Times*,
    20 December.
http://www.thetimes.co.uk/article/
    canny-sturgeon-can-make-fairytale-come-true-f8sbn5kzt
Scottish Government (2016), *Scotland's Future in Europe*.
http://www.gov.scot/Publications/2016/12/9234
Sturgeon, N. (2017), 'First Minister's Speech', 13 March.
https://beta.gov.scot/publications/
    first-ministers-speech-bute-house-march-2017/
Sunstein, C. (2017), *#Republic: Divided Democracy in the Age of Social
    Media*, Princeton: Princeton University Press.

CHAPTER ONE

The UK's approach to Brexit: where will it take us?

Kirsty Hughes

AS THE UK'S Brexit talks finally get under way, what sort of future relationship with the EU does the UK look like ending up with? Will the UK, after a lot of tough talking with the EU27, end up with good access to the single market, cooperation on foreign policy and security issues, and a reasonably positive UK-EU future relationship, or will any deal be difficult to achieve and worse for the UK than what it has now? In the worse-case scenario, the UK and EU would fail to agree any deal – leading to the 'WTO (World Trade Organisation) cliff' outcomes that none but the most extreme Brexiteers think would be a positive result.

The Article 50 exit talks

Theresa May's government has few constraints on how it approaches the talks with the EU27. Labour, as the main opposition party, is in disarray – and the majority of its MPS backed the government's bill to trigger Article 50 in the House of Commons, with an overwhelming vote of 494 in favour of the bill to 122 against.

Despite efforts in the House of Lords to insert amendments on the rights of EU citizens and to ensure that the House of Commons had a real opportunity to reject the draft deal that is negotiated, these amendments were overturned by the Commons. So May has ended up rather unconstrained in how she plays the talks from the UK side. Some suggest that Nicola Sturgeon's call for a second independence referendum between autumn 2018 and spring 2019 means that May could look for a softer Brexit than otherwise. But May's red lines are clear – and difficult for her to change given her own Conservative Party internal politics.

May has set her own red lines out at various points, both in her October 2016 Conservative Party conference speech and in the government's Brexit White Paper (Department for Exiting the European Union, 2017). May has said she will negotiate a deal for the whole UK, that the UK will take back control over its migration policy, will no longer be subject to judgements of the European Court of Justice (ECJ) and that the UK will be free to negotiate its own trade deals around the world.

This means the UK will not and cannot stay in the EU's single market. Without accepting the ECJ, EU laws, and free movement of people, the EU27 has made clear there is no single market option of the sort that Norway has. So the UK is aiming at a Canada-style free trade deal, though May clearly hopes for a stronger, better deal than Canada achieved after its seven years of talks.

But before in-depth trade talks can start, the UK has to agree an exit deal with the EU27. The European Commission, with chief negotiator Michel Barnier, will lead the talks for the EU27 under the guidance of the European Council. The European Council – at 27 – will decide by a qualified majority, under Article 50, whether to agree the final deal or not, and the European parliament must also approve the final deal by a majority vote.

Article 50 sets a two-year time limit on talks, unless extended by unanimity. With European parliament elections due in May 2019, there is little political appetite in the EU27 to delay the UK's departure beyond March 2019. Article 50 talks are expected to conclude by autumn 2018 to allow time for the EU27 approval of the exit deal and the UK parliament's approval too.

Barnier has already made it clear that he wants to focus on the exit package before starting any talks on a future trade deal. The UK's outstanding budget liabilities to the EU are going to be the biggest flashpoint in the exit talks, with suggestions that the European Commission has estimated the exit bill at €60 billion.

The rights of EU citizens in the UK, and UK citizens living and working elsewhere in the EU, will also be a major issue for the exit talks. While both sides will want to tackle this constructively, there will be, as for almost all other Brexit issues, a range of tough issues to cover: what will be the cut-off date for retaining rights, will those rights be retained for the lifetime of those included, will the rights include full access to health care, benefits and more.

The exit talks will also need to cover a range of other questions including relocating EU agencies currently based in the UK, a transition set of arrangements so that when the UK leaves in March 2019 there is not an abrupt shift, and a large number of more specific issues and areas. These range from, for example, whether existing drugs recognised by the European Medicines Agency will still be able to be sold in the UK, whether and how the UK will be able to handle nuclear material (from waste and nuclear power through to X-rays) when it withdraws from Euratom, to how, when and in what form customs regulations and controls are brought in on both sides.

Any transition arrangements that are agreed as part of the exit deal will need to be based on some understanding of the final goal for UK-EU relations. A Canada-style trade deal will imply a different transition deal to a future relationship based only on WTO rules. The transition deal – if agreed – will have a fixed time limit but, within that, it is anticipated there will be different time periods for different issues (customs controls might take a year to set up, shifts to a new regulatory regime for financial services and all other products may take longer).

Some think that the talks will start with a general commitment to recognise the rights, on both sides, of EU citizens living in the UK and UK citizens living elsewhere in the EU. But then the talks may hit their first big battle – whether to first discuss the big exit bill, and other related exit issues, as the Commission wants or whether to discuss a future trade deal in parallel, as the UK wants.

Article 50 is clear that there should be some discussion of future UK-EU relations. It states the exit deal should take 'account of the framework [of] its future relationship with the Union'. But a framework is not a trade deal, and as the Commission says, legally it cannot negotiate a trade deal with the UK until it is a third country outside the EU.

Could the UK change its mind on Brexit?

However the row over parallel or sequential talks is resolved, any final Article 50 deal should set out some goals or aims for future relations. How shallow or detailed these goals will be is, for now, an open question. The less detail there is on future relations in the exit deal, the harder it will be for the House of Commons to decide its view on the package.

The Lib Dems have argued for a second referendum on the deal – but the fact that the exit deal may have relatively little to say on the scope and nature of any future UK-EU comprehensive trade deal could make the argument for a second referendum before the UK leaves the EU in March 2019 harder to sustain. It is also an argument that, so far, has not been supported either by Labour or the Scottish National Party.

Until now, opinion polls have shown little change in public views on whether, in hindsight, Brexit was the right or wrong decision. But if public opinion swung back towards the EU in the coming year or more, arguments over a second EU referendum – whether on the deal or on the general principle – could become stronger.

Views differ as to whether the UK could withdraw its Article 50 notification unilaterally before the two-year time limit for talks is up – a number of EU experts have suggested that it is revocable, while one UK lawyer is attempting to get an ECJ judgement on that question (Maugham, 2017). If the House of Commons were to vote against the Brexit deal, Theresa May has said the UK would simply leave without a deal. This does not look like a credible threat, and she may be forced back to the negotiating table, but there would be little time at that point, and probably little EU27 appetite, for reopening talks.

How hard a Brexit?

If the exit talks under Article 50 break down, then the risk is that the UK would crash out of the EU into uncertain legal territory and be reliant on WTO rules and tariffs for its future trade with the EU27. This would be the most damaging for the UK, but it would be damaging for the EU27 too. Not only would it impact very negatively on economic and trade relations but the acrimonious political standoff, that a breakdown in talks would imply, would make it very hard to develop new and effective foreign policy and security relations between the two sides.

If the UK is seen as having reneged on some of its legal obligations to the EU and if it is not en route to a new trade deal with the EU27, this may seriously damage the UK's ability to negotiate new trade deals around the world – not least with those 60 countries with which the EU currently has trade deals.

Both sides will look to avoid such an outcome, but one former permanent under-secretary at the Foreign and Commonwealth, Lord Kerr, told the Lords during its Brexit debate in February that he considered there was a 30 per cent chance of the talks breaking down.

If the WTO cliff is avoided, then the most likely outcome for future UK-EU27 relations is that there will be a Canada-style trade deal – with a wider set of relationships covering foreign and security policy cooperation (Hughes, 2017). While the latter is seen by many as the easier part of the future relationship to agree on, Brexit means that the UK will inevitably have a much less intense interaction with its EU partners on foreign policy issues than it currently does. Through the myriad of EU meetings, committees and summits on issues ranging from EU policy towards Russia, the EU's Africa policies, transatlantic relations, climate change, relations with China and much more, the UK is currently a significant EU player. No EU27-UK foreign policy consultative framework will replicate this existing intense interaction and the UK's influence on these issues will surely shrink considerably.

If the UK and EU27 negotiate a Canada-style trade deal, this is likely to take several years – Canada's took seven years and almost failed to clear the ratification hurdle when Wallonia's parliament initially rejected the deal last year. Theresa May's optimism that the fact the UK will start out on the same regulatory footing as the EU27 – due to its current EU membership – could make talks much shorter and easier is not shared across the EU27.

The Great Repeal Bill will, initially, ensure EU laws are brought into UK law when the UK leaves the EU – but this plan is difficult in itself, since many EU laws depend on membership of, and oversight from, EU institutions and agencies. More important still, the UK's laws will inevitably diverge over time from EU laws and it is this regulatory divergence that is always challenging in negotiating trade deals.

Even if an outline framework for future trade and economic relations is agreed under Article 50, some in Brussels think it could easily take three to seven years after March 2019 to conclude a new trade deal, with the potential for ratification difficulties always there.

Agreeing tariff-free trade in goods is seen as one of the more straightforward parts of any future deal to agree. The real challenges in modern trade deals are how to deal with regulatory differences, how to supervise any deal on mutual recognition of different regulatory regimes and how to manage any disputes. With the UK agreeing its own trade deals around the world, UK and EU companies will also face 'rules of origin' customs procedures to ensure that goods from third countries imported into the UK or EU do not then benefit from tariff-free trade where UK and EU tariffs exist and are different.

Any future UK-EU trade deal will involve more bureaucracy, customs procedures, and in effect a whole series of non-tariff barriers, that EU membership removes. The UK will, once it leaves the EU, diverge from EU regulatory rules to some extent, and will no longer recognise rulings of the ECJ. So the future UK-EU trade deal will need to agree procedures for so-called 'regulatory equivalence' and some new, non-ECJ oversight body.

The introduction of non-tariff barriers into UK-EU trade will increase costs of trade, reduce trade levels below what they would otherwise have been, and make it hard, if not impossible, to manage or run many existing cross-border and just-in-time supply chains. How damaging this may be will depend on the nature of the trade agreement. One of the gloomiest assessments comes from the National Institute of Economic Research who estimate – using other trade deals as a guide – that UK trade in goods to the EU under a trade deal could fall by 35 per cent and services trade by a massive 61 per cent (Ebell, 2017).

Theresa May has suggested that she will look for some sector-specific deals that could mimic current single market access, and that while the UK will not remain part of the EU's common commercial policy, and so its trade deals, it may look for some form of beneficial customs deal for some sectors. Brussels in return has made clear that there can be no cherry-picking of the single market by sector (something the EU27 look, for now, united on), while the idea of a favourable customs deal while being outside the Customs Union is often met simply with bemusement.

Is a soft Brexit still possible?

A soft Brexit, whereby the UK stayed in the EU's single market and possibly also its Customs Union, looks highly unlikely.

Even Norway, in the EU's single market through its membership of the European Economic Area (along with Iceland and Liechtenstein), is not in the EU Customs Union. And while Turkey has a customs union agreement with the EU, it is partial – covering mainly industrial goods. The Lib Dems and the SNP and Greens have argued for the UK to stay in the EU's single market. This would require respecting all four freedoms of movement – of goods, capital, services and labour – and respecting the remit of the ECJ.

It is clear that Theresa May has no intention of going down this path. It would be in many ways less damaging for the UK to remain a full member of the EU's single market. But to do so as a rule-taker – like Norway – rather than as a rule-maker with substantial influence, as the UK is in the EU today, would be in many ways a very odd political choice, not least for a country of the UK's size.

The reason soft Brexit has become a rallying cry for some of the UK's opposition parties is that there has been a reluctance to argue against the referendum result and to aim to persuade voters to change their minds. The Lib Dems are indeed arguing for a second referendum on the deal once negotiated but they have not taken the stronger step of arguing that the decision to leave the EU is so damaging that their central political project is to persuade the UK public (or specifically the English and Welsh public) to change their minds now, irrespective of the deal.

Equally, the SNP do not want to tie their own hands on when to hold a second independence referendum by waiting for a second UK EU referendum. Meanwhile Labour, in accepting the result of the referendum – with no push-back – has stepped away from this debate entirely.

Getting to a deal

The UK has to get to two main deals with the EU27: firstly, it must agree an exit deal, including a transition arrangement, and secondly, it must agree an economic and trade deal – and future cooperation relationships in foreign and security policies.

If all these talks are successful, in that they lead to a deal rather than breakdown, then the UK will leave the EU in March 2019, with some sort of transitional arrangements in place while a longer-term trade deal is negotiated and ratified over subsequent years. At the most optimistic, a new trade deal might be agreed by the end of 2022 and be ratified two years later by 2024.

In the process of implementing these deals, the UK will face the major task of transferring existing EU laws into UK law, agreeing with the devolved administrations which laws are repatriated to where, implementing a new migration policy, replacing many existing EU regulatory and monitoring agencies with its own bodies, and of establishing bureaucratic and customs compliance processes and personnel to implement the new UK-EU trade deal (which will also be a major task for all exporting and importing companies). It will also need to negotiate trade deals to replace – and go beyond – those the EU has with 60 countries around the world.

It is a huge task and a major challenge even if all goes smoothly, which it may not. The end-point, if successfully reached, will be a UK that is more distanced – economically and politically – from the EU and European continent than at any point since 1945. It will be a UK where citizens, companies and many other organisations all face more barriers, more bureaucracy, more costs and more restricted access in dealing with the EU27 than they do today. It will be a hard road to a hard Brexit.

References

Department for Exiting the European Union (2017), *The United Kingdom's exit from and new partnership with the European Union*, CM 9417, UK Government.

Ebell, M. (2017), 'Will New Trade Deals Soften the Blow of Hard Brexit', *National Institute of Economic and Social Research*, 27 January. http://www.niesr.ac.uk/blog/will-new-trade-deals-soften-blow-hard-brexit#. WLlmHhD5ZPM

Hughes, K. (2017), 'Canada-dry: where next for UK-EU Brexit talks', *Constitutional Change Centre*, University of Edinburgh.

Maugham, J. (2017), 'Is Article 50 Reversible? A Primer On The Dublin Case', *Waiting for Godot* website, 17 January. https://waitingfortax.com/2017/01/17/ is-article-50-reversible-a-primer-on-the-dublin-case/

CHAPTER TWO

A differentiated Brexit for Scotland?

Tobias Lock

Introduction

THE EU REFERENDUM of 23 June 2016 revealed a stark difference between the preferences expressed by voters in Scotland – 62 per cent of whom voted to remain in the EU – compared with those in the UK overall, where 52 per cent voted to leave. As an integral part of the UK, Scotland is therefore on a path to exit the EU. That is unless the Scots vote for independence in a re-run of the 2014 vote, in which the 'No' side won with 55 per cent. This contribution is trying to assess whether there is scope for a middle way between these two extremes. In other words, would it be possible for Scotland to stay both in the UK and either in the EU or, at least, in the EU's single market?

A middle way?

A middle way would require legal engineering at two levels: external and internal. On the external side, the EU can currently only be joined by independent states. The same is true for the European Free Trade Association (EFTA), membership of which would enable Scotland to become part of the European Economic Area (EEA) and thus stay in the single market. One way of doing this could be by way of a change to the relevant treaties opening them up to membership by sub-state entities. Politically this may be difficult to achieve, however, in particular where the EU is concerned, as it may be reluctant to allow in sub-state entities as a general rule.

Thus more creative solutions need to be considered. The EU has a certain track record of accommodating complex internal situations in Member States. For instance, it allowed East Germany to become part of the EU upon German reunification; it made it possible for Greenland to be given a more detached status following greater internal autonomy for Greenland within Denmark; and it found a way of enabling the whole of Cyprus to join, even though its government does not have control over the northern part of the country. In a similar vein, the EEA Agreement allowed Norway to exempt the territory of Svalbard from its application. None of these precedents can simply be adopted by Scotland, but they could serve as an inspiration for a bespoke solution.

The key difference between the Scottish situation and the precedents mentioned here is that in all of them the titular Member State was to the largest extent covered by the treaty concerned. Only a small part of it – in population and economic terms at least – is affected by the special status. In the case of Scotland and the UK, this would be reversed. For instance, if the Scottish government's proposal (Scottish Government, 2016) were followed and a 'reverse Svalbard' solution were adopted, the UK would be a member of EFTA and the EEA in name, but the agreements would not apply to England, Wales, and possibly Northern Ireland. While this would certainly produce the desired legal effect of these agreements only applying to Scotland, it might prove difficult to get this accepted politically and it would need the full support of the UK government.

On the internal side, a differentiated solution would require a further devolution of powers to Scotland. As a member of the single market Scotland would need to be able to comply with EU regulatory standards on goods, services, and capital. Furthermore, it would require Scotland to be able to allow free movement of people, which includes, for example, the recognition of qualifications and the coordination of social security, such as pensions. The relevant legislative powers would need to be devolved. If Scotland wanted to be in the EU, even more powers would have to come to Scotland, in particular to enable it to take part in the Common Foreign and Security Policy.

This shows that a differentiated deal for Scotland would be legally possible, but would require good will on all sides (for a discussion of the UK-internal situation, see the chapter by Fletcher and Zahn). The Scottish government (Scottish Government, 2016) was therefore wise to only ask for EFTA/EEA membership as full EU membership as a non-independent country would probably be too ambitious.

The practicalities of a differentiated arrangement

This then raises the question whether a differentiated arrangement would be practically feasible. The practicalities of any differentiated arrangement for Scotland very much depend upon the future relationship between the EU and the UK. We know from the UK government's white paper (UK Government, 2017) that it wants the UK to leave both the single market and the EU's customs union (more on the future EU-UK arrangement in the contribution by Kirsty Hughes).

The UK government will probably aim for a comprehensive free trade agreement with the EU, which would mean zero tariffs on most, if not all, goods and rules on mutual recognition of regulatory standards concerning goods and services. There are no indications that there will be a special deal for migration from the UK or into the UK. At the same time, the UK government's white paper on Brexit states as a guiding principle that 'no new barriers to living and doing business within our own Union are created'.

Trade

If Scotland stayed in the EU's customs union, this would transform the English-Scottish border into a customs border even if there are zero tariffs on all goods. This is because customs tariffs would still need to be paid for goods (or parts of goods) imported into the rest of the UK (rUK) from abroad and then sold on to Scotland. Traders will need to declare the rules of origin for the products traded across the border. In physical terms, the customs border could be almost invisible with electronic surveillance and facilities for spot checks in place. If Scotland stayed in the customs union, it would therefore be restricted in terms of the trading arrangements it could have with rUK. For this reason, the Scottish government proposes (Scottish Government, 2016) that Scotland should leave the EU customs union and stay in the same customs zone as rUK.

At the same time, it proposes that Scotland should stay in the single market as a member of EFTA/EEA. This may be legally difficult, however. Ordinarily, membership of EFTA requires a new member to sign up to all of EFTA'S 27 trade agreements (Hughes, 2017). This requirement would be incompatible with Scotland staying in a customs union with the UK as it would mean different external customs tariffs for Scotland by virtue of these trade agreements compared with rUK, which would not be party to these agreements. At the same time, it could be possible to negotiate that Scotland would not need to accede to these trade deals.

Assuming there is enough good will on the part of the EFTA countries to allow Scotland to remain in a customs union with the rUK, would this mean unimpeded trade between Scotland and rUK? A consequence of rUK outside the single market, but of Scotland inside it, would be that Scottish products would need to comply with the regulatory standards of the single market, whereas rUK products would not. So would there be barriers to trade if product standards diverged between Scotland and rUK? For instance, vacuum cleaners traded within the Single Market must comply with EU environmental standards and not use more than 1,600W of energy. Imagine rUK changes its product rules in this regard and allows more powerful vacuum cleaners to be sold there. If an English producer of vacuum cleaners wanted to sell its vacuums into the EU, it would have to comply with the 1600w limit. But what if it wanted to sell its vacuums to Scotland? The Scottish government's paper says that the trader would be allowed to do so (i.e. sell 2,000w machine in Scotland) under the principle of 'parallel marketability' (Scottish Government, 2016). This principle is currently in place for Liechtenstein, which is in the EEA but also in a customs union with Switzerland (not in the EEA). It allows products to freely circulate in Liechtenstein fulfilling either the EEA or Swiss product requirements. Crucially, however, it restricts access of products to other EEA countries marketed under diverging Swiss product requirements and vice versa.

If adopted for Scotland, this would mean that the English vacuum cleaner could be sold in Scotland, but traders would not be able to circumvent the rules of the Single Market by importing sub-standard products from England and then selling them on to the Single Market. This would require some form of surveillance, however. Scottish exporters to the EU would have to designate the products they sell to the Single Market and show that they fulfil EU product standards. Given that Scotland would be outside the EU customs union, exporting goods would require some paperwork to be filled-in in any event – even if there were zero tariffs – in order to show compliance with rules of origin, so that this additional bit of red tape created might not prove to be too burdensome.

Migration

If Scotland were part of the single market, it would have to accept free movement of people from the rest of the EU and EEA. Free movement of people to Scotland only would mean that EU citizens could work and reside in Scotland, but not anywhere else in the UK. Provided that rUK will continue to allow visitors like tourists and people visiting on business to enter rUK from the EU without a visa, there would not need to be immigration checks on the border between Scotland and England. This is because it is possible, and already practice, to have remote checks in place – through employers, landlords, etc. – to ensure that the person concerned is entitled to live and work there (Miller Westoby and Shaw, 2016).

True, an EU citizen who took up employment and residence in England regardless, would do so illegally. But the prevention of this eventuality does not necessitate border checks between England and Scotland: after all, some non-EU citizens (e.g. Americans) can already enter the UK without a visa without having the right to work and live here. If they do so regardless, they act illegally, and there are sanctions and enforcement mechanisms in place to prevent this. However, it should be noted that this restriction on EU citizens working in rUK would work only up to the moment that they naturalise as UK citizens: once this is accomplished (the qualifying period is currently six years), they will be able to move 'south' and work there. Nonetheless, it would most probably mean a significant reduction in the levels of EU migration to the UK overall.

What about the flipside of free movement then? How would one determine which British nationals count as 'Scots' and are allowed to live and work anywhere within the single market? A criterion would doubtless need to be found. The Scottish government's paper mentions 'domicile' – a more permanent status than mere residency, but this would need to be negotiated with the other EEA countries. Critically, 'Scots' so determined would need a document, for example a special form of passport or ID card, to prove that they enjoy this entitlement. This is something that would not be too difficult to create, but might not go down well with some parts of the population.

Conclusion

A differentiated deal for Scotland does not look easily achievable. While lawyers can certainly find legal solutions that would work in practice, much would depend upon political goodwill on all sides: Scotland, the UK government, as well as the governments of 27 EU Member States and three additional EEA members. The crucial actor in this would seem to be the UK government. Without its support for a differentiated solution, and willingness to put its full diplomatic weight behind it during the withdrawal negotiation process, there is not much hope this can be achieved.

References

Hughes, K. (2017), 'Scotland's EU Single Market Options: Some challenges from the trade side', *Centre for Constitutional Change*.
http://www.centreonconstitutionalchange.ac.uk/blog/scotland's-eu-single-market-options-some-challenges-trade-side

Miller Westoby, N. and Shaw, J. (2016), 'Free Movement, Immigration and Political Rights', *Scottish Universities Legal Network on Europe*.
https://sulne.ac.uk/

Scottish Government, (2016), *Scotland's Place in Europe*.
http://www.gov.scot/Publications/2016/12/9234

UK Government (2017), *The United Kingdom's exit from and new partnership with the European Union, 2017*.
https://www.gov.uk/government/publications/the-united-kingdoms-exit-from-and-new-partnership-with-the-european-union-white-paper

CHAPTER THREE

Brexit and belonging: empathy, voice and moral authority

Laura Cram

Introduction

WHAT CONSTITUTES 'us' and 'them' in the multi-level UK polity, and how a sense of belonging is created or eroded, are key questions for policy-makers facing the Brexit challenge. For the UK, and its devolved polities, this applies as much at home as abroad. Any new settlement between the UK and the EU will have legal, financial and practical implications not only for the future relationship between the UK and the EU, but also for the relationships between the constituent parts of the UK. The challenge of unpicking the UK's complex EU settlement is itself gargantuan. This is exacerbated by the very different attitudes to the process in the components of the UK. In addressing these challenges, empathy with the lived experience of others and an understanding of how they frame issues is vital. The legal and technical changes may come to seem negligible when compared with the long-term psychological shifts in the positions of key protagonists, and viewed through the long lens of history.

In managing the major transition to a post-Brexit UK, decision-makers must seek to get inside the minds of the key actors and movements involved and understand what belonging means to different individuals, groups and nationalities in the UK. At the heart of the debate about the UK's membership of the EU, and Scotland's relationship with both the UK and the EU, are issues of voice and influence. The motivating power of resentment as a result of perceived exclusion from decision-making should not be underestimated. A sense of 'relative political deprivation' (Connor, 1994) can be a powerful mobiliser.

Empathy, voice and moral authority

Social cohesion is a major concern for all governments and policy-makers. Experimental studies from cognitive neuroscientists have demonstrated that the pain associated with social exclusion and rejection activates the same brain regions as those responding to physical pain (Eisenberger et al, 2003). Our feelings really can hurt. We are hard-wired to avoid social exclusion and a sense of social exclusion motivates us powerfully. The Brexit vote, in England particularly, provided a stark reminder of the implications of leaving a section of society unheard, hurt and resentful of their exclusion from the seats of power.

The UK's EU referendum campaign highlighted the growing distrust of 'others'. Immigration issues, fear of terrorism, even a wider fear of foreigners took central stage. The campaign also highlighted the depth of internal divisions – between ethnic and religious groups, rich and poor, young and old, educated and less educated. Like ships passing in the night, there is little interaction or engagement between groups with different perspectives. Shouting over one another, repetitive sloganising and accusations of misinformation in a post-truth world has emerged as the prevailing mode of discourse, rather than discussion and debate. As losers (often labelled by opponents as 'Bremoaners' in the Brexit context) refuse to accept the positions of the winners – marching and petitioning to overturn results, questioning the intelligence and personal qualities of opponents – the extent of these divisions and the lack of mutual comprehension have been revealed. The current debate over the Scottish position on Brexit is illustrative.

It was always an error to portray the Scottish independence debate as primarily driven by an emotional nationalism. The debate on independence was less about an impassioned vision of a free Scotland and more about a mode of delivery of valued goods and services. The debate was always more about *voice* than about *identity*. In similar vein, the current discussions on Scotland and Brexit and the Scottish government's demands as articulated in its document 'Scotland's Place in Europe' (Scottish Government, 2016c) have voice at their heart. *Democracy*, the need to ensure that Scotland's voice is heard and its wishes respected, was at the top of the list of the Scottish government's five Brexit tests. *Influence*, making sure that Scotland does not just abide by the rules of the Single Market but also has a say in shaping these, completes the list.

In the consultation document on a second draft referendum bill, the UK government's approach to Brexit was presented as limiting the democratic voice of the Scottish public, posing 'unacceptable risks to our democratic, economic and social interests' (Scottish Government, 2016b). Concerning the need to engage Scotland meaningfully in the Brexit process: 'We will put forward constructive proposals that will both protect Scotland's interests and *give an opportunity for the* UK *government to demonstrate that Scotland is indeed an equal partner'* (emphasis added). In a press release (Scottish Government, 2016a) prior to his first meeting with David Davis, the UK Minister responsible for exiting the EU, Michael Russell, Scottish government Brexit Minister, stressed the importance of engagement with Scotland in the negotiation process: 'During our discussions about the future with the nations of these islands, we continue to stress the absolute necessity of *Scotland's voice* being an integral and meaningful part of the negotiating process' (emphasis added).

A key psychological difference between the red lines emerging from Scotland on the Brexit issue and those from other parts of the UK, including London and Northern Ireland which both also voted remain, is that the Scottish government holds the independence wild-card in its deck. The Scottish government's claim to moral authority on the EU issue is strong, even amongst some erstwhile opponents of independence. The image of Scotland being dragged out of the EU against its will is powerful. In Scotland, not only did 62 per cent of the vote support remain, but there was also a majority for remain in every local authority referendum counting area throughout the country. The result reflected a unique consensus amongst the Scottish political party leaders that EU membership was important for Scotland. Following the referendum, the Scottish parliament gave First Minister Sturgeon a mandate to hold direct talks with European institutions and with other member states, to seek to protect Scotland's place in the EU. On February 7th, the Scottish parliament voted by 90 to 34 to oppose the UK government starting the Brexit process. A motion lodged by Michael Russell stated that the UK government had failed to consult the devolved administrations properly on an agreed UK position on Brexit. It also argued that the government had refused to give a guarantee on the position of EU nationals in the UK, and had not answered a series of questions regarding the full implications of withdrawal from the single market. Holyrood does not have a legal right to block the Brexit Bill. However, given the markedly different position of Scottish voters in favour of remaining in the EU, a vote in Holyrood has considerable symbolic significance. Our analysis of Twitter conversations about the EU referendum found the hashtags #indyref and #indyref2 to be two of the top ten hashtags most used by those tweeting about the Brexit referendum in Scotland during the referendum campaign (Llewellyn and Cram, 2016).

Prime Minister May, recognising the already precarious relationship between Scotland and the rest of the UK and the potential for the Brexit decision to exacerbate this, made a very speedy visit to Scotland – within days of taking office. She stated that the UK government would adopt a UK-wide approach to negotiations on Brexit before triggering Article 50 and that she wanted the

Scottish government to be fully engaged in those discussions. Early comments from the new Chancellor, Philip Hammond, however, stated that there would be no special deal for Scotland and were reinforced by Prime Minister May at the Conservative Party conference. Subsequent actions, such as the creation of the PM's Brexit cabinet committee, with no permanent representation for the devolved nations, swiftly gave the lie to the commitment to fully involve Scotland in Brexit negotiations. The role allowed to the devolved bodies in the Joint Ministerial Committee (EU negotiations) has been strongly criticised. The UK government's White Paper on 'The United Kingdom's exit from and new partnership with the European Union' promises 'a good deal that works for all parts of the UK' and acknowledges the Scottish and Welsh proposals on Brexit but, in practice, raises as many questions as it answers on the future powers and responsibilities for Scotland in a post-Brexit UK (HM Government, 2017). As has become clear, providing forums in which Scotland's representatives are formally entitled to participate is not the same as being heard, understood or influential. Raised and dashed expectations can breed resentment even more powerful than simply being ignored and are likely to further fuel the sense of relative political deprivation amongst Scottish voters.

The ability to empathise is critical in enabling someone to take another's perspective (Decety, 2007; Bernhardt and Singer, 2012; Engen and Singer, 2012). Empathy, however, requires recognition that the other person is equally human – effectively, that they have a mind with the same capacity for thought, emotion, desire, intention, and self-awareness as ourselves (Fiske 2009). The ability to make complex recursive judgments about the knowledge of others and about their knowledge of our knowledge – the ability to get inside someone else's head – is fundamental to our social functioning (Frith and Frith, 2012).

Dehumanisation of another person, exaggeration of differences and demonisation of others' motives, allows us to downgrade or trivialise others' demands and to build a false perception of the virtue of our own position. The denial mindset that has emerged in social liberal circles has strong elitist undertones. Huge effort has been expended to explore scenarios in which Brexit could be avoided. As the formal status of the referendum is only advisory, the prospect of a parliamentary veto, a second referendum or of a general election nullifying the Brexit referendum are all options considered. However the political ramifications of any of these would be far reaching. Many of those who voted leave did not vote on EU membership as such but as an expression of their anger, disaffection and sense that their voices are not heard in elite circles. The iniquities of austerity are not evenly distributed. Riding roughshod over popular opinion and stigmatising Leave voters, as ignorant or racist, is a risky option. Attempting to override the democratic process by making these people vote again – because those who claimed to be listening to the public did not like what they heard – would simply reinforce and affirm the sense of alienation that was being articulated.

Similarly, Theresa May's portrayal of Scotland's governing party, in her speech to the Scottish Conservative conference, as 'divisive nationalists' who never stop twisting the truth and distorting reality 'whose single purpose in political life' is 'to denigrate our United Kingdom and further their obsession of independence' while perhaps shoring up support in her own backyard, and engendering moral authority for her position to a British nationalist or even English-nationalist audience, cannot facilitate dialogue or mutual understanding between these groups (May, 2017). Demonisation or stigmatisation of another makes dialogue impossible and stokes a sense of exclusion and unfairness in the target group that feels its character and position have been misrepresented. On the other hand, the genuine sense of fear and hurt on the part of British nationalists who wish to maintain the integrity of the UK and see withdrawal from the European Union as a positive move to 'take back control' also has to be understood and taken into account. The common thread is a desire to have greater voice and influence whether by increasing autonomy within the UK and gaining the power to conduct external relations suited to the Scottish contexts or by addressing the concerns of disaffected swathes of the wider UK electorate by withdrawing from the EU. This is not the zero sum game that it is portrayed as when dehumanisation is the dominant negotiating strategy. Dehumanisation as a strategy is fraught with long-term risks for the entrenchment of positions based on grievances and imbued with a moral authority on that basis.

Conclusion

Now that the decision that the UK will leave the EU has been taken, understanding what shapes a sense of societal belonging will be integral not only to the future of the wider European Union and the UK's relations with it, but for internal relations within the UK in this new context. Understanding why some individuals, groups and nations are willing to engage more whole-heartedly in the EU project, and why some hold back or actively resist, is essential to the management of internal UK relations. In the same vein, understanding why attachment to the UK is linked for some to the EU settlement is key. The ability to have an influential voice is at the heart of these understandings and failure to recognise this is likely to have lasting implications for the psychological positioning and sense of moral authority of future protagonists in the ongoing renegotiation of the UK constitutional settlement in a post-Brexit world.

References

Bernhardt, B. C. and Singer, T. (2012), 'The neural basis of empathy', *Annual Review of Neuroscience*, 35: 1-23.

Connor, W. (1994), *Ethnonationalism: The Quest for Understanding*, Princeton, N.J., Princeton University Press.

Decety, J. and Jackson, P.L. (2004), 'The functional architecture of Human Empathy', *Behavioral Cognitive Neuroscience Review*, 3:71-100.

Engen, H. G. & Singer, T. (2013), 'Empathy circuits', *Current Opinion in Neurobiology*, 23(2): 275-282.

Eisenberger, N. I., Lieberman, M. D. and Williams, K. D. (2003), 'Does rejection hurt? An FMRI study of social exclusion', *Science (New York, N.Y.)*, 302(5643), 290-292.

Fiske, S. T. (2009), 'From dehumanisation and objectification to rehumanisation: Neuroimaging studies on the building blocks of empathy', *Annals of the New York Academy of Sciences*, 1167, 31–34.

Frith, C. D., and Frith, U. (2012), 'Mechanisms of social cognition', *Annual Review of Psychology*, 63, 287–313.

Llewellyn, C. and Cram, L. (2016), 'What Did Social Media Tell Us About the UK's EU Referendum?', 27 June 27.

http://www. europeanfutures.ed.ac.uk/article-3534

Scottish Government (2016a), 'Press Release: Scotland's Future in Europe', Scottish Government, 14 September.

http://news.gov.scot/news/scotlands-future-in-europe

Scottish Government (2016b), *Consultation on a Draft Referendum Bill.*

http://www.gov.scot/Resource/0050/00507743.pdf

Scottish Government (2016c), *Scotland's Place in Europe.*

http://www.gov.scot/Resource/0051/00512073.pdf

May, T. (2017), Speech to Scottish Conservative conference, 3 March.

http://www.scottishconservatives.com/2017/03/theresa-may-speech-to-scottish-conservative-conference/

HM Government (2017), *The United Kingdom's Exit from and New Partnership with the European Union.*

https://www.gov.uk/government/uploads/system/uploads/attachment_data/file/589191/The_United_Kingdoms_exit_from_and_partnership_with_the_EU_Web.pdf

CHAPTER FOUR

Scottish public opinion and Brexit: not so clear after all?

John Curtice

Introduction

SCOTLAND VOTED VERY differently from much of the rest of the UK in the referendum on Britain's membership of the EU held in June 2016. North of the border, 62 per cent voted in favour of remaining in the EU, while only 38 per cent voted to leave. In contrast, only 47 per cent of voters in England and Wales backed remaining, while 53 per cent voted to leave. That narrow outcome south of the border was easily enough to tip the balance across the UK as a whole in favour of leaving, even though Northern Ireland also voted (by 56 per cent to 44 per cent) in favour of staying in the EU.

From the perspective of nationalists, nothing could have provided a clearer illustration of how, as part of the Union, Scotland is at risk of having its 'democratic' wishes overturned by votes cast south of the border. It is then, perhaps, little wonder that the result should have sparked new life into the debate about whether Scotland should become an independent country, especially as those arguing against that proposition had suggested in the independence referendum held in September 2014 that it was a vote for independence that would put the country's EU membership at risk. In any event, no sooner had the EU referendum votes been counted, Scotland's First Minister, Nicola Sturgeon, was indicating that the possibility of another referendum on independence was now 'on the table'.

But, to what extent should the outcome of the EU referendum be regarded as evidence that Scotland is keen on maintaining a close relationship with the EU? In particular, is it sufficiently keen that it might now vote for independence should a second referendum now be held on the premise that independence would create a pathway to keeping Scotland within the EU? This is the proposition that this chapter addresses. We begin by examining why Scotland voted as strongly as it did in favour of remaining in the EU. We then turn to attitudes in Scotland towards the possible shape of Brexit. Finally, we consider the impact of this debate so far on attitudes towards Scotland's constitutional status.

Why did Scotland vote to remain?

The most obvious explanation as to why Scotland voted so heavily to remain in the EU is, of course, that more people in Scotland believe in the merits of the institution. However, this is only true up to a point. This becomes apparent when we compare the pattern of responses on the two sides of the border to a question that was included in the 2015 Scottish and British Social Attitudes surveys – high quality annual surveys conducted each year by NatCen Social Research (Curtice, 2016a). The question about the EU posed by these surveys invites respondents to choose one of a number of possible options for Britain's relationship with the EU, ranging from leaving the EU at one end of the spectrum to creating a single European government at the other.

Table 1. Attitudes towards Britain's relationship with the EU in (a) Scotland (b) England and Wales, 2015

Britain's long-term policy should be to...	Scotland	England and Wales
	%	%
Leave the EU	17	23
Stay and try to reduce the EU's powers	43	43
Leave things as they are	20	18
Stay and try to increase the EU's powers	11	7
Work for a single European government	6	3

Sources: Scottish and British Social Attitudes Surveys

Table 1 shows that in the second half of 2015 (when the readings in the table were obtained, that is, before the referendum campaign got underway), 17 per cent of people in Scotland said that the country should leave the EU, rather less than the 23 per cent of those in England and Wales who expressed that view. In contrast, while 17 per cent of people in Scotland backed one or other of the options that imply a closer relationship with the EU, only 10 per cent of those in England and Wales did so. Thus on balance – and the results were much the same in previous years (Ormston, 2015; Curtice, 2016a) – public opinion in Scotland on the eve of the referendum campaign appears to have been some-what more sympathetic towards Britain's membership of the EU than the climate of opinion elsewhere in Great Britain.

But at the same time, the difference is not so great that one would anticipate these two parts of the UK would go on to vote so differently on the question of EU membership. In particular, we might note that in both parts of the UK the most popular view by far was that while Britain should probably remain a member of the EU, it would be preferable if the EU were a less powerful institution. In that sense public opinion in Scotland was at one with that in England and Wales, and thus might be sympathetic to the attempt that David Cameron made before the referendum to negotiate a looser membership for the UK.

During the referendum campaign itself, public opinion north of the border again revealed itself to be somewhat more sympathetic to the case being put forward by those arguing in favour of remaining in the EU, but no more than that. In the first three columns of Table 2 we can see that in the month before the referendum rather more people in Scotland accepted the arguments being put forward by the remain campaign that if Britain left the EU the country's economy would suffer, unemployment would go up, and that it would have less influence in the world. Conversely, rather fewer backed the claims of the leave campaign that exiting the EU would create an opportunity for improving the NHS and lowering immigration, while fewer also supported the proposition that the UK's current membership undermines Britain's distinctive sense of identity.

Table 2. Evaluations of the Consequences of Leaving the EU: Scotland and England and Wales

	Less Influence in world	Economy Worse	Unem-ployment Higher	NHS Better	End Threat to Identity	Immi-gration Lower
	%	%	%	%	%	%
Scotland	40	41	34	22	39	50
England and Wales	34	34	27	33	47	55

'End threat to identity' refers to the proportion who said that being a member of the EU undermines Britain's distinctive identity.

Source: British Election Study 2015 Internet Panel Wave 9 May-June 2016

However, the differences are only ones of degree. On average across the six items in the table, respondents in Scotland were seven points more likely than their counterparts in England and Wales to take the remain side's point of view, so less likely to agree with the leave side. That is rather less than half the 15-point difference in the level of support for remain registered in the ballot boxes. Moreover, even in Scotland, as many as a half of all voters thought that immigration would fall if the UK left the EU, while the proportion who thought the economy would be worse was still well under half.

As we would anticipate, what voters thought about the consequences of leaving the EU was reflected in their referendum vote. As Table 3 shows, over 90 per cent of those who thought that the economy would get worse as a result of leaving voted to remain, irrespective of where in the UK they lived. Conversely, throughout Britain 90 per cent of those who thought that the economy would be better voted to leave. What, however, distinguishes voters in Scotland from those in England and Wales is the vote choice of those who thought that leaving would not make much difference either way to the economy. In England and Wales only around three in ten of this group voted to remain, whereas in Scotland over two in five did so.

Table 3. *Support for remain by Perceptions of the Consequences of Leaving the EU for the Economy and for Immigration, Scotland and England and Wales.*

% voted remain in:	Expect Brexit to make the economy			Expect Brexit to mean immigration would be	
	Worse	About the same	Better	Lower	About the same/ Higher
Scotland	94	43	10	43	80
England and Wales	92	29	10	29	78

Source: 2015 British Election Study Internet Panel Waves 8 and 9. Non-voters excluded from the denominator

A similar pattern is in evidence on the issue of immigration. On both sides of the border those who thought that the level of immigration would be unaffected by leaving the EU (or in a small number of cases thought that it would actually be higher) were quite likely to vote to remain. However, whereas in England and Wales only around three in ten of those who thought that immigration would fall backed staying in the EU, in Scotland over three in five did so. The prospect of lower immigration was apparently less likely to be regarded by voters in Scotland as a reason to vote to leave.

How might we account for these differences? One possibility is to bear in mind that the vision of independence that has been promulgated by the SNP since the late eighties has been one of 'independence in Europe'. Thus, whereas in England and Wales membership of the EU has often been portrayed as a constraint on the sovereignty of the UK, in Scotland it has been presented as helping to facilitate the realisation of Scotland's sovereignty. The SNP advised its (substantial body of) supporters to vote to remain in the EU, thereby providing a cue to voters as to which way to vote that was absent south of the border.

This distinctive message would not necessarily make a difference to the behaviour of those with a clear view on the economic consequences of leaving the EU (though it might help to explain why rather more people in Scotland believed that those consequences would be deleterious). But the distinctive framing of the issue by the SNP could have made a difference to the vote choice of those who were neutral on the economic consequences of leaving the EU. This is precisely what we find. According to the British Election Study internet panel, amongst those who voted Yes in September 2014 and who thought that leaving the EU would not make any difference to the economy, as many as 52 per cent voted to remain. In contrast, the equivalent figure amongst those who voted No was just 35 per cent. A similar analysis of those who thought that immigration would fall produces much the same pattern.

True, discerning readers will have noticed that even No voters who thought the economic consequences of leaving the EU would be neutral were somewhat more likely to vote to remain in the EU (35 per cent did so) than were those with similar views in England and Wales (29 per cent). Nevertheless, it would seem that the higher level of support for remaining in the EU north of the border was, in part at least, a consequence of the link that had been forged by the SNP between EU membership and the prospect of independence.

The shape of Brexit

One possible implication of this analysis is that the outcome of the referendum overstates the enthusiasm in Scotland for maintaining close ties with the EU. Nevertheless, in December 2016 the Scottish government published a White Paper in which it not only argued that, following Brexit, Scotland should remain in the single market even if the rest of the UK did not, but also that it should continue to accept the freedom of movement provisions of the EU (Scottish Government, 2016). It was a stance that pointed to a much closer relationship with the EU than that apparently envisaged by the UK government (HM Government, 2017).

Unfortunately, to date, only one poll has attempted to ascertain what shape voters in Scotland would like Brexit to take. Conducted by Panelbase for *The Sunday Times*, it suggests that trading freely with the EU has widespread support. As many as 65 per cent agree that 'Companies in other EU countries should be allowed to sell goods as easily in Scotland as they can in their own country', while just 11 per cent disagree. But in truth, support for free trade is at least as widespread south of the border, and, of course, is not necessarily synonymous with remaining part of the single market (Curtice, 2016b).

What the EU at least believes is integral to being part of the single market is maintaining freedom of movement. This appears to be much less popular. According to the same poll, only 40 per cent agree that 'People from other European countries should still have an automatic right to come to Scotland to live and work should they so wish', while almost as many, 36 per cent, disagree. Even amongst those who voted Yes in the independence referendum, a little over a quarter (27 per cent) disagree. Given the evidence presented above on perceptions in Scotland of the consequences of leaving the EU for immigration, this should not come as a surprise. But it does suggest that the enthusiasm of voters in Scotland for this integral feature of the EU is rather less than the referendum result might lead one to expect.

The independence debate

Although the SNP's long-term advocacy of 'independence in Europe' may have served to boost the remain vote in the EU referendum, this does not mean that supporters of independence were united in favour of remaining in the EU. Far from it. The British Election Study data suggest that only two-thirds of those who voted for the SNP in 2015 – as did only two-thirds who voted Yes in the independence referendum – voted to remain. Other sources paint a similar picture (Ashcroft, 2016). The EU referendum divided the nationalist movement in Scotland, just as it did almost every other political movement in Britain – UKIP apart.

This alone is sufficient to raise doubts about any expectation that the outcome of the EU referendum would serve to increase support for independence. For a minority of Yes voters, at least, a UK that is heading out of the EU might now look like a more attractive prospect. But what also is crucial is whether those who voted No in the independence referendum (of whom 58 per cent voted to remain in the EU) value continuing membership of the EU over staying in the UK. According to evidence collected by YouGov, the proportion that do so is relatively small. In a poll conducted in July 2016, the company found that as many as 68 per cent of No voters would rather live in a UK that was outside the EU and only 18 per cent in an independent Scotland that was in the EU. The potential for persuading voters to switch from No to Yes because of the outcome of the EU referendum might then be quite limited.

Indeed, apart from an initial flurry of hastily conducted opinion polls immediately after the EU referendum, there is little evidence to suggest that the outcome of the EU referendum has had much impact on the balance of opinion on independence. In twelve polls conducted in the six months leading up to the EU referendum, on average 47 per cent said that they would now vote for independence (after leaving aside those who said Don't Know), while 53 per cent indicated that they would back staying in the UK. Meanwhile, in a dozen polls conducted between July 2016 and February 2017 the figures were exactly the same. Evidently the apparent inequity of Scotland being forced to leave the EU against its will has not been felt strongly enough by sufficient voters to change the overall level of support for independence.

True, some voters do appear to have changed their minds. According to YouGov (Curtis, 2017), while 93 per cent of those who voted No in September 2014 and for leave in June 2016 would now vote No again, only 74 per cent of No voters who backed remain have remained loyal to the Union. Support for the Union amongst some of those in the latter group seems to have been eroded. However, at the same time, while 86 per cent of those who voted Yes in the independence referendum and remain in the EU referendum still support independence, only 65 per cent of Yes voters who supported leave have maintained their view about independence. The net effect of this pair of patterns has been to leave the overall level of balance of opinion unchanged.

Conclusion

Since the EU referendum, SNP spokespersons have been keen to point out that not only did Scotland as a whole vote decisively to stay in the EU, but also that a majority voted to remain in each of the country's 32 local authority districts in which the count was conducted. The impression is created that there was a strong consensus north of the border in favour of staying in the EU.

The reality seems to be a little more complex. Some of the support for remain in the EU referendum was seemingly the product of the way in which EU membership has been linked by the SNP with the attainment of independence, and does not necessarily indicate unalloyed enthusiasm for the EU itself. On the issue that proved so toxic for the remain side everywhere, freedom of movement, it appears that voters in Scotland are divided. Meanwhile what certainly was divided in the EU referendum was the nationalist movement, one in three of whose supporters voted to leave. As a result, for every voter that has switched in favour of independence in the wake of the EU referendum, another has switched in the opposite direction.

That does of course mean that Scotland continues to be divided almost exactly down the middle on the question of independence, just as it has been ever since the independence referendum. It would not take many voters to switch sides either to generate an even larger vote in favour of staying in the UK than was obtained in September 2014 or to produce an overall majority in favour of independence. In practice, much may turn on whether Brexit itself comes to look like a success or a failure – but that is an even bigger unknown.

References

Ashcroft, Lord (2016), 'How the United Kingdom voted on Thursday… and why'.
http://lordashcroftpolls.com/2016/06/how-the-united-kingdom-voted-and-why/
Curtice, J. (2016a), *How deeply does Britain's Euroscepticism run?*, London: NatCen Social Research.
http://whatukthinks.org/eu/analysis/
how-deeply-does-britains-euroscepticism-run/
Curtice, J. (2016b), *What do voters want from Brexit?*, London: NatCen Social Research.
http://whatukthinks.org/eu/analysis/what-do-voters-want-from-brexit/
Curtis, C. (2017), 'Why have the polls not shown a shift towards Scottish Independence?'
https://yougov.co.uk/news/2017/01/27/
why-have-polls-not-shown-shift-towards-scottish-in/
HM Government (2017), *The United Kingdom's exit from and new partnership with the European Union*, Cm 9417, London: Cabinet Office.
https://www.gov.uk/government/uploads/system/uploads/attachment_data/
file/589191/The_United_Kingdoms_exit_from_and_partnership_with_the_
EU_Web.pdf
Ormston, R. (2015), *Disunited Kingdom? Attitudes to the EU across the UK*, London: NatCen Social Research.
http://whatukthinks.org/eu/analysis/
disunited-kingdom-attitudes-to-the-eu-across-the-uk/
Scottish Government (2016), *Scotland's Place in Europe*, Edinburgh: Scottish Government.
http://www.gov.scot/Publications/2016/12/9234

CHAPTER FIVE

What's law got to do with it?

The Scottish parliament and the independence referendum
Matthew Qvortrup

"If the law supposes that," said Mr. Bumble, squeezing his hat emphatically in both hands, "the law is a ass – a idiot".
Charles Dickens, Oliver Twist, Chapter 61

THIS ARTICLE SUGGESTS that the British Supreme Court may require the Scottish government to get permission to hold another referendum. Ambiguity in the Scotland Act forces us to go back to the intention of the sponsor of the original Bill, and Donald Dewar was clear that a referendum was not in the Scottish parliament's gift. Still, cases from abroad suggest there might be leeway and moreover there are several cases from international law of countries gaining recognition even if domestic law has forbidden secession.

The problem

Once again the Scottish government is toying with the idea of a second referendum on becoming an independent country. This raises the issue of whether such a referendum would be legal under the existing statutory framework as set out in the *Scotland Act 1998*. If a referendum on Scottish independence is *ultra vires*, will it be necessary for the Scottish government to seek a Section 30 Order, which would allow them to legislate on 'reserved matter'?

The issue of the legality of a decision by the Scottish parliament has been hotly contested. On the one hand Scottish First Minister Nicola Sturgeon argued that Holyrood had a right to decide to hold a referendum. On the other hand Theresa May, the UK Prime Minister, has argued that such a referendum would be illegal as it is outside the powers of the Scotland Act 1998. The Westminster government has even suggested that the issue could be decided in the Courts. Who is right? It is a bit tricky, so hold on…

Whether a legal challenge is politically likely, is an open question, but from a legal point of view, deserves attention. Would the Courts, or even the Supreme Court, block a decision to hold a referendum like they pronounced on the (il) legality of the government's decision to force Brexit without consulting parliament in R (Miller) v Secretary of State for Exiting the European Union? And would it matter that a referendum on independence was the centre-piece of the Scottish National Party's election manifesto which secured the SNP a third term?

For starters, winning an electoral mandate will not sway the judges, and has little appeal to black-letter lawyers. This might seem undemocratic, but that is how things work under the rule of law.

So, given this, how would the judges adjudicate if the decision to hold a referendum on Scottish independence were to be challenged in the Courts? Knowing what determines the decisions of their Lordships – and their more junior colleagues – is a speculative business. Yet, while – in the words of American legal scholar Jerome Frank 'the ultimately important influences in the decisions of any judge are the most obscure, and are the least easily discoverable' (Frank, 1930: 114), we can make educated guesses on the basis of precedent, but no more than that.

The legal position under UK *law*

The overall problem for the Courts is that the legislation is unclear. The Scotland Act does not mention referendums, let alone the right to hold an independence referendum, and the fact that a referendum has been held before does not change matters. Indeed, the fact that David Cameron allowed a referendum might create a negative precedent from the point of view of Nicola Sturgeon. In other words, it might have created a precedent – that the decision as to whether a referendum should be held is determined by the UK Prime Minister.

So let's for a moment look at the bare legal bones of the problem. The Scotland Act 1998, states Section 29(1), 'an Act of the Scottish parliament is not law so far as any provision of the Act is outside the legislative competence of the parliament'.

The Act goes on to say that the parliament at Holyrood cannot legislate in certain 'reserved matters'. These consist of '(a) the Crown, including succession to the Crown and a regency, (b) the Union of the Kingdoms of Scotland and

England, (c) the parliament of the United Kingdom' (Paragraph 1, Schedule 5). But the Act is silent on the issue of a referendum, especially an advisory one.

This poses a problem. How can the courts decide if the power to hold a referendum falls under the 'reserved powers'? Legally speaking, this issue can be resolved if we take – what lawyers call – a *purposive approach* to the issue.

Since the often cited case of *Pepper v Hart*, the Supreme Court (or House of Lords as they were then) has held that when primary is ambiguous then, under certain circumstances, the court may refer to statements made in the House of Commons in an attempt to interpret the meaning of the legislation.

It is thus likely that the Courts could use the statement in the House of Commons by the then Secretary of State for Scotland, and promoter of the Bill, Donald Dewar, who rather unequivocally stated:

> A referendum that purported to pave the way for something that was *ultra vires* is itself *ultra vires*. That is a view that I take, and one to which I will hold. But, as I said, the sovereignty of the Scottish people, which is often prayed in aid, is still there in the sense that, if they vote for a point of view, for change, and mean that they want that change by their vote, any elected politician in this country must very carefully take that into account. I do not believe that they will vote for that change, or that there is enthusiasm or a wish for that change. We shall no doubt argue about, debate and analyse that many, many times (House of Commons Debates 5 December 1998: Column 257).

This would seem to have settled the matter. But the issue is a bit more complicated and convoluted. Presumably, the decision to hold a referendum would, legally speaking, be *ultra vires*, that is beyond the powers conferred on the Scottish parliament by the Scotland Act. Some SNP supporters – and perhaps others besides– might be tempted to conclude that the 'law is an ass'!

But, the Supreme Court has not unequivocally supported such an interpretation. In AXA v Lord Advocate, Lord Hope said on appeal, 'the elected members of [the] legislature… are best placed to judge what is in the country's best interests as a whole'. Given that the Scottish National Party won the 2016 elections on a manifesto commitment to hold a referendum in the event of the British government taking the UK out of the EU, it could seem that the judges in London, have accepted that a referendum on independence is legally acceptable.

But it is not a cast iron certainty. Given the dearth of comparable cases it is conceivable – though this is speculation – that the Supreme Court in London could look to the case of Canada.

In 1998, in a reference about the legality of a referendum for the French-speaking province of Quebec, the Canadian judges held in *Re Quebec* that the rest of

Canada 'would have no basis to deny the right of the government of Quebec to pursue secession' (*Re Quebec* 1998: 7101).

True, the Canadian judges did state that negotiations would have to follow to define the terms under which Quebec would gain independence, and the referendum would have to be compatible with the principles of democracy, protection of minorities and the rule of law. Specifically, the argument was that referendums are only permitted in countries where all democratic avenues are closed.

Admittedly, constitutional law is not an exact science, nor one that lends itself to certainties and unequivocal statements, but based on the historical examples and legal precedents, it is far from certain what the outcome of a legal challenge would be.

Perhaps, the various political parties would be well advised to reflect on this passage in the Canadian judgement before they hire their lawyers:

> The reconciliation of the various legitimate constitutional interests is necessarily committed to the political rather than the judicial realm precisely because that reconciliation can only be achieved through the give and take of political negotiations (*Re Quebec* 1998: 7101)

So this is only true in national or domestic law. Is the position different under international law?

Independence referendums in international law

The issue of the legality of independence in international law is no less important, but it too has received a somewhat stepmotherly treatment by international lawyers (Radan, 2012: 17).

This is somewhat surprising as it is very pertinent to the issue. International law generally holds that two conditions must be met. First of all, the people on the territory must express a wish to secede. This was recognised by the *International Court of Justice* (ICJ) in the Case Concerning East Timor and in the ICJ's Advisory opinion on Western Sahara, in which it was held that independence 'requires the free and genuine expression of the will of the peoples concerned' (ICJ 1975: 55). To use but two examples, Malta did not have to ask Britain to secede in 1964, nor did Estonia seek the Soviet Union's permission to become independent in 1991, and clearly permission would not have been granted.

But this is not sufficient. According to the second principle of international law, countries must also be recognised by the international community. In matters regarding recognition, most countries follow the so-called *Estrada Doctrine*

– named after the Mexican Foreign Secretary, Genaro Estrada, in the 1930s (Kaczorowska, 2008: 83).

According to this doctrine, a country should be recognised when it has control over its own territory. Though in some cases, it should be noted, the international community has recognised a state after a referendum and without ascertaining that the state in question controlled the territory (as happened in the case of Croatia (Cassese, 2005: 74).

If, for example, Scotland votes for independence (and if the Scottish government is in control of the territory), then the international community will in all likelihood recognise the new state, just like in the cases of former Soviet states in the 1990s.

Thus referendums on independence in international law tend to result in recognition if it is clear that there is a popular mandate for statehood among the voters. This might save a Scottish referendum from being rendered invalid. A second Scottish referendum might be deemed illegal by the British Supreme Court – indeed, it is all but certain that it will. However, under international law, Scotland may have a case. And this, after all, is what matters. If the rest of the world recognises the independent state of Scotland after a majority has voted for independence then the opinion of the British Supreme Court – or Theresa May, for that matter – is of mere academic interest. The law may not after all be an ass!

References

Books and Articles

Cassese, A. (2005), *International Law*, Oxford: Oxford University Press.

Frank, J. (1930), *Law and the Modern Mind*, New York: Brentano's.

Kaczorowska, A. (2008), *Public International Law*: London, Routledge.

Radan, Peter (2012), 'Secessionist Referenda in International and Domestic law', in *Nationalism and Ethnic Politics*, 18, No. 1.

Primary Legislation

Scotland Act 1998

Legal Cases

Advisory Opinion, International Court of Justice, (1975) 16 October, ICJ Report 12-68, 55.

AXA v Lord Advocate [2011], UK Supreme Court, 46.

Pepper (Inspector of Taxes) *v Hart* (1992), UKHL 3.

Portugal v. Australia, International Court of Justice (1995), 30 June, ICJ Reports, 90-106.

Reference re Secession of Quebec (1998) 2 S.C.R, 7.

CHAPTER SIX

Living in interesting times: Scotland's economic development trajectory post-Brexit

Andrew Cumbers

Introduction

SCOTLAND AND THE UK are living through 'interesting times', to quote the old Chinese curse. Although the origins of this saying are unclear, the underlying sentiment that it is better to live in a boring and thereby peaceful era, rather than a dynamic and chaotic one, is apposite. The global economy has been through a period of upheaval since the start of the financial crisis in 2007, made worse by policies of austerity, pursued most energetically by European governments and institutions, with the UK in the vanguard (Blyth, 2013). Even before Brexit, the government's flawed deficit reduction strategy has served to both deepen the recession following the financial crisis and constrain recovery (Scottish Government, 2014).

In the wake of all this, in what follows, I offer an assessment of Scotland's economic development prospects post-Brexit. In doing so, I interpret the economy as an open, dynamic system, influenced as much by human behaviour, and political and social dynamics as by some immutable economic laws (Dow et al, 2017). Past legacies and ongoing trajectories shape contemporary events and future pathways, mediating, if not determining, the power and capacity of economic and political actors. Such an analysis recognises that Scotland's existing economic pathway is largely dominated by external processes and policies set in train by UK governments. As a heavily globalised national region, it is particularly susceptible to the UK government's current approach of a 'hard Brexit'. Despite devolution, Scotland lacks the key economic decision-making powers to shape its own economic trajectory and mitigate the likely negative impacts of the course currently being pursued.

Scotland's existing economic development trajectory

A region or country's economic development pathway is ultimately shaped by political and institutional forces, as much as narrowly conceived economic ones. In this sense, it is a combination of conventional economic factors that determine competitive abilities to compete in a global economy (e.g. productivity, human capital, innovation, entrepreneurialism, access to capital), although these are also subject to specific cultural and institutional contexts; and the political agency to mobilise resources and assets in pursuit of a particular economic strategy over a sustainable period.

Faced with the prospect of Brexit, Scotland is at an important junction in its economic development, with different pathways open to it that depend on the political choices made and the actors (both economic and political, national, sub-national and global) that influence those choices. At present, Scotland's position in this respect is a heavily dependent one, tied to the broader UK economy and the policies being pursued by the Westminster government, but also dependent on the decisions made by its key business sectors, many of which are externally controlled.

I have argued elsewhere that the UK's economic geography – the economic relationships between the country's cities and regions – is an increasingly dysfunctional one (Cumbers, 2014). There are different aspects to this, but the most important is the chasm in economic wealth between London and the south east of England, and the rest of the UK. This is a longstanding problem that goes back to the 1960s, resulting from deindustrialisation and the unbalanced geographical nature of the shift towards a more service-driven economy (Martin et al, 2015).

Since the late 1990s economic growth in the London region has dramatically outstripped the rest of the UK (Figure 1). The main factor has been the capital's pre-eminence as a global financial centre, largely facilitated by the UK's economic model (principally pursued by both Labour and Conservative governments since the 1970s) centred upon neoliberal market deregulation (of the financial sector in particular), a retreat from industrial (or perhaps more accurately economic modernisation) policy, and cuts in personal and corporate taxation. Such policies have privileged finance and the corporate sector and their elites (heavily concentrated in London and the south east) over the interests of other social groups and regions (Savage, 2013).

Since 2010, both Coalition and Conservative governments have added the strategy of austerity-driven cuts in public sending to this existing trajectory. The self-induced pain, and its consequences of continued economic decline and social marginalisation for many of the UK's most deprived areas and poorest

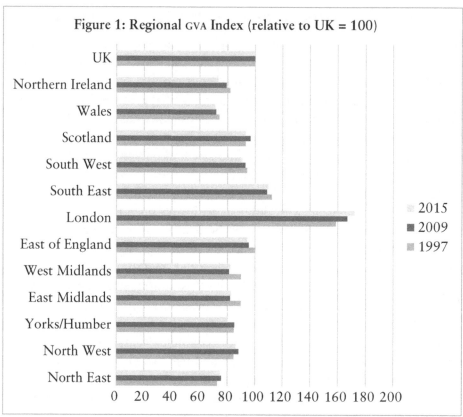

Figure 1: Regional GVA Index (relative to UK = 100)

Source: Office for National Statistics: https://www.ons.gov.uk/

citizens, were evident before anyone dreamed up the term Brexit. As has widely been reported, some of the highest votes for Brexit were in parts of the UK such as south Wales, Yorkshire and the north east of England, long affected by deindustrialisation and the lack of effective economic regeneration. Austerity and swingeing cutbacks in welfare and social services have also been experienced hardest in these areas due to the importance of the public sector in anchoring these local economies.

Set against this, Scotland as a whole is faring better than many other UK regions (Figure 1). It has pockets of above average economic growth and wealth; notably Aberdeen, but also Edinburgh, Perth and Stirling.[1] Indeed, devolution and greater autonomy in some areas of welfare and education policy seem to have cushioned the effects of austerity on household incomes compared to other northern and peripheral regions (Figure 2). Nevertheless, levels of poverty and economic marginalisation remain high in many parts of Scotland, particularly in Glasgow, Lanarkshire and parts of Ayrshire.

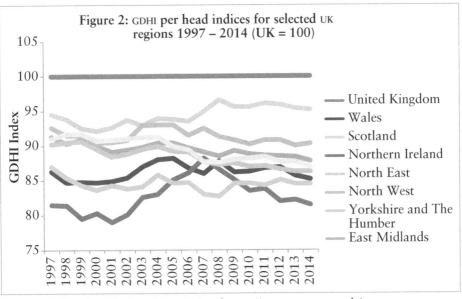

Figure 2: GDHI per head indices for selected UK regions 1997 – 2014 (UK = 100)

Source: Office for National Statistics: https://www.ons.gov.uk/

External ownership of the Scottish economy, by foreign and other UK firms, has recently been estimated as accounting for one third of the country's non-financial economy (Scottish Government, 2014). Although the SNP government has recently been criticised for this, the globalisation of the Scottish economy is the result of processes and policies established well before the period it started to rule as a majority government from 2011–6. Since the 1970s, UK regional development policy under all governments has largely been about attracting foreign direct investment into Wales, Scotland and the North of England at the expense of a coherent economic modernisation or diversification strategy for existing businesses and workforces.

Ultimately, much depends on the quality of that investment and the success of local actors in embedding FDI (foreign direct investment) in place. Foreign capital can lead to an influx of expertise and know-how that can help to enhance and upgrade the local economy. If local firms are successful in integrating themselves into the supply chains of larger foreign customers, this can also lead to them piggybacking into export markets over the longer term. Both Scotland's oil industry and life sciences sectors are examples of sectors that have benefited from such processes. However, too much external dependence, particularly on routine and low skilled activities can make places vulnerable to capital flight in an economic downturn, or to competition from other regions. Silicon Glen discovered this to its cost in the early 2000s with the closure of Motorola and the loss of 3,000 jobs, and the movement of other electronics branch plants to cheaper locations in central and Eastern Europe. Brexit could of course facilitate a similar outflow over the next decade.

Economic trajectories post-Brexit

Brexit, as a dramatic political and institutional reconfiguration of economic governance, is likely to have an extremely negative impact on Scotland's future economic development if the UK government's stated position of a 'hard Brexit' (as of the beginning of March 2017), which involves no access to the European Single Market and some form of bilateral trade deal, is pursued. Subjected to this state of affairs, and without the power to control and shape its own economic development pathway – particularly with regard to trade, business and market regulation, corporate governance, innovation and technology policy, employment relations, lending, finance and banking regulation, all of which reside in Westminster - Scotland will be hostage to whatever economic model is adopted by the UK government.

Different scenarios are of course possible depending on the nature of the UK's eventual exit from the EU. Given Scotland's position as an open globalised economy, and the importance of cross-border flows of goods, capital and labour, as well as the importance of international knowledge networks to many of the country's more advanced and high performing research and development activities, including its leading universities, a hard Brexit is likely to have very negative effects on the country's long term economic wellbeing. EU markets currently make up 43 per cent of total exports (Scottish Government, 2016) and recent estimates from the Fraser of Allander Institute have estimated that Brexit might reduce Scottish GDP by as much as £11bn by 2030 with a worst-case scenario of a 13 per cent effective cut in the government budget resulting from the loss of tax revenue (Scottish Government, 2016).

The most harmful effects are not related to tariffs on trade per se but the non-tariff boundaries that stem from the institutional and procedural benefits that companies currently enjoy from operating across the European Union. To take a particularly prominent example, under European Union rules, Scotch whisky has protected geographical status, which means that no other country's whisky can be labelled as 'Scotch' within European markets. The EU also has bilateral recognition of this status with the US, one of the largest markets for whisky outside Europe. But such status can no longer be guaranteed with new trade agreements that are yet to be constructed.

Additionally, what is often forgotten is that the economy is not static but evolves in an incremental fashion through time with technological, cultural and institutional changes. As various remain proponents noted during the Referendum campaign, being outside the EU, and, as looks increasingly likely, outside the Single Market, means that UK firms and workers will have no say in the rules for how this market develops, across a whole range of areas relating to

product standards and quality; consumer affairs; employment rights and standards; technology, innovation and knowledge formation; competition policy, to
name but a small selection. Equally damaging will be the increased estrange-
ment of UK based firms from the 'soft power' networks of the EU economy; in
other words all the many informal routines and customs that shape economic
decision-making and behaviour.

All of this is bad news in itself, before one considers the kind of UK political
economy that is likely to be forged out of the ashes of Brexit. Recent statements by the Chancellor of the Exchequer threatening a new low tax economic
model away from the European model of a welfare state completely, with all
the dire implications for further public sector cuts, will be felt particularly in
Scotland's more deprived areas. The dominance of the financial services sector
over the economy, the importance of property based growth, and credit-fuelled
consumption, are likely to increase even further, given the absence of a coherent alternative economic strategy and the lack of public investment needed to
change paths. The UK's existing role as a tax haven that helps corporations
escape regulation elsewhere is likely to be greatly amplified, whilst also undermining international attempts to create fairer tax regimes (Shaxson, 2012). This
will further dampen any goodwill in the European Union to look favourably
upon Scottish business interests,

Tantalising steps towards an alternative path

Spurred on in part by the last independence referendum, the past few years
have seen an outpouring of alternative ideas and fresh thinking from various
progressive think tanks about how Scotland could embark upon a very different
economic development strategy. Such proposals advocate a departure from the
current financialised, rent seeking model of British capitalism towards a more
progressive trajectory, governed by social need and the productive use of capital and resources. Greater collective ownership of renewable energy resources,
a thoroughgoing industrial strategy, greater protection and empowerment of
workers, and a revolution in banking and finance to repurpose these existing
skills and capital for the common good.

While the Scottish government has made a few cautious nods in this direction
with its living wage policy, proposals to expand social housing, community
empowerment and land reform bills, and could arguably be more radical, under
the current devolved settlement, it lacks the necessary economic powers to
chart a different course. Not only does it have no control of the key economic
decision-making powers identified earlier, but it lacks the borrowing powers of

the Basque region in Spain or the state-owned regional banks of the German Länder, to harness the patient capital needed for longer term public projects.

Despite some warm words from Theresa May about governing on behalf of the whole of society, rather than a privileged elite, there is little sign thus far that the UK government intends to change tack on the central policy of austerity and deficit reduction. There is even less evidence that May's government has any appetite to devolve real economic decision-making power to the Scottish government or any of the other sub-national governments that would allow them to chart a different economic course post-Brexit. Without some form of radical political reconfiguration, Scotland seems destined for yet more 'interesting times' and considerable economic disruption in the years ahead.

References

Blyth, M. (2013), *Austerity: The history of a dangerous idea*, New York: Routledge.

Cumbers, A. (2014), 'The Scottish Independence Referendum and the dysfunctional economic geography of the UK', *Political Geography* 41, pp. 33-36.

Dow, S. Cumbers, A. and McMaster, R. (2017), *Sine praejudicio? Economics and the 2014 Scottish independence referendum*, Glasgow, Adam Smith Business School Working Paper.

Emmerson, C. Johnson, P. and Joyce, R. (eds) (2017), *The IFS Green Budget*, Institute for Fiscal Studies, London.

Martin, R. Pike, A. Tyler, P. and Gardiner, B. (2015), *Spatially Rebalancing the UK Economy: the Need for a New Growth Model*, Regional Studies Association, Seaford.

Savage, M. (2013), *A new model of social class? Findings from the BBC's Great British Class Survey experiment. Sociology* 47, 2, 219-50.

Scottish Government (2014), *Annual Business Survey 2014.*

http://www.gov.scot/Topics/Statistics/Browse/Business/SABS/KeyFacts

Scottish Government (2016), *Potential Implications of the UK Leaving the EU on Scotland's Long Run Economic Performance*. Scottish Government, Edinburgh.

Scottish Government (2017), *Export Statistics Scotland 2015*, Scottish Government, Edinburgh, 2017.

Shaxson, N. (2012), *Treasure Islands: Tax Havens and the Men Who Stole the World*, Random House, London.

CHAPTER SEVEN

Brexit and Scotland's public spending

Richard Kerley

IT IS SURPRISINGLY difficult to define 'public spending' in Scotland – that which is generally assumed to be spending on public services. It is even more difficult to disaggregate funding from the European Union in this analysis. It is therefore necessary to look wider than the most obvious public spending to get some sense of the reach and scale of the EU contribution. It is about trying to build a picture – whether impressionistic or realistic – that illustrates the impact that the EU has on spending and taxing in Scotland.

Let's start with the obvious. Most of us will have seen signage – with the familiar multi star flag – that tells us the European Union has some financial involvement in a project such as the M74 extension in Glasgow/Lanarkshire. Such support arises as a function of attempts to redress long-term economic disadvantage (and often environmental degradation) in areas of former heavy industry. Historically it reflects policy choices that date back to the original antecedents of the EU, the European Coal and Steel Community.

Less obvious for most people will be the involvement of EU organisations in, for example, the support of film and cinema. In some venues, the opening screen will often show a logo for 'Media – Creative Europe' a EU programme to support film. The EU flag is also on the website of events such as the Glasgow Film Festival. Edinburgh University (2016) describes itself as the largest HE recipient of European research and other Funds in Scotland, fifth largest in the UK, and in 2014–2015 it received £31.2M from the EU. Most of this will be the successful outcome of competitive bidding for research grants against other similar European HE institutions. These three examples illustrate how complex it can be to unravel the skeins of public spending that permeate our social and economic fabric. Clearly roads such as the M74 are public assets and public provision. The cinemas supported by the 'Media' programme are both charitable bodies and trading companies; universities are technically private, not public bodies, and usually charities as well.

The flow of tax-generated funds into Scotland is influenced by, and contributed to by, the European Union, but in forms that extend to a wide range of organisations, and the greatest volume of such public spending is not to public services. The referendum campaigns of both sides made claims and counter claims that ranged across legislative options (post-Brexit, different immigration controls *could* be introduced); the economic impact (leaving might lead to a dramatic collapse in house prices) and different options on public expenditure (£350M per week extra *would* be spent on the NHS). I italicise these words above to suggest such claims were rarely qualified, and at worst were simply wrong.

What is worth noting is that on both sides of campaigning, little was made of the direct consequences for public expenditure other than the now derided £350 million a week for the NHS. In one partisan paper, 'We'll get our money back' was listed as the number 1 reason of 20 reasons to leave the EU (*Daily Telegraph*, 2016). What all such claims usually omitted to mention was the manner and extent to which any ending of funds from the EU might be replaced.

Whatever the balance of arguments that figured in the referendum campaign the programmatic transfer of public monies into and back from the EU has on an *aggregate* level been a relatively minor part of the relationship with the EU and has declined in recent years compared to the first two decades of membership. Both the UK, and Scotland, itself make direct contributions to European budgets over and above the return value of cash benefits. Of course, in specific parts of each of the four home countries of the UK, the transfer of EU funds has often been highly significant, such the more economically deprived areas like Cornwall, West Wales and parts of Scotland. This is why there is EU support for the M74 extension, but not the Aberdeen by pass.

Over time this form and level of transfer has been affected by relative improvements in the economy of the affected areas; in the accession of poorer countries into the EU as it expanded to 28 states; and through internal shifts within the Scottish economy. Indeed, were the UK or Scotland separately to remain in the EU, on the currently defined statistical boundaries most parts of Scotland might not benefit much longer from such a transfer of funds.

Currently the range of mainstream public spending in Scotland that derives from the EU in one form or another covers a number of different publicly funded initiatives. For example, consider those channelled through local government (and partner organisations in the third sector). Over the EU programme period of 2014–2020, the Convention of Scottish Local Authorities (COSLA) reports this to include €105 million to invest in potential growth businesses; €15 million to support the Cities Alliance; in the order of €50 million for business loan substitutes and €200 million for various forms of employability support. There is also support in the order of €120 million for low carbon and green

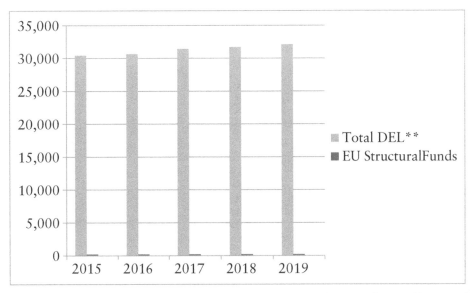

Figure 1 Comparison of EU support for 'public spending' and overall Scottish budget. DEL** is Departmental Expenditure Limit
(Source: Scottish Government 2016b & 2016c)

initiatives, along with €50 million for action on social exclusion. We have to take account of the fact that such figures cover a multi-year programme period and when we assess the totality of EU Structural Funds for Scotland they amount to approximately €1.3 billion over the period 2014–2020, or somewhere over €200 million per year.

These seem large figures when stated in that way; however, the relative impact of EU spend is not a large part of total public spending. Figure 1 below shows how the transfer of funds from the EU into Scotland – and allocated to what we might describe as mainstream public spending through the Scottish parliament – compares to overall actual and projected budgets over the period 2015–2020. As can be seen, the EU figures are just dwarfed by the overall scale of other elements of Scottish government spend on the mainstream of public services in Scotland.

The EU funds associated with various forms of agricultural support show a somewhat different picture. 'Pillar 1' is quasi-automatic support for farm incomes, awarded because of being a farm; this money comes directly from the EU. 'Pillar 2' is jointly supported by the Scottish government and the EU through matched funding and is discretionary, covering a range of rural activities from forestry to encouraging new farming entrants. When these two elements are added together, the figures begin to register more prominently on the chart of our overall finances as Figure 2 below.

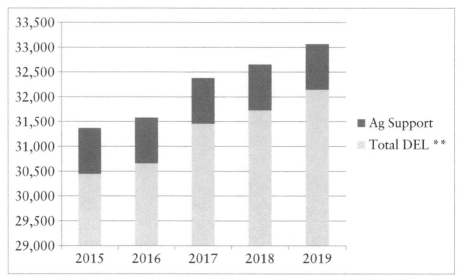

Figure 2 Comparison of EU support for agriculture and overall Scottish budget (Source: Scottish Government 2016b & 2016c, Auditor General 2016)

I am therefore suggesting that the act of leaving the EU will not – of itself – impact negatively on mainstream public spending across Scotland as a whole. Notwithstanding this, Scotland does receive a disproportionate share of EU funding within the UK and different areas of Scotland and different sectors also receive disproportionate levels. So we receive about eight per cent of Structural Funds (close to population) and 44 per cent of Fisheries monies.

This aspect of our departure from the EU on 'the public finances 'has been analysed by Beg and Mushövel who published a paper entitled 'The economic impact of Brexit: jobs, growth and the public finances'. I assume their title was chosen to reflect the complex inter-relationship between the three elements listed and as they explain, those different elements interact in different ways. Their first observation of the impact on 'public finances' is as follows:

> The direct effect of Brexit on the public finances will be to allow the UK to save on its current payments into the EU budget. (p. 1)

For Scotland, like the UK as a whole, we are net contributors to the EU budget, which the Scottish Parliment. Information Centre (SPICe) calculates to be in the order of £500 million p.a. However, that does not mean that all is well, as the authors immediately observe in the next sentence:

> Any savings from direct contributions to the EU budget would be erased if Brexit results in a GDP loss of as little as one percentage point and the public finances would be worse if the loss were greater, despite no longer paying into the EU.

These two linked observations also reflect the views expressed by the Scottish government (2016a), most recently in their pre-emptive publication 'Scotland's Place in Europe'. In that position paper it is stated that:

> … under a 'hard Brexit' Scottish GDP could be up around £11 billion per year lower by 2030 than it would be if Brexit does not occur. Such an adverse shock to our economic performance would reduce tax revenues, and in turn the funding available for public services. The Scottish government analysis estimates that resources for public spending could be up to £3.7 billion a year lower under a 'hard Brexit'. (p. 10)

In this passage they clearly identify the scale of a possible decline in economic activity and that this will impact on public spending. Elsewhere in the document some tendency to overstatement is observed:

> The impact of a changed relationship with the EU will be variable across sectors and regions. Higher impacts will potentially be felt… where we rely on EU structural funds, for example, for infrastructure projects…

Such a claim of 'reliance' on EU funds for infrastructure is simply not borne out by the available evidence. As mentioned above, some road projects receive support from EU funding streams; some do not. The Queensferry Crossing and the Borders Rail Link (the largest Infrastructure projects recently completed) do not appear to have benefitted from direct EU financial support.

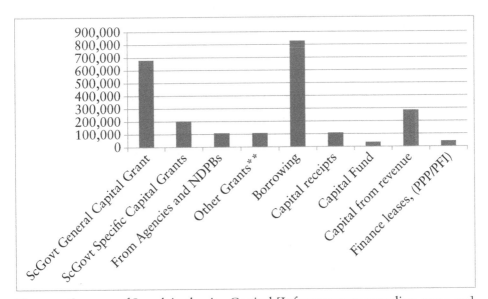

Figure 3 Sources of Local Authority Capital [Infrastructure spending 2014-15] (Source: Scottish Government 2016d ** Other Grants includes EU sourced funds)

Examination of local government capital spending (Scottish Government 2016d) shows the level of EU support to be low, broadly on a par with National Lottery support in some years, and not explicitly detailed in the narrative description of available capital funding as Figure 3 shows.

Conclusion

On both sides of the EU debate, protagonists have often fallen into the correlation/causation trap. 'Because we have been in the EU (good or bad) X has happened' when any such change or development might well have been otherwise introduced by domestic government legislation. Across all EU members, forms of public spending and their proportion as part of GDP (Ireland high 30s, Finland mid 50s) are determined solely by domestic governments (though arguably not currently in Greece) (OECD, 2017).

There may be many undesirable consequences for Scotland of leaving the European Union; however the direct impact on public spending will not be the most significant of them. It seems likely that possible limitations on the movement of labour, and the overall shock to the economy that is projected by many post-Brexit will have a far greater impact than cash reductions alone and may be more debilitating in their impact. With changes in the financial arrangements that exist between the UK government and the Scottish parliament, it is hard to project what inter-related forms these various impacts might take; currently and in combination they do not look positive.

References

Auditor General for Scotland (2016), *Common Agricultural Policy Future Programme – an update*, Audit Scotland, Edinburgh.

Begg, I. and Mushövel, F. (2016), *The economic impact of Brexit: jobs, growth and the public finances*, European Institute, London School of Economics, mimeo, London.

Convention of Scottish Local Authorities (2016), *Briefing document for Scottish Parliament Local Government and Communities Committee*, 14 December, Edinburgh.

Daily Telegraph (2016), '20 reasons you should vote to leave the European Union', 22 June, London.

Edinburgh University (2016), *News Release*, 23 September, Edinburgh.

Organisation for Economic Cooperation and Development (2017), National Accounts of OECD Countries.

Scottish Government (2016a), *Scotland's Place in Europe*, Scottish Government, Edinburgh.

Scottish Government (2016b), *Draft Scottish Budget 2017-2018*, Scottish Government, Edinburgh.

Scottish Government (2016c), *Government Expenditure and Revenue in Scotland*, Scottish Government, Edinburgh.

Scottish Government (2016d), *Scottish Local Government Financial Statistics, 2014-2015*, Scottish Government, Edinburgh.

SPICE [Scottish Parliament Information Centre] (2016), *European Union Funding in Scotland*, Scottish Parliament, Edinburgh.

CHAPTER EIGHT

Troubled waters: Scottish fisheries and the EU

Griffin Carpenter

THE COMMON FISHERIES Policy is one of the most controversial EU policies, attracting much criticism for its failure to end overfishing while many fishing ports around the EU decline in significance. Scotland, perhaps more than almost anywhere else in the EU, knows this well. Fishing is a more prominent part of the economy in Scotland than elsewhere (Scotland has only 8 per cent of the UK population but 60 per cent of the total UK catch) and much (92 per cent) of the fishing industry would like to leave the EU (McAngus, 2016). In this context, it is not surprising that the infamous 'Brexit flotilla' that led to the clash on the Thames between then UKIP leader Nigel Farage and singer-activist Bob Geldof was organised by a group of Scottish skippers wanting to make their voice heard in the lead-up to the referendum.

What is not clear, however, is whether leaving the EU will address many of the underlying issues in fisheries. In fact, if the benefits of shared management are ignored, there is a risk of returning to rampant overfishing as individual nations pursue their own self-interest to overexploit common resources. This article will explore the history and current state of the Scottish fishing industry, the major areas of interaction between Scottish fisheries and the European Union, the attitudes that have led to calls for Brexit from much of the fishing industry, and some key issues that will shape Brexit negotiations and the way forward.

A tale of expansion and limitation

Beginning with the earliest settlers, fishing around the Scottish coast has undergone constant expansion into the industrial age. Starting in the early 19th century, fishing boats began to be subsidised for industrial production, particularly herring boats, which exported much of their catch to continental Europe. By the end of the century, 'active' fishing techniques, such as trawling, were in full force, dramatically changing the structure of the industry and its impact on the marine environment. In terms of employment and activity, the beginning of the First World War marked a high point in Scotland, as the industry began a major shift during the inter-war period. By the end of the Second World War, the industry had begun a gradual decline in economic significance, in particular as the limits of continued expansion were tested.

The most obvious of these limitations is environmental, through overfishing of key fish stocks. While a shift in the composition of catches had already begun to occur in the post-war period, overfishing further contributed to a shifting of catches towards whitefish (mainly cod and haddock) and then on to shellfish (mainly Nephrops and scallops). There were also economic constraints on the industry, particularly in attracting labour and investment, as other Scottish sectors such as North Sea oil boomed and as many young people moved away from fishing communities to seek employment in urban centres.

This combination of limitations on the supply of fishing opportunities and the demand for them constrained the Scottish fishing industry from the second half of the twentieth century onwards. These limitations also had compounding factors, such as technological developments and licensing schemes, resulting in fewer vessels and fishers in the industry. In recent decades, a market for fishing quotas (tradeable catch limits by quantity and fish stock) has developed, leading to a continuously smaller and more consolidated industry.

The changing face of Scottish fisheries

Today, both the quantity and value of Scottish catches are fairly stable, with a recent uptick as stock improvements are followed by increases in catches. In 2015, just over 2,000 Scottish registered vessels landed 440 thousand tonnes of fish, with a value of £437 million (Marine Scotland 2016). These vessels employ just under 5,000 fishers, most of whom are regularly employed.

The status of Scottish fish stocks is improving, but is still precarious. Marine Scotland notes that there is still overfishing (fishing mortality higher than what would produce the maximum sustainable yield) for key species including North Sea cod, several Nephrops stocks, mackerel, as well as cod and haddock to the west of Scotland (Marine Scotland Science, 2016b). Significant changes to Scottish fisheries are therefore limited by what these stocks can sustain – an important consideration in the shaping of post-Brexit fisheries. This trend is also true across the EU: stock assessments show that many stocks are in recovery, although not at a sufficient rate to meet the EU's deadline of ending overfishing by 2020 (STECF, 2016).

The employment situation in Scottish fisheries has also changed significantly over the previous decades. A substantial proportion of crew are foreign-born

(28 per cent), with crew from the Philippines making up the largest share of non-UK fishing crew (Marine Scotland Science, 2016a). What has not changed is the precarious nature of fisheries employment, with long trips at sea and wages often paid as a share of revenues or profits – by no means guaranteed.

Adding technological changes and the substitution of labour for capital to environmental limitations and the employment of foreign labour and a picture emerges of multiple, interwoven factors that have meant a sharp decline in Scottish fishers over the past decades, and a separation of fisheries from coastal communities in Scotland.

A sharing of waters, fish stocks, and management

Since the ascension of the UK to the EU in 1972, it is EU management that has been the focus of most of the attention regarding Scottish fisheries. At that time, countries around the world – starting in Peru, Chile and famously Iceland with the 'cod wars' – began to declare exclusive fishing zones around their coasts. The Member States of the EU followed suit, and while the waters of Member States stretched to only twelve nautical miles upon EU ascension, in 1972 a common area out to 200nm was available for fishing for all EU Member States.

The sharing of waters is a different question to the sharing of fish stocks. In 1983, with the passing of the EU's Common Fisheries Policy, EU Member States agreed to jointly set total allowable catches (TACS) to limit the amount of fishing, while also distributing these fishing quotas between Member States in fixed shares. It took six years to negotiate these shares that are based largely on historic fishing patterns (termed 'relative stability'). These shares continue today, where ministers of EU Member States meet to negotiate an overall catch limit for each fish stock (sometimes in coordination with third countries like Norway, Iceland and the Faroe Islands) and then quotas are split between Member States based on relative stability.

Shared waters and shared catch opportunities have inevitably given way to shared management of fisheries. Shared management involves technical measures such as the size of mesh for certain gear types, to far-reaching policies like the recent discard ban ('landing obligation') to end the practice of discarding (throwing fish overboard) due to low commercial value or catches above quota allowances.

What motivates support for Brexit from Scottish fishers?

Much of the fishing industry is opposed to EU management and supported the Brexit campaign. A survey of fishers in the lead-up to the referendum by researchers at the University of Aberdeen found that 92 per cent of fishers planned to vote to leave (McAngus, 2016). Fish processors and retailers, however, were not so keen. There is little relation between the fish consumed in the UK and fish caught locally as 80 per cent of UK catches are exported and 70 per cent of fish for UK consumption is imported (Marine Management Organisation, 2016).

Many fishers became active spokespeople for Brexit and were particularly notable in Scotland, due to the contrast with the majority of groups and industries that backed the campaign to remain a member of the EU. The reasons for fishers taking up this position are varied but can roughly be characterised by a sense of unfairness (with access to waters and how quotas are divided) and a view that decisions about fisheries are being made remotely without the interests of Scottish fishers at heart. More broadly, there is also a sense that fisheries have been in decline over the period of EU management, a trend most visually obvious by the declining number of people and fishing vessels in harbours, and that fisheries are a forgotten industry.

The Aberdeen University survey reflected these sentiments, as not only did 92 per cent of fishers indicate that they would vote to leave, but 93 per cent indicated that they thought that leaving the EU would improve the industry's fortunes (McAngus 2016). On fishing quotas, 77 per cent of respondents thought that the amount of fish they would be allowed to catch would increase outside of the EU (only 1 per cent thought they would decrease). On the issue of fisheries trade, only 6 per cent of fishers thought leaving the EU would harm future prospects (77 per cent – no impact and 17 per cent – increase).

What does the future hold?

These survey results point to optimistic attitudes but a potentially troubling future for Brexit and Scottish fisheries. While negotiations will determine the extent of changes regarding shared waters, shared quotas and shared management, there are a number of issues that are not likely to change as a result of Brexit alone.

The first truism in fisheries is that there are only so many fish in the sea, and only so many that can be harvested sustainably. The UK taking a greater share of fish quotas by definition means that the rest of the EU must take less – something easier said than done. The great worry here is failure to agree on quota shares could lead to overfishing as both sides aim to increase their catch. This continues to be the case with many tumultuous fishing relationships involving non-EU countries like Iceland, the Faroe Islands and Norway (Carpenter, 2016a).

There is also the important issue of trade-offs in negotiations with the EU, between different sectors, but also within fisheries itself. This point was made clearly in the House of Lords report on Brexit and fisheries where it was emphasised that there would likely be a trade-off between access to waters and access to markets, as was the case when Greenland left the EU, and continues to shape the EU's current relationship with Norwegian fisheries (House of Lords European Union Committee 2016). This likely trade-off also presents a worrying conflict with the expectation of more quota but no impact on trade, as revealed in the University of Aberdeen survey (McAngus, 2016).

Many of the economic trends are driving Scottish fisheries towards a concentrated high-capital, low-labour fleet, which will remain post-Brexit, just as fishing industries outside of the EU and other industries within the UK have experienced (Carpenter, 2016b). That is not to say, however, that this restructuring is inevitable. Innovative policy approaches, such as allocating quota to the fishing fleet based on social and environmental criteria so as to incentivise the creation of wider public benefits, have not been fully pursued in the UK or abroad.

It is also worth noting that several criticised aspects of fisheries management are already national competencies, such as how quotas are distributed by Member States within their fleet. News reports about Dutch and Spanish vessels hoovering up UK quota are actually describing UK-flagged vessels that were sold to foreign owners under the rules of the UK's own system for allocating quota. It is a source of significant confusion, but issues of foreign ownership are a result of national management, as are complaints about the continued concentration of UK quota through market transactions.

This track record of national management, combined with the fact that already 56 per cent of fishers in the University of Aberdeen survey responded that they do not think their voice counts in the UK (McAngus, 2016), points to similarly troubled waters for the industry under national management for existing and new competencies. Ultimately, whether Brexit delivers for Scottish fishers will depend in large part on the issue of how fisheries management is shared. This is true in the international sense, that progress in managing fish stocks sustainably requires shared management that prevents individual countries from charting their own course and overexploiting the resource. This is also true in a more localised sense, as at every level of management, fishers feel distant and like their voice doesn't matter. Regardless of the level of management post-Brexit, a radical rethink in participatory approaches and co-management is needed to create a system of fisheries management that is truly shared.

References

Carpenter, G. (2016a), 'The EU Common Fisheries Policy has helped, not harmed, UK fisheries' Opendemocracy, 12 January.
https://www.opendemocracy.net/can-europe-make-it/griffin-carpenter/eu-common-fisheries-policy-has-helped-not-harmed-uk-fisheries-0

Carpenter, G. (2016b), *Where did all the fishers go?*, cfooduw.

House of Lords European Union Committee (2016), *Brexit: fisheries: 8th Report of Session 2016-17*, Authority of the House of Lords, London.

Marine Management Organisation (MMO) (2016), UK *Sea Fisheries Statistics 2015*, Marine Management Organisation, London.

Marine Scotland (2016), *Scottish Sea Fisheries Statistics 2015*, The Scottish Government, Edinburgh.

Marine Scotland Science (2016a), *Scottish Sea Fisheries Employment 2015*, Marine Scotland, Edinburgh.

Marine Scotland Science (2016b), *Fish and Shellfish Stocks: 2016 Edition*, Marine Scotland, Edinburgh.

McAngus, C. (2016), *Report on initial analysis of a survey of UK fishermen ahead of the referendum on the UK's membership of the EU*, University of Aberdeen, Aberdeen.

Scientific, Technical and Economic Committee for Fisheries (STECF) (2016), *Monitoring the performance of the Common Fisheries Policy (STECF-16-05)*, Publications Office of the European Union, Luxembourg.

CHAPTER NINE

Farming, Scotland and Brexit

Pete Ritchie

The truth of the matter is that if we left the EU there would be an £18bn a year dividend, so could we find the money to spend £2bn a year on farming and the environment? Of course we could. Would we? Without a shadow of a doubt. George Eustice, *Speech to National Farmers Union conference,* 23 February 2016.

If subsidies equal direct payments, of course we want to move away from that. George Eustice, *Farming Online,* January 2017.

MORE THAN HALF of farmers in Scotland voted for Brexit. What were they thinking? Cash subsidies from the Common Agricultural Policy equate to around 65 per cent of net farm income in Scotland (and the wider UK). Livestock farming (which is over-represented in Scotland because of geography and climate) is particularly dependent on direct payments for its viability.

In 2014, 20 per cent of farms in Scotland made a loss after subsidy, and a further 27 per cent didn't make enough money to pay the farmer an agricultural minimum wage. So most farmers weren't voting against EU farm subsidies, but against European 'red tape'. They wanted the future to be much like the past, same money but with less paperwork. That's not going to happen. What is?

There's certainly a current of autarky within the broad Brexit church – 'British food for British people' – but since the vote, the 'free trade' ideology has become increasingly dominant. For agriculture, this is a replay of the 'repeal of the corn laws' debate from the 1840s, where removing tariffs on imports was promoted ostensibly to reduce the price of bread for working people. (UKIP originated in part from the 'Anti-Federalist League' of the 1990s, a conscious nod to the Anti-Corn Law League.)

Just as the Corn Laws had their origin in the Napoleonic war, the Common Agricultural Policy (CAP) was a response to wartime food shortages, increasing domestic production through subsidies and tariffs. The policy has broadly served farmers well, slowing down the process of consolidation of small farms and transferring income from urban to rural areas. It also has multiple perverse impacts, not least encouraging high levels of livestock production to consume high levels of grain production, with all the associated negative externalities. Reform has been painfully slow.

Much of the subsidy washes through into artificially high land prices and rents, particularly benefiting (like the Corn Laws) large landowners in the UK (which unlike Napoleonic Europe never undertook land reform).

So how will Brexit affect food prices and farm viability in Scotland and the UK – and, as importantly, how might the political debate about food and farming play out in a much more fragile UK than under Robert Peel?

Although the CAP still represents almost 40 per cent of EU spending, agriculture will be an economic sideshow in the forthcoming UK-EU divorce proceedings. S. van Berkum et al (2016) model a range of trade scenarios, mostly showing a small increase in consumer prices due to increased cost of trade and a loss of access by the UK to tariff-free imports from some third countries.

For most commodities, these price movements are considerably smaller than the impact of sterling's decline since the Brexit vote (which has already helped farm incomes bounce back slightly after a three-year decline, and will lead to food price rises). However, it is also possible that the UK – whether as a negotiating tactic or simply as an ideological 'free to trade globally' imperative – will move towards further trade liberalisation, cutting external tariffs and encouraging imports of commodities from countries outside the EU.

This would lead to sharp falls in domestic prices for beef, lamb, pigs and poultry – and would have knock-on effects on cereal prices as domestic demand for livestock feed contracts. The option of selling more into the EU would no longer be there, as tariff quotas would put a ceiling on UK exports. At the same time, the UK government's longstanding objection to direct subsidies would mean a further reduction in farm incomes, and make many, if not most, livestock farms non-viable.

So how does this play in Scotland? Agriculture has been largely devolved, with Scotland able to tweak local application of the CAP: but the unitary UK mood music and the need for a 'single market' in the UK will now both push towards powers moving towards Westminster rather than Holyrood.

While in practice, UK food and farming regulation will shadow Europe to maintain trade, the UK's fondness for GM along with the likely focus on marketing 'British' rather than 'Scottish' food would increase policy tensions. Apportioning the UK's net contribution to the EU budget of around £20bn to the CAP suggests almost £8bn going to support agriculture while only around

4.1bn is spent on agriculture and agri-environment in the UK. Arguably, under a devolved regime, Scotland's share of this £7.9bn contribution (about £670m) would be repatriated, allowing Scottish government to maintain the current level of spending, both on direct farm payments and on environmental schemes. However, this 'Brexit bonus' has been spent many times over and in practice, whether devolved or not, the budget for farm support is likely to reduce in the face of continuing austerity and competing demands.

In any case, reform of farm support in Scotland is long overdue, and an agricultural policy which aligns farm support much more clearly with progressive policies on land reform, climate change, biodiversity and public health would see a marked shift in the 'social contract' between farmers and the public. There is surprisingly little overlap between what we grow in Scotland and what we eat, and considerable scope for shifting to more sustainable production and consumption patterns, with shorter food chains and a reduction in processing intensity.

However, Brexit is about perceptions, not reality and as IndyRef 2 unfolds, narrative matters more than nitty-gritty. On one side, the nasty neoliberals importing hormone-fed beef while destroying our hard-working family farms, with the spectre of tumbleweed in Tighnabruaich. On the other side, a Scottish government with a progressive food policy, supporting farmers to produce sustainable healthy food for all, along with environmental stewardship.

In a tight referendum, the rural areas that voted No last time are a key battleground. The promise of cheap food is less attractive than it was in 1846, but the food and farming vote could yet bring down a government.

References

S. van Berkum, R.A. Jongeneel, H.C.J. Vrolijk, M.G.A. van Leeuwen and J.H. Jager (2016), *Implications of a UK exit from the EU for British agriculture*, LEI Wageningen.

CHAPTER TEN

The importance of Scotch whisky

Richard Marsh

Industry background

THE SCOTCH WHISKY industry is an iconic part of Scotland's economy as much as ship building or banking. At the start of the twentieth century there were 159 active distilleries across Scotland (Craig, 1994). The 1960s and 1970s represented a golden age for the Scotch whisky industry. By the late 1970s the industry accounted for just over 20,000 jobs across Scotland supporting nearly 100,000 jobs in total through its supply chains across Scotland (4-consulting, 2012). The 1980s saw a dramatic reversal of fortunes for industry. Some of the difficulties were compounded by overproduction in the previous decade. The last decade has seen significant inward investment into the Scotch whisky industry with high value brands performing particularly well. Last year exports of single malt whisky passed £1 billion for the first time (Fraser, 2017).

Economic impact

Today, the latest estimates suggest the Scotch whisky industry directly contributes over £3.2 billion in Gross Value Added (GVA) to the Scottish economy (Scotch Whisky Association, 2017a). In 2015 there were 115 distilleries licensed to produce Scotch whisky (Scotch Whisky Association, 2015)

The operating expenditure of Scotch whisky producers is mainly spent on Scottish suppliers (81 per cent) including cereals, water, packaging and energy (4-consulting, 2015). The deeply embedded supply chains raise the overall impact on the Scottish economy to £4.7 billion GVA with the Scotch whisky industry supporting a total of 37,000 jobs across Scotland.

Scotch whisky exports stood at £3.9 billion in 2016 and made the largest contribution to the UK's net balance of trade of any commodity across the UK (Scotch Whisky Association, 2017a). This mainly because most Scotch whisky is exported outside of the UK and ingredients and supplies to produce Scotch whisky are sourced from within Scotland. The industry plays an important role in rural communities across Scotland supporting around 7,000 jobs (Scotch Whisky Association, 2017a). Additionally, Scotch whisky industry jobs tend to be reasonably well paid (4-consulting, 2015).

Tourism

Scotch whisky distilleries attracted around 1.5 million visitors during 2015 (Scotch Whisky Association, 2015), with clusters of tourism and culture-related activities linked to distilleries across Scotland (4-consulting, 2011). The distillery effect was found to support jobs in accommodation, recreational and cultural industries.

China represents one of the fastest growing tourist markets for Scotland. Scotch whisky was the Scottish product most commonly cited among potential Chinese tourists (Scottish Government, 2007a). Whisky was more likely to be cited among those with university education and those with higher incomes.

When the number of tourists to Scotland increases from different countries, there is a corresponding rise in the average price of a bottle of whisky exported back to those countries. The average price of a bottle of Scotch whisky exported abroad has risen more quickly among countries where tourism to Scotland has also risen more quickly (4-consulting, 2011). The tourist who visits Speyside to watch the wildlife and visit a distillery may take a bottle home. Having a reminder of Scotland on the shelf may encourage them, or friends and family, to return or visit Scotland in future years.

The implications of leaving the EU for scotch whisky

Exports

The European Union (EU) represents the Scotch whisky industry's biggest export market with £1.2 billion sold to member states during 2015 (Scotch Whisky Association, 2017b). This compares to over £900 million to North America and just under £800 million to Asia.

The Scotch Whisky Association (2017c) has suggested that Scotch whisky should benefit from zero tariffs to the EU and US under World Trade Organisation (WTO) rules. But there is some concern if the UK ends up outside the EU's network of bilateral trade deals, with a risk of losing lower tariffs and market share. It will be important to establish trade agreements with countries like India, China and Brazil.

Legal protection of Scotch Whisky

The Scotch whisky industry has invested considerable resources to ensure legal recognition as a product that must be produced in Scotland according to traditional methods. If the UK leaves the protected EU Geographical Indication (GI) scheme, the Scotch whisky industry will have lost an important tool to prevent imitation products.

The Scotch Whisky Association (2017c) has recommended the development of a UK GI register and has also suggested there should be reciprocal recognition between the UK and EU GI schemes.

Inward investment

Some of Scotland's largest companies are EU-owned Scotch whisky producers, including Chivas Brothers, (Business Insider, 2017); arguably it is inward investment and the development of international networks that have helped performance in recent years. The Scotch Whisky Association has called for 'business certainty and consistency' by moving relevant EU single market legislation into UK law (Scotch Whisky Association, 2017c).

EU workers account for around one in every eight pounds (11.9 per cent) paid in wages in Scotland's manufacturing industry. The Scotch whisky industry has seen significant capital investment in recent years and the reopening of previously mothballed distilleries. If the industry's ability to attract skilled workers were restricted this would be likely to have an impact on future growth.

References

4-consulting (2011), *Scotch Whisky and Tourism*, Scotch Whisky Association.
4-consulting (2012), *Scotch Whisky & Scotland's Economy a 100-Year-Old Blend*, Scotch Whisky Association.

4-consulting (2014), *The Economic Impact of Scotch Whisky Production in the UK*, Scotch Whisky Association.

4-consulting (2016), *Economic Impact of Leaving the European Union*, 4-consulting.

Business Insider (2017), Vol. 34 No. 1, Jan/Feb Issue.

Craig, H.C. (1994), *The Scotch Whisky Industry Record*, Index Publishing.

Fraser, D. (2017), 'Single malt Scotch whisky exports top £1bn for first time', BBC *Scotland News*, 20 February.

Scotch Whisky Association (2015), *Facts and Figures May 2015*.

Scotch Whisky Association (2015), *Scotch Whisky distilleries attract around 1.5 million visitors*.

Scotch Whisky Association (2017a), *The Economic Impact of Scotch Whisky Production in the UK*.

Scotch Whisky Association (2017b), *Scotch Whisky Statistical Report 2015*.

Scotch Whisky Association (2017c), *Scotch Whisky and Brexit*.

Scottish Government (2007), *Scotland's International Engagement and the China Strategy*.

CHAPTER ELEVEN

Scotland's higher education

Andrea M. Nolan

SCOTLAND'S HIGHER EDUCATION system is a precious national asset. Five of our universities are ranked in the top one per cent in the world, with another seven in the top five per cent (*Times Higher Education*, 2016). Our reputation for research and teaching attracts students and academics to Scotland. Mobility of students, staff and alumni to and from Scotland builds a network of ambassadors and friends, strengthening Scotland's international reputation, relations and trade. The sector contributes £11bn gross value added to the Scottish economy, supports 38,000 jobs directly and another 142,000 indirectly (Universities Scotland, 2016). Our institutions work with thousands of organisations in Scotland to support innovation in the economy and the development of new products and processes (Higher Education Statistics Agency, 2016). They play a vital role in the development of individuals, communities and the nation's cultural life.

Scottish higher education has become closely integrated into European Union structures over a long period. In 2014/15 institutions received £94 million of research funding from European Commission programmes, EU charities and businesses (Higher Education Statistics Agency, 2016). They have also been successful in securing European Regional Development Funds and European Social Funds. This funding and freedom of movement rights within the EU have greatly helped institutions to participate in, and lead, international collaborations in research and teaching. Students and staff coming from EU countries to Scotland have enriched our academic life and the diversity of our institutions, and the Erasmus programme has provided opportunities for many Scottish students and staff to study and gain experience in Europe.

Deep integration and engagement across the EU, supported by EU institutions but driven by the essentially international and collaborative outlook of HE, means that Brexit and questions over future engagement, collaboration and funding have unavoidably been disruptive to the sector as it has to plan for new, as yet unknown scenarios. In time, the disruption will settle, but how will the sector change to succeed in the post-Brexit world?

The question will be answered incrementally over a period of many years. Much is not yet knowable about the future of the relationship between the UK and the EU, nor of Scotland's position in relation to it. At the time of publication, we have a sense of the dimensions of the uncertainty and of higher education's own role in charting a way through it.

There are over 13,000 undergraduate students (Full Person Equivalent) studying in Scotland (Higher Education Statistics Agency, 2016). The status of these students for fees and funding has been guaranteed for the duration of their studies by the Scottish government. Their future immigration status, should their intended study run beyond the date of the UK's departure from the EU, is not determined. Prospective students from the EU considering study in Scotland from 2018 onwards have no certainty about either aspect of their future status should they make that choice. In January 2017, UCAS reported initial evidence of a decline in undergraduate applications from EU countries (Universities and Colleges Admissions Service, 2017).

The attractiveness of Scotland as a study destination for EU students will be affected by decisions to be made by the UK and Scottish governments on post-Brexit domestic policy on immigration and student fee regulation respectively. It will also depend on institutions' own ability to promote study in Scotland in the post-Brexit environment. The outcome will have consequences. Beside the cultural and economic contribution that EU students make directly, they are also more likely to be studying certain subjects, particularly science, technology, engineering and maths – areas where Scotland currently faces shortages of graduates and where EU graduates exercising their current free movement rights are able to make an important contribution to Scotland's skills needs. Changing demand as a result of Brexit has potential to change the shape and volume of the provision institutions can offer in the longer-term and the skills provision for the future.

Seventeen per cent of Scotland's academic staff and 25 per cent of research staff are from the EU (Higher Education Statistics Agency, 2016). This represents an enormously important talent pool, which has faced personal uncertainty since the referendum in June 2016. The short-term risk this poses for Higher Education will be determined by whether the UK government is able to move reasonably quickly, either as part of the exit negotiations or unilaterally, to provide a framework of reassurance which will give individuals confidence as to their future status as residents in the UK and their entitlement to healthcare and schooling for their dependents. If this is not achieved, individual decision-making may see the talent pool in Scottish Higher Education eroded even before the UK has determined its future relationship with the EU.

Funding can arguably be replaced and it is within the capabilities of the UK and Scottish governments to continue to support research, and other activity which is currently supported by the EU, if they deem it to be of sufficient priority. Sustaining collaboration is a different matter and one where Scottish institutions themselves will have to work hard to maintain their profile, connections and reputation as the centre of gravity in EU academia inevitably moves following Brexit. These challenges will be less if the UK government is willing and able to negotiate continued participation in programmes such as Horizon 2020 and its successors, and Erasmus, as part of the UK's new relationship with the EU. The greatest challenge to achieving that may be where these considerations sit in the list of priorities to be resolved in a complex and time constrained negotiation.

In this and other matters our higher education system has understanding, insight and expertise to offer on the implications of the UK's departure from the European Union and an opportunity to offer answers, disseminate understanding and inform priorities, and it has a responsibility to do so. The consequences of the many choices and decisions to be made in the next two years will be with us for decades to come.

References

Higher Education Statistics Agency (2016), *Finance Record 2014/15*.

Higher Education Statistics Agency (2016), HE *Business and Community Interaction Survey 2014/15*.

Higher Education Statistics Agency (2016), *Staff Record 2014/15*.

Higher Education Statistics Agency (2016), *Student Record 2014/15*.

Universities and Colleges Admissions Service (2017), 'Applicants for UK higher education down: 5% for UK students and 7% for EU students'.

https://www.ucas.com/corporate/news-and-key-documents/news/applicants-uk-higher-education-down-5-uk-students-and-7-eu-students [accessed 28 February 2017]

Universities Scotland (2016), 'Ten Things to Know About Scottish Higher Education'.

http://www.universities-scotland.ac.uk/scotlands-universities/ [accessed 28 February 2017]

CHAPTER TWELVE

Financial Services

Owen Kelly

THE FINANCIAL SERVICES industry is diverse. But whatever it is doing, from providing car insurance to funding government debt, it intermediates between different interests. This makes it exceptionally pragmatic. Some parts of the industry make money out of instability but are small and specialised. It does not seek political controversy and it does not, as an industry, have a uniform view – it is rational, empiricist and, some might say, cold-blooded.

The industry has never been in favour of Brexit, although a relatively small number of voices have been raised in support. These have come mainly from the independent investment sector, rather than large corporations or companies with significant numbers of customers. This difference might be explained, depending on one's point of view, by corporate pusillanimity or by the prudence that comes with responsibility for large numbers of customers and employees; by the scope for independent investors to get richer from volatility, or by their buccaneering spirit. Whatever one's view, it is not contentious to characterise the industry as sceptical about Brexit and more inclined to see risks than opportunities.

Given this general caution, the statements of leading banks during the campaign, and since (Reuters, 2017), should receive careful attention. They are more likely to be understatements than exaggerations, and confirm that sizeable elements of international banking operations will move away from the UK.

These moves are at the hand of international banks, operating mainly out of the City of London. Financial services in Scotland are an integral part of the UK industry, complementing activities based elsewhere. Exchanges of various kinds are in London, making it one of the world's leading centres for financial trading, and Scottish-based investors are major participants. While few financial institutions are headquartered in Scotland, many international companies operate here, principally in Edinburgh, Glasgow, Dundee and Aberdeen. Scotland's financial services industry provides about a tenth of its total employment and about 7 per cent of Scotland's GDP.

Most of those working in Scotland's financial services industry are serving customers in the UK. There are successful investment managers and asset servicers (who price, administer and protect financial assets) in Scotland, with clients all around the world. But the largest employers are banks, insurance companies and pension providers, predominantly serving commercial and retail customers in the UK. That will continue after Brexit. Most customers for Scottish providers will continue to be in England, Wales and Northern Ireland. (This, incidentally, is one of the main reasons why independence for Scotland, outside the UK, is not an obviously attractive alternative to Brexit, for the industry as a whole.)

The UK will almost certainly cease to be part of the EU single market (HM Government, 2017). That market, for financial services, is not well developed. Some services, such as investment management, can be provided across borders and investment vehicles, like funds and trusts, can be sold throughout the EU. But retail services like bank accounts, insurance and pensions are provided within the regulatory and taxation jurisdiction of a member state. This means that the consequences for the UK as a whole are likely to be more significant than for Scotland, in proportionate terms, because Scotland's main market is the rest of the UK whereas the UK industry exports more to the EU, mainly from the City of London. These City exports include 'big ticket' items like capital markets and currency and bond trading.

It seems unlikely that new, unexplored, overseas markets for financial services will open up, even if the UK succeeds in securing new bilateral trade agreements quickly. This is partly because trade agreements generally do not encompass services and partly because markets for financial services are largely jurisdictionally determined, as noted above. Regulation and taxation shape the demand for services and, except in some quite specialised areas, they are not provided across jurisdictional boundaries. Two Scottish strengths, asset management and asset servicing, are exceptions to this general rule, although they do not employ, compared with sectors like banking and insurance, large numbers of people. They are the most exposed to Brexit-related risks, beyond the general risk of a faltering UK economy.

The UK's departure from the single market will add a further degree of complexity to the business of asset management and servicing but it should be manageable. It is possible to serve clients from another jurisdiction, with appropriate local regulatory compliance. The bigger risk comes from restrictions on the free movement of people, as countenanced by the UK government (HM Government, 2017).

These two sectors of the industry are the most international and the most dependent on agility in response to changing demand. The asset-servicing sector, which is predominantly operational in nature and dominated by large banks with multiple operating locations, is keenly responsive to changing client demands. Flexibility over staffing is therefore a competitive advantage and the UK is undermining its own, while adding to that of other locations that can maintain or even enhance it.

Asset management is at the cerebral end of financial services. It is dependent on attracting and sustaining concentrations of talent in places like, for example, the Edinburgh New Town. While the numbers of staff may be low in comparison with other sectors, their jobs are high-value and their decisions are influential on financial markets around the world. The reputation of Edinburgh as a financial centre rests heavily on its investors and asset managers.

Both of these cosmopolitan sectors of the investment industry are international in outlook and in operation. They are part of the very mechanism of globalisation. If, as some do, we interpret the vote for Brexit as a protest against that phenomenon, they might emerge as a part of the target that has, for better or worse, actually been hit.

References

Reuters (2017), 'Morgan Stanley, Citi plan Brexit job moves: sources'. http://www.reuters.com/article/us-britain-eu-banks-idUSKBN1542KZ
[Accessed 8 February 2017]
Her Majesty's Government (2017), *The United Kingdom's exit from and new partnership with the European Union*, Cmd. 9417.
https://www.gov.uk/government/uploads/system/uploads/attachment_data/
file/589191/The_United_Kingdoms_exit_from_and_partnership_with_the_
EU_Web.pdf (Accessed 7 February 2017)

CHAPTER THIRTEEN

Brexit, Scotland and tourism

Kevin Hannam

SINCE THE FALL of the Berlin Wall, the integration of former socialist countries into the EU, as well as wider economic processes of globalisation, has made borders more porous allowing people and goods to move more freely, developing what the sociologist Bauman (2000) termed 'liquid modernity'. The theoretical concept of mobilities has been developed to make sense of the increased and uneven geopolitical and everyday mobilities and immobilities of people and things under processes of neoliberal globalisation (Hannam, Sheller and Urry, 2006). Following Brexit, and the election of President Trump in the USA, is arguably a new geopolitical world order of re-bordering where the movement of people and things will be subject to new controls, making travel more difficult. These events will undoubtedly affect 'tourism mobilities' – the integration of tourism with other practices of mobility such as migration and its infrastructures (Sheller and Urry, 2004; Rickly, Hannam and Mostafanezhad, 2016).

The popular vote in favour of Brexit in the UK (although not in Scotland specifically) has been seen to be a reflection of UK residents or hosts (as tourism researchers would term them) being worried about immigration, particularly the wrong types of immigrants. Much of this sentiment was supported by media emphasis on the economic impact of potential migrants who might become a burden on UK taxpayers (Vollmer, 2016). In Scotland, however, the popular vote was to remain part of the EU, perhaps reflecting the lower levels of net migration. In 2011, an estimated 14,000 EU citizens, or 37 per cent of total inflow, entered Scotland as migrants. In the same year, citizens from non-EU countries (Commonwealth and other countries) represented 47 per cent of international immigrants to Scotland, while 16 per cent were British citizens (Allen, 2013).

This situation had given rise to a somewhat difficult and challenging political scenario for the UK and Scottish governments respectively, and increased

uncertainties. Whilst the aim of Brexit may be to regulate the freedom of movement of those that wish to migrate in search of a better or even different life-
style, these regulations will also have consequences for those that wish to move
for tourism and cross-border leisure. While the weakening of the British currency is an incentive for overseas visitors to visit the UK as costs of travelling and
shopping become cheaper, this may only be in the short-term unless a robust
tourism plan is put in place.

From a demand-side perspective, tourism as a social and cultural practice
relies upon the idea that people have the freedom to move. A passport literally
signifies the ability to move across national boundaries unhindered, but with
Brexit this ability will lead to new real and perceived frictions of travel where
border crossings are slowed and the movement of people and things for tourism and leisure become more regulated and subject to surveillance and sorting
(Adey, 2002). It has been recognised that the 'freedom' to travel already involves
many obligations or 'unfreedoms' (Freudendal-Pedersen, 2009) such as getting
to the airport in time, queuing, and so on and these will undoubtedly increase
as passengers are subjected to more 'checks' by those in control. Such 'incon-
veniences' may be magnified by social media and negatively impacting tourist
arrivals. Scottish (and all British) travellers are unlikely to enjoy the same type
of benefits they previously enjoyed from existing bilateral agreements related to
travel across countries in the EU (Lim, 2017). With a significant number of age-
ing Scottish migrants resident abroad in the EU, this could become a long-term
and significant issue as many rely on reciprocal health agreements.

From a supply-side perspective there is a recognised global 'war for talent'
of skilled workers (and volunteers, interns and students) in knowledge-based
economies that processes of re-bordering will directly impact. It has been recognised that migration has had a positive impact on the recruitment of skilled
and unskilled workers into the tourism and hospitality industries (Janta and
Ladkin, 2013). Furthermore, migration has been noted as having a key role to
play in meeting the Scottish government's economic strategy as Scottish employers value migrants and international students (Rolfe and Metcalf, 2009).

If we examine urban and rural differences, cities which have their own economic hinterlands, such as the global centres of London, Paris, New York and
so on, will remain globally self-sustaining in terms of tourism. However, the
social and economic consequences of Brexit will be more severe for those urban
areas on the global periphery. The affects will also be uneven between, and
within, urban areas and between urban and rural areas.

Data of migration to Edinburgh, a city which relies on events, tourism
and hospitality as its economic cornerstone, reveals that Edinburgh has more

registered workers from Spain than from Poland (Edinburgh City Council, 2016). As a consequence, the cosmopolitan culture of the city may be negatively affected by regulations and limits placed on tourism, hospitality and events workers, as well as students who fill many of these seasonal and part-time occupations. Furthermore, the related impact on international student recruitment to Scottish universities also needs to be taken into account in any impact analysis of tourism mobilities.

Scotland's rural tourism economy will also feel the pressure from reduced EU investment in tourism and leisure based industries in the future. However, the weakening of the British currency as a result of Brexit has increased the cost of travelling overseas for British citizens and may lead to more 'staycations' as a result (as happened during the previous economic recession) thus boosting the Scottish rural tourism sector in the short-term at least.

The shock of the event of Brexit can be described as more than the sum of its parts, leading to greater uncertainties and processes of re-bordering. The effects will undoubtedly be geographically and socially uneven across Scotland. A detailed evidence base needs to be further developed to ascertain both the overall and the specific impacts on particular sectors of the Scottish tourism economy, from tourism demand as well as tourism supply perspectives, so that a long-term plan can be put in place.

References

Adey, P. (2002), Secured and Sorted Mobilities: Examples from the Airport, *Surveillance and Society*, 1(4): 500-519.

Allen, W. (2013), *Long-Term International Migration Flows to and from Scotland*, Oxford: The Migration Observatory.

Bauman, Z. (2000), *Liquid Modernity*, Cambridge: Polity.

Edinburgh City Council (2016), *Edinburgh by Numbers*, Edinburgh: Edinburgh City Council.

Freudendal-Pedersen, M. (2009), *Mobility in Daily Life*, Aldershot: Ashgate.

Hannam, K., Sheller, M., and Urry, J. (2006), 'Editorial: Mobilities, immobilities and moorings', *Mobilities*, 1 (1), pp. 1-32.

Janta, H. and Ladkin, A. (2013), 'In search of employment: online technologies and Polish migrants', *New Technology, Work and Employment*, 28(3), 241-253.

Lim, W. L. (2017), 'Exiting supranational unions and the corresponding impact on tourism: Some insights from a rejoinder to Brexit,' *Current Issues in Tourism*, DOI: 10.1080/13683500.2016.1272555

Rickly, J., Hannam, K. and Mostafanezhad, M. (eds) (2016), *Tourism and Leisure Mobilities: Politics, Work and Play*, London: Routledge.

Rolfe, H. and Metcalf, H. (2009), *Recent Migration into Scotland: the Evidence Base*, Edinburgh: Scottish Government Social Research.

Vollmer, B. (2017), 'Security or insecurity? Representations of the UK border in public and policy discourses', *Mobilities*.
http://dx.doi.org/10.1080/17450101.2017.1278970

Sheller, M. and Urry, J. (eds) (2004), *Tourism Mobilities*, London: Routledge.

CHAPTER FOURTEEN

How might Brexit impact the UK energy industry?

Grant Allan and David Comerford

THE IMPLICATION OF Brexit for Britain's energy future was not an important point of contention during the referendum debate. 'Environmental' issues were only identified as important in influencing their vote for 1 per cent of individuals surveyed before the referendum vote (Ipsos Mori, 2016). Since the vote to leave, environmental and energy issues have remained outside the central focus of the debate.

That being said, Brexit has the potential to have profound effects on both environmental and energy policy in the UK in the months and years ahead. As the debate moves on from the merits or demerits of the referendum outcome to the actual practicalities of the terms of the UK's exit and our future economic relationship with the EU, such issues are likely to gain significant attention.

Allan (2016) says that 'critical to avoiding a more negative outcome [from Brexit] will be ensuring access to the internal energy market and the benefits of access and market integration that will help drive Scotland and the UK towards its long-term environmental ambitions'. Here we outline developments since July 2016, and focus on items raised in February 2017's Brexit White Paper (UK Government, 2017). We can group these under two headings. Firstly, the UK government's vision of the energy and environmental policy trajectory; and secondly, its vision of future participation in an integrated European energy market.

Future energy policy

The Brexit White Paper makes clear the UK government's commitment to the 2008 Climate Change Act. New nuclear power, further decarbonisation of electricity through renewables and electricity storage, and electrification are all necessary to meet environmental obligations committed, and considerable investment will be required. (The UK Government made the decision to proceed with Hinkley Point C since June's vote, and it was formally awarded a Contract for Difference in September 2016.)

New generation capacity will continue to be built and the overall carbon consequences will depend on the technological mix. Investment decisions in the energy sector (worth a total of £100 billion over 15 years (HM Treasury, 2016) will be taken in the next five years and will determine the profile of that generation fleet. November's Autumn Statement saw no increase to the Contracts for Difference lifetimes, a consultation on the Levy Control Framework, and the confirmation of Carbon Price Support to 2020/21. With these 'steady as she goes' actions in the last few months, it is clear that the detail of the UK's exit from the EU will be important for the UK energy industry, and is likely to have long-lasting consequences on the UK's energy future.

Integration with the EU's energy market

The detail of the UK's energy exit from the EU will determine how the UK energy system links into the wider European energy landscape. These links are both physical and regulatory. Exiting membership of the various regulatory bodies that govern the EU's internal energy market (IEM) is almost certain to remove any direct input for the UK in their governance and objectives. Being outside the IEM and its regulatory frameworks may then dilute the ability of the UK to finance and facilitate the development of the future physical infrastructure and networks that may underpin energy security.

A good example of the regulatory links that the UK currently has with the EU is its membership of the Euratom organisation. The White Paper makes an explicit reference to the UK leaving Euratom, as this organisation uses the EU institutions of the European Commission, Council of Ministers and the European Court of Justice. There are two key implications of the UK leaving Euratom. First, there is the need to replace and fund the inspection duties on existing nuclear generation and waste facilities. For instance, Froggatt (2017) writes that a quarter of time spent on nuclear inspections in the EU occurs within the UK. Second, there is the potential impact on significant existing nuclear R&D activities in the UK funded by EU programmes. The UK Nuclear Industry Association has raised further concerns about ensuring transitional arrangements with EU member states and third countries (NIA, 2017).

Another EU institution that the UK is currently party to, and which forms a key part of meeting its environmental goals, is the EU's Emissions Trading

Scheme (EU ETS) (Committee on Climate Change, 2016). The EU ETS is a 'cap and trade' scheme which covers emissions from electricity generation and heavy industry, and which has the potential to be a least-cost approach, as firms with the lowest cost of carbon emissions reductions can make these changes, trading permits with firms who face higher costs of carbon emissions reductions. The quantity of permits in existence is reduced over time so that total emissions fall. The non-EU EEA countries are members of EU ETS, so perhaps the UK will not leave this organisation upon Brexit. If it were to leave EU ETS, then the UK could of course set up its own emissions trading scheme, but its reduced geographical scope would limit the universe of possibilities for low cost emissions reductions to be made by trading with players who face higher cost reductions. Additionally, setting up its own scheme will entail setup, administration and regulatory costs. On the other hand, the EU ETS has been subject to criticism, especially for over-allocation of permits and consequent low prices (which provide minimal incentives for emissions reductions), and an alternative UK scheme could learn from the mistakes of the EU ETS.

The White Paper notes that the UK benefits through lower prices and improved security of supply from 'coordinated energy trading arrangements' with EU member states through its current membership of the IEM. These arrangements consist of, for example, arbitrage opportunities for trading, a larger grid to support the balance of power flows, and the opening and extending of liberalised energy markets. A report for National Grid calculated that exclusion from the IEM could cost consumers up to £500 million per year (Vivid Economics, 2016).

Recent figures show that net imports equate 40 per cent of the UK's energy supply, making it the twelfth most import-dependent of the 28 EU member states (Eurostat, 2016), so physical connection to the IEM is vital for the UK energy needs and security of supply. Although currently a net importer of electricity through the existing interconnectors, the UK also has some of the best resources in Europe for variable renewables capacity. The viability of projects to develop these resources is enhanced the more the UK is able to export surplus electricity in periods of high generation. The EU's IEM is a basis for such an export market, and the EU is actively helping in the creation of the trans-continental infrastructure required (see e.g. BBC, 2017). The White Paper does state that the UK government 'is considering all the options for the UK's future relationship with the EU on energy' (UK Government, 2017, p. 43), but fundamentally, the economic benefits from interconnection between the

UK and the EU may be weaker when there is uncertainty about the ability of generators and consumers on each side to trade via such links.

In summary, whilst energy has yet to feature heavily in the Brexit debate thus far, the implications for investment, energy security and the future challenges and opportunities in operating outside existing EU regulatory structures mean that it is only a matter of time before some big decisions – with significant consequences – are likely to be required.

References

Allan, G.J. (2016), 'How might Brexit affect the supply of energy in Scotland?', 5 July 2016.
https://fraserofallander.org/2016/07/05/
how-might-brexit-affect-the-supply-of-energy-in-scotland/
BBC (2017, 'EU funding boost for Scotland-Norway power cable', 24 February 2017.
http://www.bbc.co.uk/news/uk-scotland-scotland-business-39080305
Committee on Climate Change (2016), 'Meeting Carbon Budgets – Implications of Brexit for UK climate policy'.
https://www.theccc.org.uk/wp-content/uploads/2016/10/Meeting-Carbon-Budgets-Implications-of-Brexit-for-UK-climate-policy-Committee-on-Climate-Change-October-2016.pdf
Eurostat (2016), 'Energy dependence'.
http://ec.europa.eu/eurostat/tgm/table.
do?tab=table&plugin=1&language=en&pcode=tsdcc310
Froggatt, A. (2017), 'Brexatom: the UK will now leave Europe's nuclear energy authority', article on *The Conversation* website, 30 January 2017.
https://theconversation.com/
brexatom-the-uk-will-now-leave-europes-nuclear-energy-authority-72136
HM Treasury (2016), '*Autumn Statement 2016*', published 23 November 2016.
https://www.gov.uk/government/publications/autumn-statement-2016-documents/autumn-statement-2016
Ipsos Mori (2016), *Ipsos MORI Political Monitor – June 2016*.
Nuclear Energy Association (2017), 'NIA comment on EU withdrawal bill', press release issued 1 February 2017.
https://www.niauk.org/media-centre/press-releases/nia-comment-eu-withdrawal-bill/
UK Government (2017), *The United Kingdom's exit from and new partnership with the European Union.*

https://www.gov.uk/government/uploads/system/uploads/attachment_data/
file/589191/The_United_Kingdoms_exit_from_and_partnership_with_the_
EU_Web.pdf
Vivid Economics (2016), 'The impact of Brexit on the UK energy sector: An
assessment of the risks and opportunities for electricity and gas in the UK',
29 March 2016.
http://www.vivideconomics.com/wp-content/uploads/2016/03/VE-note-on-im-
pact-of-Brexit-on-the-UK-energy-system.pdf

CHAPTER FIFTEEN

Brexit and the Scottish digital technologies industry

Svea Miesch

SCOTLAND IS HOME to a vibrant digital technologies industry with companies engaged in a variety of activities from software development and IT services to digital agencies, games development and telecommunications. This includes well-known businesses like Skyscanner and Rockstar North and offices of multinationals such as Microsoft, Amazon and Oracle, but the majority are small and medium sized companies and start-ups. Together they contribute more than £4.5 billion GVA to the Scottish economy (Mackay 2016). This is likely to increase as, according to KPMG's Tech Monitor, the number of tech sector enterprises in Scotland grew by 43.3 per cent between 2010 and 2015, second only to London (54.6 per cent) (KPMG, 2015: 22).

The pervasive nature of digital means that wider Scottish business is increasingly adopting digital technologies to deliver new products and services, drive productivity and open up fresh markets. More than 83,000 people work in digital technologies roles across the Scottish economy (Mackay, 2016). Digital technology occupations offer above average salaries with a median gross annual full-time pay of £39,810 in 2015, compared to £27,710 across all occupations in Scotland (ScotlandIS, 2016: 4). A wealth of career opportunities are available – with 11,000 vacancies arising every year (Skills Development Scotland, 2014: 5).

The digital technologies industry is of growing strategic importance to the future growth of the Scottish economy. A 2015 study by Deloitte, commissioned by the Scottish Futures Trust, concludes that if the optimum scenario of enhanced digitalisation were to be realised, Scotland could increase GDP by £13 billion by 2030, including over £2 billion in additional export income, an increase of almost 10 per cent from 2014. This would generate 120,000 new jobs across the economy (Deloitte, 2015: 31-35).

These contributions to the Scottish economy and growth scenarios risk being damaged by the outcome of the EU referendum in June 2016 and the political and economic changes this decision entails. The main challenges for Scotland's digital technologies industry related to Brexit are around access to skilled staff, market access, research and collaboration with universities and regulations. However, Brexit could also offer some opportunities for the sector and the wider economy with regards to productivity and skills development.

Access to skilled staff

In recent years, Scotland has been impacted by the well-documented digital skills shortage experienced across the wider UK, Europe and the US. Firms struggled to recruit the staff needed to build and deliver their products and services, with software development skills being in particularly high demand. Talent from other EU countries is a valuable asset to many digital technology businesses across the UK and helps to alleviate this skills shortage.

Many businesses are now concerned about the retention of their existing staff and their ability to recruit in the future. Three quarters of respondents to a ScotlandIS member consultation conducted in July 2016 (ScotlandIS, 2016a: 4) predict that the EU referendum result will negatively impact their access to skilled staff. Several companies have already experienced a decline in applicants from EU countries and EU citizens rejecting job offers because of the uncertainty of their status in the UK.

A continued supply of talented individuals is critical to the continued growth of the digital technologies industry in Scotland. If the skills shortage is aggravated by changes to immigration rules, salary levels will increase, disadvantaging smaller companies and particularly the start-up community. Future investments in Scotland could be put at risk if businesses cannot be sure of finding the staff they need to deliver their growth ambitions.

Market access

The EU is important for the digital technologies industry with 44 per cent of companies reporting in the Scottish Technology Industry Survey 2016 that Europe is one of the most attractive markets for them. (ScotlandIS, 2016c: 12) The developing EU Digital Single Market has the potential to make this market even more attractive.

The results of the ScotlandIS Brexit survey of July 2016 suggest that a Norway-type relationship with the EU, with continued access to the EU Single Market would be the preferred option for the majority of companies. A Brexit scenario including no trade deal with the EU was rejected by the vast majority of respondents (ScotlandIS, 2016a: 10-12).

The business consequences of exiting both the EU single market and the customs union, as announced by the Prime Minister, will depend on the terms and conditions of any free trade deal that can be struck with the EU. It will be crucial for services to be included in such an agreement as Scotland's digital technologies industry offers both services and products. This is not necessarily the case for every trade agreement. The free trade deal between Canada and the EU, for example, does not cover services.

Research and collaborations with universities

Scotland's universities provide an exceptional research base in computer science, software engineering and informatics, underpinning the digital technologies industry. This research excellence has a positive impact on undergraduate and postgraduate teaching and offers significant opportunity for commercial exploitation.

With Scottish universities being potentially excluded from EU research support programmes such as Horizon 2020 after Brexit, digital technologies companies will be impacted as well. The associated diminished access to funding, international cooperation and knowledge exchange could damage the research base's capability to innovate together with businesses and produce cutting edge start-ups and spin out companies.

Regulations

The digital technologies sector is affected by various rules and regulations determined by the EU or British laws that have been influenced by EU directives. Examples include trademarks, copyright, database regulations and data protection rules.

If Scottish companies want to continue doing business with EU countries, they will have to continue to comply with European rules in many cases. The new General Data Protection Regulation, for example, will have to be followed by every company that is handling EU residents' data regardless of the location of the business. However, in some cases it will not be up to companies themselves to continue to follow EU rules but will depend on the UK government's willingness to do so.

Divergence from EU rules could make it more difficult, time consuming and costly for UK companies to sell to EU customers. Careful consideration of the advantages and disadvantages of regulatory changes after Brexit is therefore required to enable the freest trade possible with the important EU market.

Opportunities

Despite these potential challenges, there is also an opportunity to counter the effects of uncertainty and stimulate the economy by making Scotland a more competitive and productive place to do business. Digital technologies can help all sectors of the economy to increase productivity through, for example, business and process transformation, ecommerce and the increased use of data analytics to inform decision-making. This represents an exceptional commercial opportunity for the digital technologies industry that could counter balance some of the negative effects of Brexit.

Brexit and the associated changes to immigration rules represent an opportunity to refocus efforts to ensure we have enough home-grown digital professionals in the years to come. Increased spend and commitment to digital technology skills education, both upskilling those already in the workforce and giving young people the ability to thrive in the digital world, would help addressing the skills gap which is holding the digital technologies industry back.

To seize both these opportunities fully, adequate government funding and policy reforms are required to incentivise investments and commitment by both the public and private sectors.

References

Deloitte (2015), *The economic and social impacts of enhanced digitalisation in Scotland*.
http://www.scottishfuturestrust.org.uk/files/publications/Impact_of_digitalisation_in_Scotland.pdf [Accessed 1 March 2017]

KPMG (2015), *Tech Monitor UK*.
https://assets.kpmg.com/content/dam/kpmg/pdf/2015/12/tech-monitor-december-2015.pdf [Accessed 1 March 2017]

Mackay, D. (2016), *Building Scotland's digital economy*.
https://blogs.gov.scot/scotlands-economy/2016/11/03/building-scotlands-digital-economy/. [Accessed 1 March 2017]

ScotlandIS (2016a), *ScotlandIS Brexit Survey Results*.
http://www.scotlandis.com/media/4492/brexit-survey-results.pdf. [Accessed 1 March 2017]

ScotlandIS (2016b), *ScotlandIS Salary Report 2016.*
http://www.scotlandis.com/media/4544/salary-report_vfinal.pdf. [Accessed 1
    March 2017]
ScotlandIS (2016c), *Scottish Technology Industry Survey 2016.*
http://www.scotlandis.com/media/1565/scottish-technology-industry-sur-
    vey-2016.pdf. [Accessed 1 March 2017]
Skills Development Scotland (2014), *Skills Investment Plan for Scotland's ICT
    and Digital Technologies sector.*
https://www.skillsdevelopmentscotland.co.uk/media/35682/ict___digital_tech-
    nologies_sector_skills_investment_plan.pdf. [Accessed 1 March 2017]

CHAPTER SIXTEEN

Brexit, the UK and Scotland: the story so far. A constitutional drama in four acts

Maria Fletcher and Rebecca Zahn

THE EU REFERENDUM result has led to the unfolding of a domestic constitutional drama in the United Kingdom that, on its current trajectory, could lead to its break-up. Written just prior to the anticipated trigger of the Article 50 TEU process to leave the European Union, this chapter maps that trajectory by considering the roles of the key institutional actors in the drama so far.

Setting the scene

Within the framework of the current devolution settlement, the UK's withdrawal from the EU ('Brexit') will mean that Scotland also leaves – despite 62 per cent of the Scottish electorate voting to 'remain'. In legal terms, the UK as a state recognised under international law is the signatory to the European Treaties. Withdrawal of that state includes its constituent parts.

However while relations with the EU were designed into the devolution settlement as 'reserved' to Westminster, the devolved administrations *are* required to honour the obligations of EU law; hence the Scotland Act provides that an act of the Scottish parliament is not law if it contravened an EU obligation; the Scottish parliament and Scottish ministers have powers to implement EU obligations of the UK in devolved matters (Scotland Act 1998 s.53 and s.57) and the devolved administrations have been involved in the development of the UK's EU policy via the Joint Ministerial Committee (an intergovernmental talking shop set up within the Devolution settlement and which means in various subject matter formats). In short, EU law is embedded within Scotland's devolved constitutional landscape and a UK withdrawal from the EU will have direct and significant impacts on the devolution settlement as currently designed – something that was not apparently planned for. This sets the scene for a constitutional drama which has been slowly unfolding since 24 June 2016.

Act 1

Enter – the Scottish government

The referendum result has prompted calls from Scotland's First Minister to 'take all possible steps and explore all options to give effect to how people in Scotland voted.' The Scottish government is keen to retain a strong relationship with the EU based on five key tests, set out by the First Minister in a speech in July, which will serve as a benchmark to assess the extent to which any Brexit solutions preserve key interests viewed to be related to Scotland's relationship with the EU: democracy; economic prosperity; social protection; solidarity; and influence. Short of a second independence referendum that, if successful, would allow Scotland to become an EU Member State in its own right, consideration, as promised, has been given to whether Scotland could remain in the EU without seeking independence.

The Scottish government's position has been laid out in two papers. The first, *Scotland a European Nation*, sets out the rationale for Scotland's approach to membership of the EU in terms of its political, historical and cultural orientations. It puts an argument for due process in the Brexit negotiations and the other EU Member States appear to be its intended audience. In essence, it argues that Scotland has a special relationship in Europe and has a right to be heard. The second paper, *Scotland's Place in Europe*, was published on 20 December 2016 and was intended for a UK audience. At the outset, the paper reiterates the Scottish government's wish for the whole of the UK to remain an EU Member State although it recognises that the referendum result does not permit such an outcome. In order to mitigate the impact of Brexit on Scotland, the paper therefore advocates for the UK's membership of the European Economic Area (EEA) Agreement and the Customs Union. In the event that such an option is not feasible, the paper takes a two-track and differentiated approach to mitigating the impact of Brexit.

First, it argues in favour of Scotland remaining within the European Single Market through membership of the European Free Trade Area (EFTA). However, if that also proves not to be possible and Scotland finds it is no longer a member of the European Single Market, then the policy proposals argue in favour of devolution of the necessary powers to allow the Scottish parliament to legislate on areas of primary concern. This includes 'repatriated' powers (ie those previously within the EU's competence) that are not currently within areas of devolved competence, for example employment and health and safety laws, as well as any other powers necessary to secure a differentiated relationship with Europe.

Although legally feasible, implementation of the plan set out in *Scotland's Place in* Europe would require a high level of political will and legal creativity at both the UK and the EU level. There are existing examples of the EU's considerable flexibility where it has accommodated differential territorial application of EU law within a Member State or associated territories. However, the Prime Minister has not so far shown any signs of willingness to permit Scotland to negotiate a differentiated position as part of the Brexit negotiations.

Act 2

Enter – The UK government

The UK government's reaction to its counterpart's calls from Holyrood to respect the decision of Scottish voters to remain in the EU has been muted. Aptly summarised under the title of the 'May Doctrine' the UK government is said to be proceeding on the basis of two assumptions: first, that a certain course of action, namely Brexit – however vaguely defined in its specifics – is irresistible. Second, that the UK executive alone has direct responsibility for the implementation, delineation and definition of Brexit (Blick, 2016). This assumption explains the government's assertion that it alone has the executive power through the royal prerogative to serve a notice intimating the UK's decision to leave the EU under Article 50 of the Treaty on the European Union (TEU) (see Act 3).

The 'May Doctrine' is clearly enunciated in Theresa May's Brexit speech, given on 17 January 2017, in which the Prime Minister set out her plans for a post-Brexit 'Global Britain' and made it clear that there would be no accommodation of Scotland's desire for a differentiated relationship with the EU. Doubts were also cast in this speech over the future remit of the Scottish parliament. It is often assumed that those powers currently exercised by the EU which fall within devolved competence will be repatriated to the Scottish legislature and that the removal of the requirement in the Scotland Act that the Scottish parliament cannot legislate contrary to EU law will mean a major enhancement of devolved powers. In her speech, Theresa May instead suggested that it would be left to the UK parliament (with no mention of the devolved administrations) to decide on any future changes to the law. The UK government's recently published Brexit White Paper – *The United Kingdom's exit from and new partnership with the European Union* – also suggests that complete onward devolution to the devolved legislatures and governments of EU competences is not a foregone conclusion.

The official intergovernmental forum to enable the involvement of the devolved administrations in the Brexit process is the Joint Ministerial Committee

(EU Negotiations) (JMC(EN)), a newly created format of the Joint Ministerial Committee (JMC). The JMC has never been a particularly successful forum for the exchange of views between the UK and the devolved administrations. The balance of power within the Committee is heavily tilted in favour of the UK government with a UK Minister always in the chair and with the agenda largely set by UK Ministers. It is hard to see how such a structure could deliver a genuinely inclusive debate that shapes and informs the Brexit roadmap for the UK, taking account of the differing interests and voting patterns of the devolved nations. Indeed, according to the Scottish government it has not.

Speaking in the Scottish parliament on 7 February 2017, Mike Russell, the Scottish Minister responsible for Brexit negotiations, stated that the JMC(EN) had not been involved in drawing up the 'hard Brexit' plan announced by the Prime Minister in her 'Global Britain' speech. He also stated that the devolved administrations were not party to UK government thinking. The last-minute issuing of agendas to (at least) the devolved administrations ahead of JMC(EN) meetings and non-discussion of items pertaining to the devolution of power scheduled on the agenda have also been reported. In this context, a commitment in the Brexit White Paper to further 'bilateral discussions' between the UK government and the devolved administrations 'to fully understand their priorities, which will inform the continuing discussions' might appear somewhat disingenuous.

Despite much rhetoric to the contrary the UK government's position on Brexit expounded to date appears to diminish rather than value the devolved constitutional landscape of the UK and the voices of the administrations within that. There is no legal means by which those voices can be taken into account and an already flawed intergovernmental talking shop is not providing a meaningful forum for genuine discussions based on mutual trust and respect. With the stakes so high, this is a sorry situation indeed, and in all likelihood, a constitutional collision course in the making.

Act 3

Enter – The Supreme Court

The Supreme Court has taken the place of the third actor in this constitutional drama. In R (on the application of Miller and Dos Santos) v Secretary of State for Exiting the European Union [2017] UKSC 5 the Court was asked whether the UK government had the power to give formal notice of the UK's withdrawal from the EU (to 'trigger article 50 TEU') without prior parliamentary authorisation through a legislative Act. The outcome of the case in respect of this question is well known. However, the Court was also asked to examine the role of the Sewel Convention, now given statutory form by Section 28(8) of the Scotland Act. This provision provides that the UK parliament will not normally legislate with regard to devolved matters without the consent of the Scottish parliament. Given that the decision to leave the EU directly impinges on a considerable part of the work of the Scottish parliament and Scottish government on issues ranging from agriculture and fisheries, environmental protection to higher education and research, the argument was led that the UK parliament required the consent of the Scottish parliament before it could trigger Article 50 TEU.

The Supreme Court analysed the wording of the provision to unanimously hold that it effectively restates a constitutional convention. It does not translate it into a legally binding obligation and thus does not legally enhance the constitutional position of the devolved institutions. The Court then reiterated the well understood constitutional maxim that it is not in the remit of the courts to police constitutional conventions since these are political agreements and not law. The Court then did not reach a conclusive decision on whether consent was required *as a matter of convention* but did decide that the devolved legislatures lack the legal power to block the triggering of Article 50 TEU.

Two observations are offered on this. First, the decision of the Supreme Court highlights once again how fragile the devolved settlement is, and powerless the devolved institutions are, in the face of something so intrinsically significant to it/them; Brexit. Second, while the Scottish parliament will not therefore have any involvement in the triggering of Article 50 TEU, it is likely that it will at a later stage of the unfolding Brexit process. For instance the Great Repeal Bill – which will be introduced in the next Queen's speech in order to preserve EU laws in force in the UK post-Brexit – *will* be subject to approval by the Scottish parliament through a legislative consent motion. In other words the Sewel Convention will apply in that context. Given the different voting patterns and political and constitutional dynamics in Scotland (and Northern Ireland), this may be far more controversial and may certainly contribute to the heightening of tensions within our current constitutional drama.

Act 4

Enter – The UK parliament

The Supreme Court's decision in Miller has been described as simply putting 'the Brexit ball firmly back in the [UK] parliament's court' (Elliott, 2017). Only it, through the adoption of a statute – and not the UK government – can allow Article 50 TEU to be triggered. This raised hopes in some quarters that the two

Houses of Parliament would vote down the draft legislation – EU Withdrawal Bill – or at least vote to insert substantive amendments to it, such as to secure parliament a 'meaningful vote' on the Brexit deal early in the process, effectively giving MPs and peers the chance to send the government back to seek a better deal. Unwilling to 'frustrate the will of the people', and in a significant nod to *popular*, as opposed to the traditional and embedded notion of *representative* democracy, the House of Commons voted with a majority of more than 300 to give the Prime Minister the power to trigger Article 50 TEU. Perhaps unsurprisingly, all SNP MPs voted against the Bill. More surprising is that the Bill also got through the House unamended. All eyes are now on the House of Lords, with many defiant speeches anticipated (at the time of writing) but ultimately with approval expected, perhaps with several amendments (on 'meaningful' parliamentary approval of the Brexit deal and guaranteeing the rights of non-UK EU citizens living in the UK at the start of the Brexit negotiations).

Meanwhile, suggestions have been made that the Great Repeal Bill – which legislates for what will happen on the day that the UK leaves the EU – will delegate statutory powers to enable Ministers to make changes, by secondary legislation, to give effect to the outcome of the negotiations with the EU 'as they proceed'. These so-called 'Henry VIII clauses' cause concern as they would allow the government to circumvent the full legislative process, which the executive would otherwise need to use in order to enact primary legislation. The role of the devolved administrations in the scrutiny of such legislation is also not clear. On 7 November 2016, during a debate in the House of Commons on exiting the EU and workers' rights, Mark Durkan MP (SDLP, Foyle) raised questions, which have yet to be resolved, concerning both Henry VIII powers and devolution:

> The right hon. Gentleman refers to the great repeal Bill, which is in essence the great download and save Bill for day one of Brexit. Who controls the delete key thereafter as far as these rights and key standards are concerned? Is it, as he implies, this House? Would any removal of rights have to be done by primary legislation, or could it be done by ministerial direction? And where is the position of the devolved Administrations in this? These matters are devolved competencies; will they be devolved on day one?

Final curtain?

Brexit has effected a shock on the UK's constitution, the consequences of which are penetrating deep and wide – including questions about the extent of the royal prerogative and the very hierarchy of law, ultimately answered by the highest court in the land. Another central tenet of the UK constitutional landscape – the devolution settlement – is similarly being tested by Brexit, but appears to lack the legal teeth and the political mechanisms to effectively assert its place (and in the case of Scotland and Northern Ireland, the will of their electorate) within the UK's constitutional landscape. Brexit will effect fundamental changes to the devolution settlement, and, given that devolution has embedded itself increasingly into the fabric of the UK constitution over its almost 20-year history, it seems unconscionable that it might be at breaking point – but on the basis of performances given thus far in the drama, it is, at least when viewed from North of the Border.

References

Blick, A. (2016), *The EU referendum, devolution and the Union | The Federal Trust*.
http://fedtrust.co.uk/our-work-on-europe/the-eu-referendum-devolution-and-the-union/ [Accessed 1 March 2017]
Elliott, M. (2017), '1,000 words The Supreme Court's Judgement in *Miller*', *Public Law For Everyone*.
https://publiclawforeveryone.com/2017/01/25/1000-words-the-supreme-courts-judgment-in-miller/ [Accessed 1 March 2017]

CHAPTER SEVENTEEN

Keeping up the pressure. Equality and human rights in Scotland post-Brexit

Angela O'Hagan

SCOTLAND SINCE DEVOLUTION has seen many significant changes in how its people lead their lives, the freedoms and rights that they now enjoy compared to a scant generation ago, and the requirements on public institutions to promote equality and human rights. While we are a long way from an equalities utopia, the protections from discrimination under the UK legislation, and the promotion of equalities under successive Scottish governments have arguably characterised political, legislative and attitudinal change in Scotland in the last 20 years.

We cannot forget the ferocity that met the proposed repeal of Section 28/Clause 2a in 1999-2000, but can now set it in the context of same sex marriage legislation, and funding support for a range of organisations engaged in the representation and support of LBGTQI people that are firmly part of civic and institutional Scotland. The discourse on gender equality in Scotland has long been shaped and informed by a vibrant feminist movement that under devolution has resulted in conceptual and practical advances in the recognition and institutional response to domestic abuse and other forms of gender-based violence. Scotland is one of the few countries in the European Union, and the only part of the UK, with a commitment to equality analysis in the national budget process and that produces an Equality Budget Statement.

In the face of withdrawal from the EU arguably none of these rights and protections are threatened. Legal protection from discrimination on a number of specified protected characteristics is provided under the Equality Act 2010: an act of the Westminster parliament. Schedule 5 of Scotland Act contains a provision to 'promote' equal opportunities but competence to legislate against discrimination in employment, for example, continues to be reserved to Westminster. Between that rock and the hard Brexit sits the Equality Act 2010 with its 'very good protections' (SP OR EHRIC, 3 November 2016) that include provisions beyond the European minima.

It has been suggested that preserving the Equality Act 2010 and the provisions extended through the Scotland Act 2016 do offer some safeguards to the status quo protections from discrimination. However, many of these provisions have come into UK law through membership of the EU. Indeed, 'EU Law [has been] the engine that hauled the development of UK anti-discrimination law' (HL 88/HC695 2016-17, p.7.) Maintaining the 'gold plated' provisions that include, for example, rights on maternity and family leave provision in the context of the daily realities of pregnancy and maternity discrimination (EHRC, 2016) and a current UK government that has offered no assurances or indication of its intentions to preserve these rights is far from secure.

Claims have been made that equalities legislation and protection have become so culturally acceptable and embedded in public attitudes in Scotland and the wider UK that any attempt to revoke or repeal existing provisions would not succeed. There are two significant caveats to that thinking. Business interests, along with what the UK or other governments are prepared to give away in the interests of profit, and the removal of any suggested impediment to employers' rights. Secondly, the thin ice of public attitudes that reflect a formal acceptance of principles of non-discrimination and indeed the desire to be protected by legislation which has, in large part, been derived from membership of the EU, while at the same time revealing enduring prejudices against non-white, non-heterosexual, non-disabled, indigenous, male 'norms'.

Analysis from the Equality and Human Rights Commission and the Social Attitudes survey reveal persistent religious intolerance, bigotry and discrimination against people of colour, non-heterosexual people, and a lack of empathy or understanding of difference from 'norms' that hark back to a Scotland that no longer exists. These prejudices, and the lack of knowledge and information on levels of immigration, access to social protections, and the contribution of migrants, for example, that characterised so much of the Brexit referendum debate cannot be dismissed. As others have eloquently questioned, did the Brexit debate fuel racism and intolerance or did it present an opportunity, or indeed a licence, to express the barely concealed attitudes and standpoints that have always been obtained? (Emejulu, 2016; Heuchan, 2016). While we would hope not to see these attitudes prevail in the future, we cannot ignore the strength of their presence at a time when the machinery of rights and protections is at such risk.

Principal among these risks is the immediate withdrawal from the European Charter of Fundamental Rights and Freedoms. Currently binding on the EU Member States and institutions, the Charter comprises a wide range of economic, social, political, cultural and civil rights. A hard Brexit would mean that this integral component of the equalities engine will be removed. This reality is the focus of real and present anxiety across civil society in Scotland, including from the Human Rights Consortium Scotland and its member organisations, and the Scottish Women's Convention among others. Add to this the further possibility of future threats to the European Convention on Human Rights (ECHR) which, while not connected institutionally or legally to the European Union, is bound up in the public mind and the political sights of the UK government and its stated intention to repeal the Human Rights Act 1998 which binds in the ECHR into UK law.

As for other ties to the EU that strengthen our public policy making through research funding and mobility; economic, human and infrastructure development through the Structural Funds, and other policy initiatives, these will be loosened off and the UK pushed to the outer limits of research funding partnerships and consortia. The prospect of extended rights for disabled people through enlarged European accessibility legislation has also been denied people in the UK, among whom of course we count citizens of other EU Member States. Their status and security has been rendered vulnerable, even while the Scottish government and civil society organisations, including the trade unions, offer assurances and highlight their economic, social and cultural contribution from which we all benefit.

In face of these uncertainties the pressure is yet again on civil society organisations and activists, including disabled peoples' and feminist organisations, anti-racist organisations and others to maintain public awareness and political pressure on the Scottish government and the political parties in Scotland. Equalities can be a will o' the wisp presence in party manifestos but faced with such vulnerabilities – and potentially opportunities for strengthening provision – political parties need to up their game. Maintaining pressure on Scottish governments throughout the exit process to embed protections, resource the realisation of rights, and secure enduring protections, calling Scottish and Westminster governments to account on their efforts in this regard, could be a full-time focus for a sector already buckling under standstill funding and increasing pressures, as years of politically motivated austerity from Westminster have whittled away public funding and the income security and autonomy of the most vulnerable people. Without protections from the EU, the Scottish government will be under pressure to provide the necessary safeguards and protections through maximising the recently devolved powers and future provisions of social security.

As a small nation in the northern margins of the EU, how much does our departure really matter to the EU and will we really miss it when it's gone? With all its flaws, not least the treatment by the EU institutions of Eurozone countries in Southern Europe and the disregard for sovereignty and economic autonomy, in the context of Scotland and the wider UK, the EU arguably has been a source of progressive rights and protections for workers, particularly women and more vulnerable workers. As well as the legal and political uncertainties of leaving the EU, we also face the prospect of isolation, adrift between the remaining countries of the EU and our Nordic neighbours, to whom we have looked so keenly on equality matters. That prospect is by turn positive, and we should look to build closer relations and better policy learning and adaptation on equality and public policy.

References

Emejulu, A. (2016), 'On the Hideous Whiteness of Brexit', in Verso Books (ed.), *The Brexit Crisis: A Verso Report*, London: Verso Books.

Equality and Human Rights Commission (2016), *Pregnancy and maternity related discrimination and disadvantage*.

file:///C:/Users/aoh1/Downloads/summary_of_key_findings_-_bis-16-145-pregnancy-and-maternity-related-discrimination-and-disadvantage-summary.pdf

Heuchan, C. (2016), 'Race, History, and Brexit: Black Scottish Identity'. sisteroutrider.wordpress.com [Accessed: 21 February 2017].

House of Lords and House of Commons Joint Committee on Human Rights (2016), *The Human Rights Implications of Brexit*, HLPaper88/HC695, 14 December.

Scottish Parliament Official Report (2016), Equality and Human Rights Committee, 3 November.

http://www.parliament.scot/S5_Equal_Opps/Meeting%20Papers/EHRiC_Agenda_and_Public_Papers_20161103.pdf [Accessed: 21 February 2017]

CHAPTER EIGHTEEN

Brexit and UK Energy Policy

Aileen McHarg

Introduction

Despite the fact that two out of the three founding organisations of what is now the European Union (EU) – the European Coal and Steel Community (which expired in 2002) and the European Atomic Energy Community (Euratom) – had energy at their heart, the EU did not acquire a general legal competence in energy policy until the Lisbon Treaty came into force in 2009. What is now Article 194 of the Treaty on the Functioning of the European Union gives the EU institutions shared competence with Member States to adopt measures to (a) ensure the functioning of the energy market; (b) ensure security of energy supply in the Union; (c) promote energy efficiency and energy saving and the development of new and renewable forms of energy; and (d) promote the interconnection of energy networks. However, Member State sovereignty over the exploitation of primary energy sources, their energy mix, and the general structure of their energy supply is expressly preserved.

Nevertheless, well before the Lisbon Treaty, the EU had begun to make significant inroads into Member States' energy policy autonomy, often in the face of considerable resistance, relying on other policy bases. From the early 1990s onwards, the European Commission sought to liberalise European gas and electricity markets, relying on general competition and free movement laws. Three successive waves of liberalisation directives, in 1996/98, 2003 and 2009, progressively opened Member States' wholesale and retail energy markets to competition, and in February 2015, the EU launched its *Framework Strategy for an Energy Union* with the aim of creating a genuinely cross-border internal market in energy. EU environmental policy, and latterly climate change policy, has also had a significant impact on Member States' energy systems. The promotion of low-carbon energy, along with transparent and integrated markets, affordability, and security of energy supply, is now a key objective of EU energy policy.

UK *and* EU *Energy Policy*

Since the 1980s, the UK has been in the vanguard of energy reform in Europe, both as regards the liberalisation of energy markets and subsequently in the transition to low-carbon energy systems. In general, the UK has been a strong supporter, and influential driver, of EU energy policy. EU law has therefore been a constraint upon, rather than a major determinant of UK energy policy, although more of the detail of UK energy regulation has been derived from EU law as the scope and ambition of EU energy policy has increased.

Given the clear alignment between EU and UK energy goals, withdrawal from the EU is unlikely to change UK energy policy significantly. In any case, other constraints – such as domestic and international climate change obligations, and the sharing of domestic energy policy competences between UK and devolved institutions – are likely to ensure considerable policy continuity. Moreover, achievement of those policy goals makes ongoing integration with European energy markets highly desirable. Nonetheless, loss of the external enforcement and accountability mechanisms provided by EU law means that Brexit will remove an important guarantor of energy policy stability. Such stability is particularly important in the current low-carbon energy transition. This requires enormous investment in energy infrastructure, which – given its long-term, capital-intensive, and 'sunk' nature – is notoriously susceptible to political risk.

Brexit and UK *Energy Policy*

So far, the UK Government has given very limited indication as to how it sees Brexit affecting UK energy policy. However key issues are likely to arise in the following areas:

Market Structures

There is unlikely to be much change in the short term in relation to energy market structures. Regulatory rules, even where derived from EU law, are mostly contained in domestic primary or secondary legislation, and where they are not can relatively unproblematically be given a domestic legal base via the Great Repeal Bill. In the longer term, Brexit will in theory allow greater freedom to reform energy markets. This might encompass detailed aspects of energy regulation, for instance in relation to the scope and content of consumer protection obligations, the technical requirements on networks and providers, or the duties of energy regulators. More fundamentally, it could also relate to the structure of the energy industries, for example, allowing more direct governmental involvement in energy decision-making, a stronger emphasis on energy planning rather than market-driven investment, a reintegration of energy networks with producers and suppliers, or restrictions on foreign ownership. In practice, alongside ongoing ideological commitments to free energy markets, the room for manoeuvre is likely to be significantly constrained by whatever relationship the UK has in future with the Internal Energy Market (IEM).

Market Integration

As a net importer of both gas and electricity, maintaining access to European energy markets is essential from a security of supply point of view. In addition, transparent and properly integrated energy markets improve energy affordability by increasing the efficient use of existing energy facilities and thereby reducing investment costs, as well as by removing opportunities for arbitrage. Finally, integration is also an important means of managing the potential balancing problems caused by intermittent renewable energy sources. This is particularly important for the Scottish Government, which has high ambitions as a producer and exporter of renewable energy.

The UK has significantly increased its interconnection with other European gas and electricity systems in recent years, and more interconnection capacity is planned. It has also played a leading role in the development of European Network Codes to facilitate genuine system integration, and not merely inter-system trade. Integration is particularly advanced in Northern Ireland, where there has been a single All-Ireland electricity wholesale market since 2007, and where work to create an All-Ireland wholesale gas market is ongoing.

In its Brexit White Paper (Department for Exiting the European Union, 2017: para 8.28), the UK Government recognises the value of co-ordinated trading arrangements, but states simply that '[w]e are considering all future options for the UK's future relationship with the EU on energy, in particular, to avoid disruption to the all-Ireland single electricity market ... on which both Northern Ireland and Ireland rely for affordable, sustainable and secure electricity supplies.' Options for continued participation in the IEM include membership of the European Economic Area, which the UK Government has already ruled out, or some kind of bespoke agreement along the lines of the Energy Community Treaty, which extends the IEM into non-EU Member States in South-East Europe and beyond. Alternatively the UK might seek access to European energy markets without being part of the IEM as such.

The House of Commons' Energy and Climate Change Committee reported in October 2016 that none of the respondents to its inquiry into the implications of Brexit for energy and climate change policy had advocated leaving the IEM (Energy and Climate Change Committee, 2016: para 95). It did, however, note considerable concern that the UK might remain subject to IEM rules while losing its current influential position in the making of those rules (ibid: para 97). It therefore recommended that the Government should seek to ensure a continued role for the UK in European energy regulatory bodies (ibid: para 103).

Low Carbon Energy

The energy industries are subject to a range of EU measures to reduce greenhouse gas (GHG) emissions. These include the EU Emissions Trading Scheme (EU-ETS), targets and measures to promote renewable energy consumption, and targets and measures to promote energy efficiency, although these are all supplemented by domestic policy measures.

It is unclear whether the UK will seek to remain within the EU-ETS after Brexit, or establish its own emissions trading scheme linked to the EU-ETS, or pursue a different approach to establishing a price for carbon, such as a carbon tax. The Energy and Climate Change Committee noted that, despite criticism of the EU-ETS, it is highly valued as a policy instrument for reducing GHG emissions, and warned that alternative measures would potentially costly and complex or politically difficult (Energy and Climate Change Committee, 2016: para 84).

In relation to renewable energy and energy efficiency, we are likely to see continuity at least in the short term in relation to specific policy measures, many of which have already been incorporated into domestic law. It is, however, unlikely that EU-level targets will be replicated at domestic level as the UK Government has in the past been critical of the distorting effects of sectoral targets, preferring to rely on overall climate change targets to drive emissions reduction. Given that the Conservative Government has already reversed some domestic policy supports for low carbon energy (including withdrawal or cuts to subsidies for renewable electricity generation, cancellation of funding for carbon capture and storage demonstration projects, and ending some energy efficiency programmes) in order to reduce energy costs, and is keen to promote shale gas exploitation, there must be considerable concern about the future direction of policy in this area post-Brexit.

Other Environmental Constraints

A host of other EU environmental laws also affect the energy industries, including atmospheric and water pollution controls; nature protection measures; and environmental impact assessment regulations. The impact of such measures can be considerable. It was, for instance, the Large Combustion Plants Directives of 1998 and 2001 (now replaced by the 2010 Industrial Emissions Directive) that were primarily responsible for the decline of the coal-fired electricity generation in the UK. The Habitats and Wild Birds Directives similarly often pose obstacles to the exploitation of renewable generation.

The majority of relevant EU environmental measures are already implemented in domestic law and will therefore be unaffected by Brexit. In the short term, there is unlikely to be much appetite for significant change in the environmental regulatory framework, given the other policy uncertainty caused by Brexit. In any case, some EU environmental laws are underpinned by international obligations, and in domestic terms much environmental law making falls within devolved competence in Scotland, Wales and Northern Ireland. Over time, however, there may be pressure from the energy industries to weaken environmental constraints, and there may be concerns about policy divergence between the UK and devolved governments.

Research and Investment Funding

Research and investment funding is likely to be both directly and indirectly affected by Brexit. Regarding the former, there are various EU funding sources for energy-related research and investment in energy infrastructure from which the UK has received very substantial sums in recent years. It is unclear whether British researchers and UK-based firms will be able to continue to access those funding sources after Brexit, or if not, whether they will be fully replaced by domestic funding sources (Energy and Climate Change Committee, 2016: paras 118 – 121).

More generally, Brexit is likely to make for a worse investment climate. Increased policy uncertainty may well raise the cost of capital for energy infrastructure; the falling pound has also made investment more expensive since much energy equipment is imported; and adverse impacts on the financial services sector could reduce the appetite for investment. The Energy and Climate Change Committee concluded in its October 2016 report that the greatest risk of leaving the IEM was higher investment costs, and that the Leave vote had reduced already weak investor confidence in the energy sector (ibid: paras 96 and 122 – 133).

Nuclear Safety

The UK Government has made clear in its Brexit White Paper that leaving the EU also means leaving Euratom (Department for Exiting the European Union, 2017: para 8.30). The Euratom treaty provides the current framework for civil nuclear power generation and radioactive waste management. Leaving Euratom has raised some alarm about potentially dire consequences for the nuclear industry if alternative regulatory arrangements are not put in place in time (e.g. Vaughan, 2017). However, the UK Government insists that seeking appropriate alternative arrangements, as well as maintaining collaboration with other EU Member States on nuclear research, is a high priority for the withdrawal negotiations (Department for Exiting the European Union, 2017: para 8.31). Potentially, this could involve continued participation in Euratom as a non-EU Member State, through a separate treaty, as a number of third parties already do (see Peers, 2017).

Conclusion

In theory, Brexit will bring greater flexibility to future UK energy policy, although depending on one's perspective, potential changes may be desirable or undesirable. In practice, given the convergence between UK and EU energy policy goals, and the clear advantages of continued participation in European energy and related markets, the scope for change in UK energy policy is likely to be fairly marginal. That being so, it is hard to see Brexit as anything other than an unwelcome distraction at a time when the energy industries are already in a state of transition and facing very significant regulatory and investment challenges.

References

Department for Exiting the European Union (2017), *The United Kingdom's Exit from and New Relationship With the European Union*, Cm 9417.

Energy and Climate Change Committee (2016), *The Energy Revolution and Future Challenges for UK Energy and Climate Change Policy*, 3rd Report 2016 – 17, HC 705.

Peers, S. (2017), 'The UK Brexits Euratom: Legal Framework and Future Developments', *EU Law Analysis Blog*, 30 January.

Vaughan, A. (2017), 'UK Nuclear Power Stations 'Could be Forced to Close' after Brexit', *The Guardian*, 28 February.

CHAPTER NINETEEN

Brexit, the SNP and independence

Marco G. Biagi

HOW TO DEAL with the UK voting for the EU's exit door? Strategists bent over laptop screens polishing drafts of the SNP's 2016 election manifesto in the party's campaign centre must have been just as sceptical as everyone else that what they were writing about Europe would ever need to be invoked. They knew they had to provide circumstances under which a new independence referendum would be held, to give the party faithful a reason to slog doorstep-to-doorstep for the party's re-election as the Scottish government. Just a year and a half after an epoch-defining vote on sovereignty caution was always going to be the watchword, and even as late as the early spring of 2016 Brexit seemed improbable.

The eventual wording put before the electorate was a masterwork of caveats. Capable of being read minimally as simply supporting Holyrood being *allowed* to hold a referendum, it balanced a clear reiteration of support for independence while freeing any re-elected SNP government from a commitment to call a vote speedily:

> We believe that the Scottish Parliament should have the right to hold another referendum if there is clear and sustained evidence that independence has become the preferred option of a majority of the Scottish people – or if there is a significant and material change in the circumstances that prevailed in 2014, such as Scotland being taken out of the EU against our will. (SNP, 2016)

The specific, unequivocal mention of the EU as a circumstance that could trigger a second referendum provided a clear democratic mandate should the Scottish government choose to hold one. Subtly it also almost compelled them. By choosing Brexit as an example – the *sole* example – of a possible 'material change' the party set up as the default expectation that if Brexit were to happen it would indeed trigger a new referendum. After making such an explicit manifesto commitment a subsequent decision not to call an independence referendum would need almost as much explaining as actually calling one. Yet at no point since the EU referendum did Nicola Sturgeon even come close to holding back.

Scotland after the Brexit vote

By the morning after the Brexit vote the implicit caution of that manifesto text was nowhere to be seen. The political tension of those hours is easily forgotten. Friday 24 June 2016 was a day of high stakes: a Prime Minister resigned in Downing Street and the Governor of the Bank of England urgently handed the economy a £250bn injection. Into this the First Minister of Scotland called a new independence referendum 'highly likely', announcing the initiation of legislation to that end. Since then, in every interview, speech and public statement by Scottish government representations the option has been played up rather than down.

While the threat of a referendum would always have been the Scottish government's strongest bargaining chip to secure a voice in the Brexit process, the possibility of empty bluff was never open to them. From the moment of her ascension to leadership in the wake of the 2014 referendum defeat, Nicola Sturgeon has been perched atop a hugely politically-charged membership that was burgeoning to over 100,000. Many members and most voters had come to the SNP from other parties and could just as easily drift away again if momentum shifted.

For a significant minority, the question within a matter of months became not whether there should be another referendum but why there had not been another referendum already. The SNP depends on its rank-and-file more than other parties, principally for finance and communications, and mechanisms exist for the membership to dispense with a leader who is not delivering. A political culture that values openness, accessibility and iconoclasm means strong expectations that leaders will be responsive to ordinary members. Institutional memories abound of the consequences of the perceived softening on independence in the early 2000s for party unity and consequent electability. Strategists knew that backing down from a new referendum that had been talked up would be costly in ways that are wholly unpredictable, and would present almost as much risk to the SNP's dominant position as would taking independence back to the electorate.

Ever since the Brexit vote there has been a growing sense in the wider movement that this is an opportune moment. Nationalist administrations run a famously tight ship when it comes to message discipline, but the standard bearers of the former regime have been forthright. Both former First Minister Alex Salmond and his former chief-of-staff Geoff Aberdein took to the newspapers and TV studios to argue that a new independence referendum is now winnable. Based on her actions since the Brexit vote the current First Minister agreed as throughout the winter of 2016–17 she very visibly marched the independence movement's troops to the top of the hill before finally passing the point of no return on the eve of the SNP conference.

Circumstances were conceivable where those troops could have been quietly marched down again. If support for independence – or willingness to entertain a second independence referendum – had plummeted, enough members of the independence movement might have shown caution to tip the balance back. An exit would also have been provided if the UK government had delivered a significant devolution of additional powers. Perhaps it still could. The Scottish government's repeated sincere offers to take a referendum off the table if the Scotland Act were revisited to accommodate the new post-Brexit situation have however been repeatedly rebuffed by the UK government. For supporters of independence moreover, Whitehall's relationship with Holyrood through the Brexit process has only highlighted the fundamental imbalance of esteem that has always provided fuel and justification to their cause.

A first call for the Brexit vote to require support in a majority of the UK jurisdictions as well as a majority of the UK's voters was after all rejected out-of-hand. A common condition for constitutional change in genuine federations, it was alien to the political culture of a UK that still, in London at least, sees itself as one country rather than four. Yet had that requirement been included, English voters would undoubtedly have reacted with the same frustration and fury at being held in the EU against their will as Scotland's leaders reacted at being pulled out.

The second concession that was seriously debated, where the Scottish parliament was given the power to retain full EU membership unilaterally, was less credible. Nicknamed 'reverse Greenland' after that jurisdiction's unique position outwith the EU while still a part of the state of Denmark, it would have required Scotland to assume functions associated with being an independent state in order to discharge treaty obligations, such as international representation even up to participation in mutual defence, that were never realistic.

The more credible Scottish government position of December 2016 however evolved from this; that the Scottish parliament should gain sufficient powers to be able to retain membership of the Single Market unilaterally, as opposed to full membership of the European Union. Such an arrangement would require devolution of powers over immigration, business regulation, health and safety and employment law. Precedents exist in other federal states around the world for each of these to be governed by component parts, rather than the central government, but while the UK government has strategically avoided ruling out this proposal, they have also displayed no obvious enthusiasm and made no concrete commitments. Instead the leader of the Scottish

Conservatives has predicted on a public platform that Brexit will lead to a turf war over whether Westminster seeks to reclaim powers over agriculture. Those powers were devolved to Scotland at a time when that responsibility, in practice, largely meant administering a public policy that originated in Europe. David Cameron's description, in the dying days of the independence referendum, that the UK is a 'family of nations' may have been an expedient soundbite at the time but now more than ever seems a flattering and inaccurate description of how differing interests within these islands are accommodated.

Much else has changed since 2014, and the actual process of Brexit itself is actually far from the most important. When Theresa May stated 'Brexit means Brexit' she presumably meant that the one certainty was that Brexit means the UK will no longer be a member of the EU – no more, no less. That change is very abstract – a narrow definition of Brexit – and alone would be insufficient to shift Scotland's politics radically. The Scottish Social Attitudes Surveys have consistently, over years, found little widespread evidence of a gut attachment to European identity. In-depth focus groups conducted by IPPR Scotland and IPSOS-Mori ahead of the Brexit referendum concurred. Scotland's EU member-ship is not, in and of itself, of definitive importance to more than a small number of citizens – certainly much fewer than intrinsically value a sense of attachment to the UK, its identity, traditions and flag. A new independence referendum that came to be a choice between pure emotional attachment to the EU or the UK would be a disaster for the Yes side.

To see Brexit in such narrow terms, however, is to overlook the wider impact of all that has now been bundled with it. This is now a political divide about much more than whether the words ' European Union' adorn passports, just as Scottish independence means much more than whether 'United Kingdom' is on them.

This 'wider Brexit' is what has fundamentally altered the political landscape.

The future of Britain now looms with doubt and even menace. In the indepen-dence referendum the No campaign, by contrast, made doubt the cornerstone of their efforts to weaken the independence cause. Introducing 'Project Fear' into the political lexicon, they ruthlessly associated Yes with uncertainty and risk and framed No as stability and security. The Yes campaign spent many months fruitlessly trying to contest that territory, portraying independence as steady-as-she-goes. As late as February 2013 billionaire Jim McColl was describing the prospect as 'a management buyout' in a well-heralded endorsement in *Scotland on Sunday*. By the end of that year the independence case had evolved into a White Paper offering social democracy with distinctly Nordic overtones but without the tax increases. Often fronted by Nicola Sturgeon as the Scottish gov-ernment's official 'Yes Minister', they sought to win votes through inspiration and conviction. The new Scotland offered by the Yes side won the support of 45 per cent of those who voted: short of victory but tantalisingly close.

A changed environment

The relative strength of these arguments has now changed utterly. The UK government is now unable to offer answers about the future. Even worse, if they followed Yes Scotland's example and instead put forward an authentic pledge of change, the worldview they would be tied to offering would be that of a Conservative-dominated little Britain. Nothing could be more guaranteed to repel rather than inspire Scotland's voters, who have been rejecting Conservative visions at the polls for over fifty years.

In 2014 the No side sought to make voters fear that they would lose their pensions with independence, never mind that the UK's pensions were already the third lowest relative to wages in the industrialised world (House of Commons Library, 2015). Today independence supporters can more easily convince that it is staying with the UK that invites the loss of employment rights as EU-wide minimums no longer compel UK governments to at least basic safeguards. They will be able to talk up the threats to public services posed by the free trade deals that the UK will have to negotiate with strong-willed countries like the United States. Even the core economic debate will take on a new tenor when the UK government has in Brexit a flagship policy most mainstream economists have publicly denounced as self-destructive. A second No campaign will have to explain to undecided voters the likely sight of office buildings in London being emptied of financial services companies 10,000 employees at a time, as they relocate to Paris, Frankfurt and Dublin, turning a 2014 spectre used against independence on its head. It is an unenviable position.

The vision of a fairer Scotland put forward by those who argued for independence could meanwhile remain broadly the same. Some aspects of policy, like currency and how to bring expenditure and revenue into greater balance through economic growth, need to be updated. To the SNP, however, the contrast that epitomised the late stages of the 2014 independence campaign – for example the 'Kirsty' broadcast that presented the two potential futures of a child born on referendum day – has only been vindicated since. To this can be added the collapse of the UK Labour Party as a force that could credibly win power in Westminster and the growing alignment in Scotland of unionism with Conservatism. The prospect of voting No in expectation of the UK being restored to its old self by an incoming Labour government, as many did in 2014, is now implausible.

Among those left voters there is also an enduring group of genuine progressives who are instinctively suspicious of any political movement that carries the name of 'nationalist'. For them the social democratic promises of the Scottish government and the support of the Scottish Green Party for independence in 2014 were insufficient to allay their fears of a dark side to nationalism, even as the Yes campaign offered nuclear disarmament, a living wage, extended childcare and protection of a public NHS. These are also though, precisely the people most likely to feel a heartfelt sense of European identity, along with the immigrants from the EU who also voted against independence by two-to-one.

Together these groups have now experienced not just Brexit but also the sight of Scottish (and Welsh) nationalists repeatedly taking up the causes of Europe and immigration. In contrast the Labour Party continues to self-consciously equivocate on both issues and the UK government increasingly looks outright like the exclusionary nativist movement they fear. Realisation of the consequences of the SNP's progressive *bona fides* being reinforced has led to ever more severe attacks from Labour, culminating in London Mayor Sadiq Khan's infamous Scottish Labour conference speech in Perth alleging that Scottish nationalists were not racists per se, but somehow also that nationalism was no different to racism. Set against the backdrop of the Scottish government's internationalist response to Brexit, such accusations only further question the credibility of the accuser.

After all of this, supporters of independence could be forgiven for surprise at polls seemingly still lodged roughly where they were on that auspicious day in September 2014. Since Brexit it seems that the cause of independence has lost as many supporters as it has gained. Why? A section of the population open to appeals to independence has always been simultaneously sceptical of appeals to Europeanism. Nigel Farage enjoys poking fun at the SNP by alleging that the party wants to win power from London only to hand it over to Brussels. Such a worldview is simplistic. The UK is not the EU. To even resemble the EU, the UK would need to have veto powers for the Scottish, Welsh and Northern Irish governments over all UK-wide legislation, a Cabinet made up of nominees from those governments and devolution of powers over tax, welfare, defence, employment rights, foreign affairs, broadcasting and currency. The UK affords less flexibility in these policy areas than even the USA affords to its states, let alone the European Union. Yet despite all of this this, some voters do see equivalence.

Those optimistic about a new independence referendum base their strategy on a simple calculation: that these voters can be won back to Yes as easily as they drifted away. This is not far-fetched. After all, the Yes campaign these voters supported in 2014 was one resolutely in favour of a Scotland in the EU. Winning these voters back, while not alienating new converts, would be a challenge for a renewed independence campaign; but holding on to these voters while not alienating more of the 62 per cent of Scots who voted remain would be a challenge for a renewed anti-independence campaign too.

This strategy is based on a belief that rather than a growth in support, what has grown is an openness to the appeals that a new independence campaign would put forward. Respondents in polls are notoriously terrible at predicting how they will vote in the future. Five polls in the run-up to the Brexit vote saw Scots responding that in the event of the UK voting to leave the EU against Scotland's will they would vote for independence – in one case 54 per cent to 39 per cent. Such polls shaped the Scottish EU referendum debate, despite the precedent of the three Yes Scotland-commissioned polls in 2014 that showed clear leads for independence in the event of the Conservatives being re-elected as the UK government. Both events happened and in neither case did the promised support for independence materialise in any real way. With the injection of former No voters, Brexit, has at the very least, enlarged the proportion of people who have been in recent times supportive of independence. Deeper research than a simple opinion poll would be needed to predict how they will react to a campaign.

As Scottish government ministers increasingly invoke the rhetoric of 'hard Britain' or 'Tory Brexit' it is clear they see the wider implications of Brexit as part of a message that will resonate with this population. They may well be right. A larger audience in the country is receptive to their arguments than in 2014 and progressive arguments now carry greater credibility. The UK government is mired in economic uncertainty and the face of union is now unreservedly Conservative. No referendum result is ever certain, but in post-Brexit UK, Scottish nationalists have reason to feel that circumstances have changed such that if they present their pro-European, social democratic vision of independence to the people once more they can be justified in hoping for a different result.

References

House of Commons Library (2015), *Pensions: international comparisons.*
http://researchbriefings.files.parliament.uk/documents/SN00290/SN00290.pdf
SNP (2016), *Re-elect the SNP: Manifesto 2016.*
https://d3n8a8pro7vhmx.cloudfront.net/thesnp/pages/5540/attachments/
    original/1461935515/SNP_Manifesto2016_-_ER.pdf?1461935515

CHAPTER TWENTY

Scotland, Britain, Europe: where now? A Conservative perspective

Adam Tomkins

CARDS ON THE table: on 23 June 2016 I voted for the United Kingdom to remain a member state of the European Union. Not with anything like the same enthusiasm as I had voted on 18 September 2014 for Scotland to remain part of the United Kingdom. My vote in 2014 was a matter of deep conviction; my vote in June 2016 was calculation rather than anything else. I am no cheerleader for the European Union. It is undemocratic, intolerant of critical voices, bullying and, since Maastricht in the early 1990s, it has taken on far too much and has lost sight of its core purpose. Maastricht was a double error. Its expansion of economic union to embrace a single currency was a mistake (and the United Kingdom was entirely correct to stay out of the Eurozone). And the expansion of the EU's role beyond the core task of economic integration, into fields of political union, was a grievous error. None the less, I thought Britain should remain a member state so that we could argue from within for a radical change of European direction.

Referendums, however, are not opinion polls whose verdicts we can celebrate or ignore as the case befits. They are formal, binding, decision-making devices. They represent not advice to government, but instructions to government. Had Scotland voted 'Yes' in 2014 the United Kingdom would not have been free to ignore or to seek to overturn the result. Likewise in 2016: having asked the people for their decision we are now duty bound to give effect to it. The UK is leaving the EU not because the Tories have willed it – both the current Prime Minister and her immediate predecessor campaigned and voted to remain, as did Sir John Major – but because parliament decided in the European Union Referendum Act 2015 to ask the people whether we should leave or remain, and the people gave their answer, calmly and clearly, just as the Scottish people gave their answer on the independence question in 2014.

That some parts of the UK voted to remain and others to leave is immaterial to the result, just as it was immaterial to the result in 2014 that Glasgow and Dundee voted 'Yes'. No local authority had a veto over the result of Scottish independence referendum; and no part of the UK has a veto over the result of the EU referendum. Scotland was not the only place where a majority of voters wanted the UK to remain a member state. London, Manchester, Leeds, Liverpool, Newcastle, Bristol and Northern Ireland all voted remain.

EEA *membership?*

Sadly – if predictably – however, the Scottish government has yet to accept this. At the end of 2016 the Scottish government published a paper, *Scotland's Place in* Europe (Scottish Government 2016), which made three arguments. Each is worthy of analysis. The first argument was that the whole of the United Kingdom should seek to become a member of the European Economic Area (EEA). This option, sometimes referred to as the softest of soft Brexits, would mean that the UK, whilst it would leave the institutions of the European Union (no more British MEPS, no more British members of the European Commission, and no more British judges at the Court of Justice), would remain a 'member' of the single market. Legally, there is no such thing as 'membership' of the single market. One can have *access to* a market; one can *participate in* a market; but markets do not have members. Clubs have members, and on 23 June we elected to relinquish our membership of the EU club. Membership of the single market has been adopted, however, as shorthand for membership of the EEA.

It is not the policy of the United Kingdom government to pursue EEA membership for the UK. Theresa May is right to have rejected this option. We all know that the most powerful slogan of the leave campaign was 'take back control'. EEA membership means full participation in all four fundamental freedoms of the European single market (free movement of goods, services, workers and capital) – so EEA membership would not enable the UK to take back control of its borders. EEA members must comply with the entirety of the Court of Justice's case law on the single market, including its case law on the supremacy of European law – so EEA members cannot take back control of their national legislation. For EEA members the sovereignty of national legislation is conditioned by, and subject to, the supremacy of European law. And, finally, EEA members must make a substantial financial contribution to the EU institutions, so there is no taking back control of national finances, either.

It could be argued that EEA membership is compatible with the referendum result, in that the referendum question was about EU membership, not about the EEA. But such an argument would be a triumph of form over substance. People voted to take back control, and EEA membership does not deliver on that democratic mandate.

A differentiated deal for Scotland?

The second argument put in the Scottish government's paper was that even if the UK as a whole was not going to become a member of the EEA, Scotland should join the EEA in its own right. This would see a 'differentiated' deal for Scotland, on the one hand, and the rest of the UK, on the other. This option was put forward by the Scottish government in order to maintain and protect Scotland's place in the single market. In its view, a differentiated deal such as this would reflect the differentiated result of the 23 June referendum (in which Scots voted 62:38 to remain, whilst the UK as a whole voted 52:48 to leave).

My party – the Scottish Conservative and Unionist Party – spent two months carefully considering this option. In February 2017 we published a paper, *Scotland's Trading Future* (Scottish Conservatives, 2017), in which we explained why we cannot accept it. On analysis, the option suffers from two basic flaws. First, it is undeliverable. Only states may accede to the EEA Treaty and Scotland is not a state. There is no precedent for a sub-state region or territory (I am using the language that European law uses) to join the EEA (nor indeed the EU) in its own right. Member states are exactly that: states. Scotland is not a state because in the 2014 independence referendum a majority of 55:45 rejected the Scottish National Party's proposal that Scotland should leave the United Kingdom to become an independent state. It was precisely Scottish statehood that was rejected in 2014. Subsequent opinion polls very clearly show that Scots do not want to be asked that question again.

Secondly, and more importantly, a differentiated deal along the lines proposed by the Scottish government would be contrary to Scotland's economic interests. Scotland trades four times as much with the rest of the UK as it does with the whole of the European Union. Since 2002 the value of Scottish trade with the rest of the UK has grown by 74 per cent (from £28.6 billion to £49.8 billion) whereas in the same period Scottish trade with the EU has grown by less than 8 per cent (from £11.4 billion to £12.3 billion) (Scottish Conservatives, 2017: 12). This is far from the only measure of the comparative importance to Scotland of the British domestic market compared with the European single market. Consider, for example, Scottish jobs. There are currently 2,790 enterprises registered in Scotland with ownership in the rest of the UK, employing more than 340,000 Scots (17.7 per cent of the Scottish workforce). This compares with just 1,000 EU enterprises operating in Scotland, employing 127,000 people (6.6 per cent of the Scottish workforce).

And here's the rub: whether we like it or not, a differentiated deal for Scotland, in which Scotland was in the EEA and the rest of the UK was not, would inevitably see growing divergence either side of the border. The nature of the border would change, as controls appeared along it. And the nature of trade in goods and services between Scotland and the rest of the UK would likewise change, becoming more complex and more expensive as the regulatory regimes developed along their own, different, paths.

Prime Minister Theresa May has made it clear that her 'guiding principle must be to ensure that, as we leave the European Union, no new barriers to living and doing work within our own Union are created'. As the Prime Minister made plain, that means, among other matters 'maintaining the necessary common standards and frameworks for our own domestic market' (May, 2017).

This does not mean that there can be no Scotland-specific elements to Britain's Brexit deal. For example, were universities in England and Wales not to want continued participation in the EU's schemes of research collaboration and research grants there is no reason in principle why Scottish universities could not do so, if that is what they wanted. (I should add: I do not think this likely. I think it likely that all UK universities will want to continue to participate in these schemes, and there is no reason in principle why that should not be the case even after Brexit.)

It is striking that, for a nationalist document, *Scotland's Place in* Europe fails to identify any Scotland-only interests that require a bespoke solution, different from that for the rest of the United Kingdom. This is striking, but not surprising. After all, the interests of farmers in Perthshire are surely the same as farmers in Yorkshire; the interests of manufacturers in Lanarkshire and Dundee are surely the same as those in Tyneside and South Wales; and the interests of the financial services sector in Edinburgh are the same as those of the City of London.

It may very well be that Britain's Brexit deal can be sensibly differentiated sector to sector. But no case has been made for a Brexit deal that is differentiated nation to nation.

Enhanced devolution?

The final argument made by the Scottish government in its paper is that Brexit should deliver a fresh round of devolved powers to the Scottish parliament.

I have no doubt that it will do so. It seems inevitable that some of the powers to be repatriated from Brussels to the United Kingdom will pass to the devolved legislatures in Scotland, Wales and Northern Ireland. But I am equally in no doubt that this will occur at nothing like the scale proposed by the Scottish government.

In Scotland we are now seeing Devolution 3.0. We are on our third Scotland Act, the 2016 legislation implementing into law the conclusions and recommendations of the all-party Smith Commission, which met in the immediate aftermath of the 2014 independence referendum (full disclosure: I was a member of the Smith Commission). Opinion polls record no desire on the part of Scots to see the devolution question opened up yet again. The priority must surely be to get on with the job of implementing the Smith powers, some of which (particularly as regards social security) will in any event not be operational until 2020 or 2021, the slowness of the pace being set by the Scottish Ministers, not by the United Kingdom government.

What the Scottish government argued for in *Scotland's Place in* Europe is actually a copy-and-paste job of what it had argued for going into the Smith Commission: namely, the devolution to Holyrood of more or less all powers except those pertaining to defence, national security, and monetary policy. It asserts the need to devolve employment law, equalities law, health and safety law, consumer protection, import and export controls, immigration law, competition law, company law, energy regulation, financial services, telecommunications and postal services. This is not devolution designed to strengthen the United Kingdom's domestic market: it is devolution designed to destroy it, to undermine its integrity and to break it apart. This is a vision of devolution that was rejected by the Smith Commission in 2014 and it will be rejected again as Brexit unfolds.

There are perhaps three main areas regulated by the European Union that would most obviously fall within devolved competence in Scotland. These are agriculture, fisheries and environmental regulation. One might add a fourth policy area: VAT. The Smith Commission agreed that a proportion of VAT receipts in Scotland be assigned to the Scottish government. VAT could not be devolved, the Smith Commission was advised, because it is contrary to EU law for a member state to set more than one rate of VAT. Brexit may liberate us from that rule, meaning that a proportion of VAT could be devolved to the Scottish parliament, rather than merely assigned. To date, this matter has not featured prominently in Scottish political debate since the EU referendum. Perhaps the Scottish Ministers are in no great rush to take control of sales or consumer taxes?

In recent months there has been more consideration given to agriculture, fisheries and the environment than there has to VAT. Early assumptions that these fields would be devolved in full and that this would be automatic given the nature of the Scotland Acts have been challenged since the turn of the year, however. The position of the United Kingdom government is that no power currently exercised by Holyrood (or, presumably, by Cardiff Bay or Stormont) will be re-reserved. There is nothing currently done by Holyrood that will be removed from its powers. But is it in the British national interest to have two (or three) regulatory regimes for fisheries policy and four for agriculture? It is surely a question worth asking, even if it risks a political row.

There is also the question of understanding just how broad an array of powers is covered by the Common Agriculture Policy (CAP). It includes regulation of the quality, grading, weight, sizing, packaging, wrapping, storage, transport, presentation, origin and labelling of agricultural products. By no means all of these matters are really about agriculture. Some are concerned with consumer protection or product safety. These fields are generally reserved to Westminster under the Scotland Act 1998, although there are exceptions for food products. Again, the question does need to be asked: is it in Britain's interests to have different rules on labelling, packaging, transport and storage in each of England, Wales, Scotland and Northern Ireland, or would it be more coherent, given the integrity of the UK's domestic market, to have a single, UK-wide regulatory regime for these matters?

Perhaps the answer is both. This leads me on to my final point. For more than 15 years we have acted as if a power is either devolved or it's reserved. If it is devolved, it is for these ministers accountable to this parliament; and if it is reserved it is for those ministers accountable to that parliament. The reality, particularly since the Smith Commission Agreement and even more so after Brexit, is more complicated than that. Of course there are devolved powers, and of course there are reserved powers. But there are also shared powers – areas where both the UK and Scottish governments have concurrent and overlapping responsibility. Social security is a good example. Universal Credit is a reserved benefit, but the Scottish Ministers have powers to make adjustments to its operation in Scotland. Likewise, child benefit is reserved, but Holyrood has the power to top it up (i.e. to make additional payments to recipients) if MSPs consider it to have been set at too low a rate.

The repatriation to the UK of powers over agriculture, fisheries and the environment presents an opportunity for the further development of ideas and practices of, and institutional apparatus for, shared rule. Could the UK establish a UK department of fisheries but base it in north-east Scotland rather than in landlocked Whitehall? Or think about it this way: the European Commission typically governs via directives, setting out broad principles of convergence but leaving to the member states the choice of form and methods of delivery. This is not a mechanism we have used in devolved Britain: it is not as if the UK sets broad principles and devolved administrations implement them in a manner best suited to local needs. But could such a system – innovative and novel as it would be in the UK context – not be the future of agriculture in Britain? These are the sorts of questions we are likely to be looking at in Scotland as Brexit unfolds.

Conclusion

Scottish political debate since 23 June 2016 has proceeded as if there is a gulf of difference of view and direction between the Scottish and UK governments. This has no doubted suited the party political aspirations of the SNP. But it really does not have to be like this. When you read the published views of the two governments and analyse them dispassionately, they have much more in common with one another than divides them. For example, the Scottish government wants continued 'membership' of the single market; the UK government wants the 'freest possible trade in goods and services between Britain and the EU' and 'the greatest possible access to' the European single market through a 'new, comprehensive, bold and ambitious free trade agreement' (May, 2017). These positions are really not that far apart.

Similarly, Scottish Ministers have said that EU nationals resident in the UK should have their rights protected. The Prime Minister has said that she wants to 'guarantee the rights of EU citizens who are already living in Britain... as early as we can'. But such a guarantee needs to be reciprocal, and it is the EU holding this up, not the British government. Again, Scottish Ministers have said that workers' rights, currently protected under European law, should be fully protected after Brexit. The UK government evidently agrees – in the Prime Minister's words: 'as we translate the body of European law into our domestic regulations, we will ensure that workers' rights are fully protected and maintained' (May, 2017).

In the end, Brexit could mean one of two things. It could see Britain turning in on itself, becoming more isolated, as protectionist walls are thrown up. Or it could mean the very opposite. It could mean that Britain recaptures something of its historic role as one of the world's great global trading nations, as one of the world's leading advocates of free trade and of the promise of economic freedom and prosperity it offers. The Scottish Conservatives are firmly in the latter camp. We are unionists, not nationalists – advocates of growing the economy through increased international trade, not of separating ourselves from our nearest trading partners. But this is a vision of Brexit that will need to be fought for – it cannot be taken for granted.

Across the western world, liberal internationalism is in retreat and nationalist protectionism is on the rise, in Trump's America, in Le Pen's France and elsewhere. The argument for free trade is not yet won. Those of us who believe in it must be ready, forcefully and confidently, to make its case.

References

May, T. (2017), *A Global Britain*, Speech delivered at Lancaster House, 17 January.
http://www.telegraph.co.uk/news/2017/01/17/theresa-mays-brexit-speech-full/
Scottish Conservatives (2017), *Scotland's Trading Future*.
http://www.scottishconservatives.com/wordpress/wp-content/uploads/2017/02/Scotland%E2%80%99s-Trading-Future.pdf
Scottish Government (2016), *Scotland's Place in Europe*.
http://www.gov.scot/Resource/0051/00512073.pdf

CHAPTER TWENTY-ONE

A better post-Brexit path for Scotland

Douglas Alexander

THE YEAR 2016 was one during which many old certainties, both in the UK and the US, died. A combination of economic anger, cultural anxiety, and political alienation upended the two most stable democracies on earth as a wave of populism swept the UK out of Europe and carried Donald Trump into the White House. Months on from these momentous decisions there are still many more questions than answers about their consequences and impacts, while Brexit continues to dominate British politics and will do so for years to come.

In December 2016, the Scottish government published its response to the Brexit vote in a document entitled 'Scotland's Place in Europe' (Scottish Government, 2016a), and the next month the Prime Minster set out the UK government negotiating objectives for exiting the European Union, and thereafter published a White Paper on February 2nd 2017 (HM Government, 2017). These documents help explain a central tragedy of our politics today: In the insightful words of Alex Massie (2016), 'the middle ground of Scottish politics is pro-union and pro-EU but neither of our governments can accept or accommodate the whole of that reality'.

These issues are not merely dry constitutional arrangements or interesting theoretical political constructs, and I do not claim academic detachment from them. For me, these issues run deep and indeed touch on deep senses of affinity and belonging. All of politics begins and ends with relationships; with our neighbour, our family, our community, with those who lead us and make decisions for us. Constitutional politics involves much more than a ledger of accounts: it speaks to who we are, how we see ourselves, and how we relate to others. It is about a common journey, a shared story and who we choose to share that journey with.

It would be easy in these circumstances to simply despair at the posturing and prejudice we have too often seen on both sides of the border in recent months:

for some, a retreat into cynicism and an embrace of old certainties seems the only appropriate response. Yet that would be a wholly inadequate, indeed cowardly, reaction in the face of the seismic developments in politics nationally and globally witnessed this past year. Nationalism, populism, and xenophobia are all on the march today. They have found voices once more, as almost always, in the context of economic uncertainty. Accordingly, this chapter is written not in denial of the re-emergence of these forces – or of the risk that politicians North and South of the border may well choose a path of division and grievance – but in defiance of that bleak choice. It suggests a politics, rooted in a commitment to solidarity and a recognition of our interdependence, demands a different and better path for Scotland: a path where, while retaining the strengths of the British partnership, we can in Scotland make different choices, including over relationships with Europe.

This chapter is written from a Scottish perspective and accordingly starts by considering the Scottish government's White Paper before considering the UK government's subsequent proposals. In acknowledging the political and economic backdrop to today's Brexit debate, the chapter concludes with policy proposals aimed at maintaining both British and European relationships for Scotland.

Scottish options

The Scottish government's Brexit proposals set out three options: one is staying inside the UK which itself stays part of the European Economic Area and the European Customs Union (Scottish Government, 2016a: vi). Another is for Scotland to stay inside the European Economic Area and the European Customs Union under specific arrangements, while the rest of the UK is outside them (Scottish Government, 2016a: p.vi). The other option is for Scotland to become a member of the EU as an independent country (Scottish Government, 2016a: vi). In contrast, the UK government's Brexit proposals assert that the UK will withdraw from the single market and seek a new customs arrangement and a free trade agreement with the EU (HM Government, 2017: 35).

The UK government (2017) addresses the issue of trade across the UK by highlighting that, 'Scotland's exports to the rest of the UK are estimated to be four times greater than those to the EU27. So, our guiding principle will be to ensure that – as we leave the EU – no new barriers to living and doing business within our own Union are created' (HM Government, 2017: 19). The gap between the two governments' sets of proposals are self-evident, but both governments make the same mistake in assuming the outcome of the Brexit negotiations can be dictated by a British Prime Minister. That is simply not the case.

There are politics, let us acknowledge, on both sides of the Channel, and one of the many ironies of a campaign run under the slogan 'Take Back Control' is that it has ensured the United Kingdom is not in control of the terms of the deal that will ultimately be struck with Europe. We don't get 'sovereignty' over the decision-making process, nor over the outcome of the negotiations. Indeed, the operation and the timetable of the Section 50 process is specifically designed to put the leaving country on the back foot. The politics of the Brexit negotiations must also be understood in the context of leaders across the continent determined to avoid an outcome that strengthens populism or encourages contagion. In 2017 we will see crucial elections in the Netherlands, in France and in Germany (alongside Theresa May's decision to call a snap UK election in June). In each of these contests populist, nationalist and xenophobic candidates will be challenging the mainstream governing parties.

While many of us in Scotland who supported 'remain' would be attracted to the option of the UK remaining part of the EEA and within the EU Custom's Union, the UK government's determination to end 'free movement' effectively takes this option off the table. Similarly, the option of Scotland remaining in the EEA and EU Customs Union, with the rest of the UK on the outside, has been explicitly rejected by the UK government. Indeed, even Charles Grant (2016) the Director of the Centre for European Reform and a member of the First Minister's Standing Council on Europe, has suggested that 'legally, politically, technically, it's extremely difficult for Scotland to stay in the single market if the UK as a whole does not, the basic point being that there would have to be one set of business regulations applying to England and another set applying to Scotland'. So, if these two options identified by the Scottish government are off the table, what of the alternative: Independence in Europe, described by the First Minister as 'the best option' (Scottish Government, 2016a: vi).

If the tumultuous weeks and months following the vote on 23 June 2016 have taught us anything, it should be to ask the difficult economic questions before deciding to disdain experts and simply walk away from our neighbours. There is little serious disagreement that one of the reasons the Nationalists lost the 2014 referendum was their failure to provide credible answers to reasonable economic questions; whether on the reliability of the oil price, the currency of a post-independence Scotland or the significant financial advantage Scotland gains from the operation of the Barnett Formula. So here are just a few relevant facts: The Scottish government's official blueprint for independence in 2014 asserted that the oil price would not fall below $113 a barrel (Scottish Government, 2014: 510); however, in 2017 oil prices are around $53 a barrel (Bloomberg Markets, 2017). The collapse in global oil prices has seen a 97 per cent fall in North Sea oil incomes between 2015 and 2016 (Scottish Government, 2016b: 21) while Scotland's estimated oil revenues fell from £1.8 billion to £60 million in the same period (Scottish Government, 2016b: 23).

The First Minister has stated that 'losing our place in the Single Market would be potentially devastating to our long-term prosperity' (Sturgeon, 2016a). However, while Scotland does indeed export goods and services to continental Europe totalling around £12 billion (Scottish Government, 2017: 1), the inconvenient truth for the nationalists is that, as Scots, we sell £49.8 billion of goods and services to the rest of the UK (Scottish Government, 2017: 19). It simply doesn't make sense to leave the UK without fully considering the impact of leaving the UK single market. If leaving the EU single market, where we export £12 billion of products and services, would be devastating for Scotland, how does leaving the UK single market where we export £48 billion make things better? If it is important for Scotland's companies to be able to trade freely with the European Single Market, then geography, history, and economic integration make it even more essential for Scotland's companies to be able to trade freely within the British Single Market.

And what of currency? In circumstances where the UK has left the EU, the choices for an independent Scotland become even more fraught with difficulty; joining the Euro with our interest rate decisions made in Frankfurt, or seeking to stay with Sterling with our interest rate decisions made in London (a foreign capital post-independence), or establishing a new Scottish currency with no reserve or any kind of petro-economy to underpin it when the currency speculators come calling, are all equally unappealing. Additionally, let us recognise the public expenditure backdrop to these decisions: Scotland spent £14.3 billion (Scottish Government, 2016b, p.46) more than it raised in taxes in 2015/16 (or 9.1per cent of GDP (Scottish Government, 2016b: 27)) – with these figures including a share of North Sea Oil revenue. EU rules mean that joining the European Union would require Scotland to cut this deficit down to 3 per cent of GDP (Treaty on the European Union, 1992), with all the cuts to public services and public expenditure this obligation would entail. Far from ending austerity, this would extend and deepen austerity.

The limits of nationalism north and south of the border

We have just witnessed one form of nationalism take us out of Europe with little thought for the consequences, so we should be wary of another form of nationalism repeating a similar mistake in Scotland. Little wonder a majority of

Scots are not demanding another independence referendum at this time and the opinion polls fail to show significantly increased support for independence since the Brexit vote last June (What Scotland Thinks, 2017). Yet, almost 100,000 supporters have joined the SNP following the Scottish independence referendum (House of Commons Library, 2016) – which helps explain why the First Minister continues to assert that for her, independence 'ultimately transcends the issues of Brexit, of oil, of national wealth and balance sheets and of passing political fads and trends' (Sturgeon, 2016b). It seems evident therefore that for the First Minister and her Party, the real issue is not so much the terms of the deal, but the level of the polls.

My honest worry is that the SNP now risks replicating David Cameron's fatal error – starting off trying to solve a party problem and ending up creating a far bigger country problem. Constantly threatening an independence referendum in the face of the economic evidence and without offering answers to reasonable questions doesn't enhance the First Minister's credibility for the discussions ahead – it diminishes it. Today we need more new thinking, and less of just the same old threats. Why would we choose to add greater insecurity and uncertainty to the insecurity and uncertainty already created by Brexit? Why would we choose an approach that guarantees division and rancour rather than an approach that could build consensus by consent?

The reality is that millions of Scots today feel squeezed between nationalist narratives north and south of the border and identify with neither. These narratives fail to recognise the grave risks posed by both governments' respective positions and they miss the opportunity that can still be seized to find a better path forward: a path towards a constitutional settlement that I believe could command broad support from both sides of the 2014 debate, and indeed on both sides of the border. So where, within the bounds of the possible can a way forward be found that would command this widespread support in Scotland?

A new British settlement

Rather than overestimating the capacity of the British government to dictate the terms of its new relationship with Europe, it is better to simultaneously look at internal arrangements within the UK – where the British government undoubtedly does have the capacity to deliver a new settlement. On these matters the former Prime Minister Gordon Brown, in a speech in August 2016 (Brown, 2016), started to chart a way forward. Then, in October, Professor Jim Gallagher produced a timely and influential paper (Gallagher, 2017) that sets out a number of these proposals in more detail.

Following the publication of the UK government's negotiation objectives there had been much speculation in recent weeks about the merits of the UK agreeing a Canadian-style free trade arrangement with the EU. This interest reflects the fact that the Canadian agreement (CETA) is the most recent and the most comprehensive trade agreement negotiated by the EU. I Chaired the UK government Cabinet Committee on Trade Policy back in 2009 when discussions between the European Commission and the Canadian government were first initiated. CETA took 7 years to negotiate, is 1,600 pages long, and does not cover services (Kassam, 2016) that make up 79 per cent of UK GDP (Office of National Statistics, 2016). It therefore seems highly unlikely that such a comprehensive free trade agreement (necessarily including services) could be negotiated within the two-year timetable anticipated by the Section 50 procedure. There is merit therefore, in the Scottish government focusing its immediate efforts on the terms of the ‹bridging agreement' that will likely emerge as the legal framework governing relations between the UK and the EU, while work continues on a final and more comprehensive agreement. Such an agreement, which we might call 'temporary cover', could potentially provide Scottish firms guaranteed access to both the British and the European single markets for years to come.

In the meantime, however, there are three other specific proposals that could benefit Scotland in the present circumstances, that impact on European relations but could be secured within the United Kingdom. First, after Brexit, areas of law previously within the competence of the European Union will be returned to the UK. In key areas within the competence of the Scottish parliament – agriculture, fisheries, and environmental protection – European law will no longer apply. It is therefore right that in these devolved areas, both power and resources should be repatriated – ensuring that important new power over key sections of Scotland's rural economy passes directly from Brussels to Edinburgh.

Second, the London Mayor, Sadiq Khan has initiated a dialogue with UK government Ministers arguing that it makes sense for London to be able to issue work permits based on the needs of the London economy. I would argue that the ability to issue work permits to skilled workers should be examined, as a route to ensuring the needs of Scotland's public services and private sector development are appropriately addressed post Brexit. Under the terms of the Scotland Act 1998, international relations are, of course, predominantly reserved to the UK government (HM Government, 1998). The Foreign Secretary is responsible for the foreign policy of the United Kingdom and as such holds responsibility for concluding treaties and other international agreements on behalf of the UK. In the case of a number of those neighbours, like Austria, Belgium, Italy and Germany, there already exists the capacity for regions to enter treaties within areas that fall within their competence, subject to review, consent or abrogation by the Nation State Government. In Belgium, under the 'in foro interno, in foro externo' principle of its constitution, Flanders has reached international agreements, for example with UNESCO, within areas of its competence such as education, infrastructure and the environment (Flanders International Treaty Competence, 1993). In light of the Brexit vote, it is clear that the majority of Scots are keen to maintain links with partners and neighbours across Europe.

Thirdly, therefore, we should now consider new constitutional arrangements here in the UK to better ensure effective engagement with the EU on devolved issues like health care, transportation, agriculture and education. That new engagement would be of particular interest to Scotland's world-leading universities sector, who benefit greatly from the attendance of European students and have made clear their appetite to remain within the ERASMUS + scheme that facilitates so many of these students coming to Scotland. Similarly, access to EU research funding has been a key element of Scottish universities' achievements in recent decades.

Whether these proposals will be argued for, or accepted, remains uncertain as Scottish and English nationalists seem more intent on myth-making than searching for solutions. Too much of the energy, time, and thinking required in these new circumstances is instead being diverted into entrenching a sense of 'us and them', whether it's denying sanctuary for unaccompanied child refugees or conflating the people of England with the politics of the Tories and UKIP. Shaping stories about ‹others› seems more the order of the day than figuring out solutions together.

For the constitutional arrangements post-Brexit to be durable they will need to be judged as in the service of, rather than in opposition to, Scotland's sense of self and the values and outlook we hold dear. Frankly, amidst the present rubble, that feels difficult but remains doable. It is vital that the proposals that emerge are interpreted as an affirmation of both the pride and partnership that has shaped most Scots' sense of who we are and how we want to be governed. They should enable our internationalism and minimise isolationism – a solution that allows Scotland both autonomy and cooperation – which let us recognise new circumstances without denying our enduring interdependence.

Of course, both the First Minister and the Prime Minister will face pressures from those within their respective parties to hold firm to a nationalism that shapes their negotiating demands: 'Patriotism needs no enemy but Nationalism demands one' (Gopnik, 2016), whether in the form of the British state or the European Union. This is an era when nationalism, populism and xenophobia are providing many with a story by which to make sense of their political choices. In a different time – in the age of the Scottish Enlightenment – our small northern European nation became a beacon to the world through its optimistic belief in the capacity of reason to guide change for the betterment of society. Neither independence nor the status quo can unite our nation or offer the best future for Scotland's people. So, let us hope, and continue to work to ensure, the spirit of reason can yet inform the negotiations which lie ahead in these troubled and troubling times.

References

Bloomberg Markets (2017).

https://www.bloomberg.com/energy [Accessed: 28 February 2017]

Brown, G. (2016), *Address to the Edinburgh Book Festival,* 29 August, Edinburgh Book Festival. Edinburgh.

https://www.edbookfest.co.uk/news/
gordon-brown-argues-we-re-better-together

Flanders International Treaty Competence (1993), *Flanders Department of Foreign Affairs,* 5 May 1993.

http://www.vlaanderen.be/int/en/flanders-international-treaty-competence

Gallagher, J. (2016), 'Brexit presents an opportunity to move towards a confederal UK', *Constitution Unit*, University College London, 10 October.

https://constitution-unit.com/2016/10/10/
brexit-presents-an-opportunity-to-move-towards-a-confederal-uk/

Gopnik, A. (2016), 'The Shape of our time', BBC *Radio 4*, 30 December. 20:50.

http://www.bbc.co.uk/programmes/b085z5jr

Grant, C. (2016), 'Nicola Sturgeon Brexit advisor pours cold water on her single market plans hours before they are unveiled', *Daily Telegraph*, 19 December.

http://www.telegraph.co.uk/news/2016/12/19/nicola-sturgeon-brexit-adviser-pours-cold-water-single-market/

Her Majesty's Government (2017) *The United Kingdom's exit from and new partnership with the European Union.*

https://www.gov.uk/government/uploads/system/uploads/attachment_data/
file/589191/The_United_Kingdoms_exit_from_and_partnership_with_the_
EU_Web.pdf

Her Majesty's Government (1998), *The Scotland Act 1998,* London: The Stationery Office.

House of Commons Library (2016), *Membership of UK political parties*, HC: SN05125, London: The Stationery Office.

Kassam, A. (2016), 'Canada's trade deal with EU a model for Brexit? Not quite, insiders say', *The Guardian*, 15 August.
https://www.theguardian.com/world/2016/aug/15/brexit-canada-trade-deal-eu-model-next-steps

Massie, A. (2017), 'Brexit delivers only a mandate for paralysis', *The Sunday Times*, 18 January.
http://www.thetimes.co.uk/article/brexit-delivers-only-a-mandate-for-paralysis-5db606bf9

Office for National Statistics (2016), *Statistical Bulletin: UK index of services: Dec 2016'*.
https://www.ons.gov.uk/economy/economicoutputandproductivity/output/bulletins/indexofservices/dec2016 [Accessed: 27 February 2017]

Sturgeon, N. (2016a), Speech in advance of Scottish Government Publication of '*Scotland's Place in Europe*, Edinburgh, ITV News, 20 December.
http://www.itv.com/news/border/2016-12-20/losing-single-market-could-devastate-scotlands-prosperity/

Sturgeon, N. (2016b), 'Decisions about Scotland should be taken by those who live and work here', *Sunday Herald*, 18 September.
http://www.heraldscotland.com/news/14749820.Nicola_Sturgeon__Decisions_about_Scotland_should_be_taken_by_those_who_live_and_work_here/

The Scottish Government (2016a), '*Scotland's Place in Europe*'.
http://www.gov.scot/Resource/0051/00512073.pdf

The Scottish Government (2016b), *Government Expenditure and Revenue Scotland 2015 – 16*.
http://www.gov.scot/Resource/0050/00504649.pdf

The Scottish Government (2017), *A National Statistics Publication for Scotland*.
http://www.gov.scot/Resource/0051/00514198.pdf

Treaty on European Union (1992), Luxembourg: Office for Official Publications of the European Communities.
https://europa.eu/european-union/sites/europaeu/files/docs/body/treaty_on_european_union_en.pdf

What Scotland Thinks (2017), 'How would you vote in a Scottish independence referendum if held now? (asked after the EU referendum)'.
http://whatscotlandthinks.org/questions/how-would-you-vote-in-the-in-a-scottish-independence-referendum-if-held-now-ask#line [Accessed 26 February 2017]

CHAPTER TWENTY-TWO

Wales and Brexit

Ed G. Poole

IN A RESULT that shocked the Cardiff political class, and will have repercussions for decades to come, Wales voted by a five-point margin to leave the European Union. This result transpired in spite of the many hundreds of millions of pounds Wales receives annually from European programmes, at far greater levels per head than in England. Wales' turnout of 72 per cent was also higher than in Scotland and Northern Ireland, with leave vote margins largest in deprived post-industrial areas that have arguably benefited the most from EU support.

A widespread perception of Wales in the aftermath of the referendum was of a country that had shot itself in the foot – if not in both feet. Not only did Wales separate from the other devolved nations in disregarding the urges of a large majority of its elected politicians in voting to leave, but the result also left the Welsh government entering intra-UK Brexit negotiations from a position of weakness. Wales cannot credibly threaten independence as can Scotland, nor can it appeal to land border or peace process concerns as can Northern Ireland. Perhaps understandably, the transition from the referendum shock to a coherent 'establishment' Welsh Brexit position was uncertain and protracted. Welsh Labour had a particular difficulty in reconciling their strong preference for continued membership of the EU with the voters' preference for withdrawal, frequently being unclear about their support for continuing membership of the Single Market and even retroactively deleting passages of a press release relating to free movement of people (BBC *News*, 2016).

Wales' weak bargaining position has, however, encouraged centre-left parties in the National Assembly to jointly develop Brexit policy in a manner that has not been replicated at Westminster or Holyrood. The sole Liberal Democrat in the National Assembly was already a cabinet member at the time of the referendum, and Plaid Cymru agreed to participate in three formal liaison committees, on finance, legislation and the constitution, with the Labour administration after the May 2016 elections. A fourth joint committee on Brexit was agreed soon after the referendum.

Eight months of transition pains ended in January 2017 in a Welsh government white paper published jointly with Plaid Cymru. In proposing the softest of Brexits along the lines of the EEA model, 'Securing Wales' Future: Transition from the European Union to a new relationship with Europe' diverges significantly from the UK government's intentions (Welsh Government, 2017). The Welsh proposals favour continued participation in the Single Market, the Customs Union, the European Investment Bank and many EU programmes. Reflecting Wales' slower-growing population and longstanding challenges in NHS recruitment, the proposals would also retain freedom of movement albeit with stronger links with employment than currently exercised in the UK.

These soft Brexit objectives reflect not only the parties' traditional pro-EU inclinations but the huge stakes for the Welsh economy in the eventual settlement. Manufacturing and tradable goods are significant economic sectors, such that Wales is far more dependent on the EU for its export markets than the UK average. Over two-thirds of Welsh exports outside the UK are currently to the EU, compared with less than half of exports from the UK as a whole. Single Market access is also far more conducive to the continuation of the Welsh government's prioritisation of Foreign Direct Investment in its economic development strategy. And because 77 per cent of HGV traffic between the Republic of Ireland and the continent passes through Welsh ports, both Wales and Ireland have a shared interest in the UK remaining in the customs union and common travel area.

Welsh and English interests after Brexit also diverge significantly in agricultural policy. The smaller-scale, upland Welsh rural economy is far more reliant on farm support payments than is the more intensive English agricultural sector: more than 80 per cent of farming income in Wales is currently derived from EU funding. Although a reduction on tariffs on agricultural products from outside the EU may reduce consumer prices, this would also be associated with increased price competition for Welsh farmers. For example, if Australia and New Zealand are among the first countries to conclude bilateral trade deals after Brexit, no-quota New Zealand lamb imports could render domestic production by small-scale Welsh hill farms unviable. Given that 90.7 per cent of total Welsh food and drink exports are to the EU, the downside risks from newly-imposed European tariffs or quotas exceed the potential opportunities to augment the small share of exports to non-EU markets.

Wales' vote to leave the European Union shunted Welsh politics into uncharted waters. But perhaps the result poses an even more fundamental challenge to Welsh politics than the rude awakening that the country was conspicuously less pro-european than had long been assumed. Devolution was meant to usher in an era of 'New Politics' (Osmond, 1998) in which Wales was envisioned as a 'model participatory democracy – one which engages all its citizens in shaping their own lives' (Wales Labour Party, 1999: 3). That Welsh voters felt disinclined to follow the almost united urgings of the Welsh political class for a remain vote suggests that devolution has singularly failed to achieve this re-orientation of political life in Wales.

Instead, devolution became what Richard Wyn Jones refers to as a 'largely defensive project... providing a degree of protection against the depredations of Westminster rather than an embodiment of an alternative politics' (2016), where political leaders were defined not by what they were *for*, but rather by what they were *against*: 'Westminster austerity' and 'Tory cuts'. But with the Welsh government lacking basic control over the size of their own budget and therefore powerless in avoiding cuts regardless of rhetoric, devolution as a defensive project was bound to fail. Instead, the macro-issue of Brexit showed the ease with which the Cardiff Bay bulwark against Westminster can be over-whelmed, and that Welsh opinion polling shows no sustained 'Bregret' since the referendum implies that these fundamentals have not changed. Not only did the Brexit vote repudiate old assumptions about Wales in Europe, but Welsh leaders will urgently need to replace these failed defences with an alternative construc-tion around a new vision. Doing so within the far less pluralistic infrastructure of the future British state will be the challenge of post-Brexit Wales.

References

BBC *News* (2016), 'Ministers admit changing post-Brexit vote press release'. http://www.bbc.co.uk/news/uk-wales-politics-37431646

Osmond, J. (1998), *New Politics in Wales*, London: Charter 88.

Wales Labour Party (1999), *New Opportunities for Wales: Labour's out-line policy statement for the National Assembly election*, Cardiff: Wales Labour Party.

Welsh Government (2017), *Securing Wales' Future: Transition from the European Union to a new relationship with Europe*, Cardiff: Welsh Government.

Wyn Jones, R. (2016), *Brexit Reflections – Why did Wales shoot itself in the foot in this referendum?* Centre on Constitutional Change Blog, 27 June 2016

CHAPTER TWENTY-THREE

Northern Ireland: the promise broken?

Duncan Morrow and Jonny Byrne

THE RAMIFICATIONS OF Brexit for Northern Ireland have taken time to dawn. On 23 June, only 62 per cent decided to vote. Participation was higher in middle class South Belfast (69.5 per cent) and North Down (68 per cent), and the lowest in the UK in Republican strongholds like West Belfast (49 per cent) and Foyle (58 per cent). All seven leave-voting constituencies had higher than average turnout. Pro-remain professionals and Unionist Brexiteers were clearly more exercised than Republicans. Yet despite the indifference, four constituencies with Unionist Westminster MPS voted to remain as did every constituency bordering the Border. Just one, North Antrim, voted by more than 60 per cent to leave.

Many reasons were given for this apparent quietude. Seven weeks after NI Assembly elections, voting was another duty. The campaigns in Northern Ireland were low key, especially the remain campaign that suffered from poor co-ordination among its Unionist, Nationalist, Liberal and Republican supporters. Republicans did not engage in what was, essentially, a UK-wide event dominated by Conservative Party politicians. Alone among the NI parties, the DUP campaigned to leave the EU, focussing entirely on their own electoral core. Although it was later revealed that the DUP was the conduit for an undeclared injection of finance for the UK leave campaign, very little was spent in Northern Ireland. The strongest warnings about the implications of Brexit came from the Taoiseach and former British Prime Ministers with a deep personal stake in the peace process – Tony Blair and John Major.

Yet, with hindsight, any proposal to 'bring back control' over borders and recast relationships with all of Europe, and therefore Ireland, was bound to have enormous implications for the internal politics of Northern Ireland and for the unstable equilibrium of its fragile accommodation. The question of 'UK – in or out?' is not exactly new in Ireland. Indeed, it has dramatically divided Ireland into incompatible enemies since the 1880s, drawing on deep roots in both imperialism and religious hostility. The ad-hoc 1920 border on a 26 Counties-to-6 blue-print pleased Unionists more than Nationalists, but it left them facing implacable, organised and potentially violent opponents in a 'Northern Ireland' where legitimacy was contested. Moreover, the internal dynamics of Northern Ireland increasingly isolated Unionists from the rest of Britain as much as Ireland. Politics took on a pattern of Unionists excluding Nationalists from power, underpinned by draconian emergency law and a culture of eternal suspicion and vigilance.

After 1969, 50 years of 'hostile tranquillity' gave way to 30 years of violent mayhem. After forlorn attempts to stabilise the ship through internal power-sharing and British Direct Rule, the Anglo-Irish Agreement ushered in two decades of inter-governmental partnership pursuing the comprehensive, if undefined, goal of 'reconciliation.' The apex of this unusual co-operation was the signing and ratification by referendum of the Good Friday Agreement in 1998, underpinned by US and European diplomatic and financial support. The Agreement allowed Irish nationalists to give conditional and historically unprecedented assent to British sovereignty in Northern Ireland.

Irish nationalism, including physical force republicanism, repudiated violence and acquiesced in UK sovereignty over a devolved Northern Ireland in return for a series of explicit guarantees. These were to prevent Unionist political and cultural monopoly, including recognition of the aspiration to Irish political unity and the acknowledgement of the legitimacy of Irish citizenship for everyone in Northern Ireland, cast-iron Unionist-Nationalist power-sharing, institutionalised cross-border cooperation including a North-South Ministerial Council, cultural 'parity of esteem', Human Rights grounded in international law, and equality in appointments and the provision of goods and services. For nationalists, the Agreement was a comprehensive deal trading the military reality that Northern Ireland could not be forced into a united Ireland yet establishing that Irish identity and Irish citizens would not be treated as second class in Northern Ireland while the border remained.

The Good Friday Agreement explicitly anticipated reconciliation. But within 9 years, the governments were backpedalling on anything other than the vaguest aspiration, calculating that requiring commitment to a shared future would actually prevent devolution and power-sharing between the Democratic Unionists (DUP) and Sinn Fein. The St Andrews Agreement therefore pursued the lowest common denominator rather than any higher common factor. Where the GFA aspired, St Andrews apparently delivered. Critically, by creating a governing coalition between the DUP and Sinn Fein, it secured the internal stability and escape from entanglement which both Dublin and London craved. Pragmatic containment trumped aspirational reconciliation.

The results were mixed, and predictable. After 2007, devolved government in Northern Ireland survived three elections. Violence was no longer the every-day commonplace of previous decades. In practice, peace in Northern Ireland remained a series of politically-managed ambiguities, locally known as fudge. Wheels came off when sharp decisions required one side to concede to the other. Repeated micro-crises replaced the old macro-crisis, as devolved government floundered over policing (2010), flags (2012), the past (2013), parades (2014), paramilitarism (2015) and the right of the British government to impose welfare changes (2015). Survival required the re-engagement of the governments, and the design of complex, and sometimes expensive, 'deals' that softened the blow of concession. Above all, reconciliation remained symbolic and largely depen-dent on the actions of British monarchs, Irish and American Presidents and EU cash.

Among the most important changes, was the emergence of the 'borderless border', an uncontroversial and seamless continuity between North and South. Opinion polls reflected a more confident sense of Irishness among nationalists but a reduced urgency around the aspiration for Unity. (Morrow, Robinson, Dowds, 2013)

Unionists were prepared to work with Irish Ministers on practical issues, including using Dublin airport as an international gateway. Border areas neigh-bouring Newry and Derry/Londonderry became increasingly integrated local economies, and key sectors like agriculture, food and tourism developed a clear cross-border profile.

It is difficult to imagine a more fundamental challenge to the stability of these arrangements than a unilateral UK departure from the European Union. While asserting undiluted UK territorial sovereignty appears to be legally cor-rect, it has huge consequences in a region that has been stabilised only by decades of nuance, subtlety and compromise. The establishment of a hard bor-der where, since the 1990s, the President of Ireland has made multiple official and semi-official visits into the territory of another jurisdiction with the infor-mal approval of the sovereign power is a dramatic political turnaround. The future of North-South bodies, the customs implications for agriculture, food and trade and the personal implications for cross-border commuters and com-munities are necessarily uncertain. And the longer-term implications for parity of esteem, human rights and reconciliation itself are now back on the table. More immediately, and in stark contrast to Scotland, polarisation over Brexit within the Northern Ireland Executive has effectively disabled the Executive as a vehicle for representing any consistent, coherent or common position during negotiations.

The Brexit negotiations are in effect also fundamental (re-)negotiations over the future of Northern Ireland. The form of Brexit, especially the rigidity of the border, has an existential relationship to the internal stability of Northern Ireland, and therefore to the future nature of both the UK and Ireland. The international partnership which brought about the Good Friday Agreement has been unilaterally set aside, and both the setting aside and the unilateralism matter in a society which is highly sensitive to anything which smacks of domination or external diktat. Inevitably, it will also mean that both Britain and Ireland must again become entangled in the affairs of Northern Ireland, and it is far from certain that the devolved institutions agreed in 1998 and 2007 can survive the pressures. Ultimately, the critical question may be: will Brexit in Northern Ireland be negotiated with a view to protecting reconciliation or will reconciliation in Northern Ireland be set aside to facilitate a Brexit which corresponds to the desires of other parts of the UK?

References

Morrow, D., Robinson, G. and Dowds, L. (2013), *The long view of Community Relations in Northern Ireland: 1989-2012*, Belfast: Northern Ireland Executive.

CHAPTER TWENTY-FOUR

Brexit and Ireland

Paul Gillespie

THE UNITED KINGDOM'S decision to leave the European Union is hugely consequential for Ireland. It represents an asymmetric shock politically and economically more intense than on any other member-state of the EU (O'Ceallaigh ed. 2017). Since the border between Ireland and Northern Ireland is the only land boundary between the UK and the EU, how Brexit works out will determine whether it remains fully open, as now, or relatively securitised as it was during the troubled decades from the 1970s to the 1990s (Hayward 2017). Returning to a more closed border for people and goods would polarise community relations in Northern Ireland and could imperil the peace process.

A UK outside the EU's single market and customs union would challenge a large section of the Republic's domestically owned economy which trades more intensely with the UK than does its more globalised international part. And the remarkable transformation in Irish-British relations over the last 15–20 years, which built on the longer normalisation of inter-state and popular relations arising from joint membership of the EEC/EU since 1973, would be equally challenged. This chapter examines these consequences and suggests ways to tackle them in the context of the greatly improved Irish-Scottish relations of recent times (see O'Ceallaigh and Gillespie (eds) 2015; Gillespie 2014a and Gillespie 2014b for more details).

Seen from Ireland, the UK is undergoing a dual crisis of sovereignty, externally and internally, both of which deeply affect Irish-British relations. The Brexit decision resurrects older imperial visions of Britain's place in the world within a new globalism of the Anglosphere in which control is supposedly wrested back from Brussels. Internally that is accompanied by a recentralisation of power in Westminster from devolved authorities in Scotland, Wales and Northern Ireland. It is a potent and volatile combination, which could provoke a breakup. To head that off some kind of federalisation is required; but it is not at all clear whether the revived nationalism of the English is willing to pay that extra political cost of union. The economics costs if Brexit goes badly also argue against that happening.

Political analysis cannot predict the outcome of this dual sovereignty crisis, but can, and should, anticipate the possible consequences for the constituent parts of the UK. Scenario mapping of these can help illuminate policy-making (Oppenheimer, 2015, Gillespie, 2015: 88). Much depends on whether the Conservative government, led by Theresa May, is willing or not to allow a special status vis-a-vis the EU for Scotland and Northern Ireland, which voted to remain, by keeping them in the single market and customs union. Her refusal, on grounds of a privileged UK sovereignty, to contemplate that ahead of the negotiations with Brussels, together with subordinate and ineffective influence of the devolved authorities on the UK negotiating stance, make an outcome which will satisfy them increasingly unlikely.

Demands by Sinn Fein, and the Social Democratic and Labour Party, for a similar special status for Northern Ireland were rejected by the two unionist parties in an assembly vote. Instead the Irish government talks of a 'unique' status for Northern Ireland, recognising the conflict that killed more than 3,000 people over three decades, and the peace process which brought the violence to an end in the 1998 Belfast Agreement. Without the Treaty of Rome there could be no Belfast Agreement, Taoiseach Enda Kenny argues, invoking the European peace process arising from two world wars to underwrite – and continue to fund – the Northern Ireland one. His point is that Irish-British reconciliation is embedded in joint EU membership, just as Irish values are (Kenny, 2017). Without that condition the political and economic complex interdependence between the two states could unravel and will need replacing by new bilateral arrangements agreed within an overall EU setting.

This could include a claim for special assistance to Ireland from the EU in managing the transition. It would cover continued peace funding and recognition that a hard Brexit would severely disrupt North-South trade (notably in dairy and beef products) and also Irish-British trade (especially if there is a failure to agree after 18 months and World Trade Organisation tariffs of up to 50 per cent apply, particularly on food and agricultural goods). The Irish government insists that the Common Travel Area between Ireland and Britain will continue to apply; but this will need EU agreement because of the effect on migration. Protecting that free movement of people may be easier to achieve than of goods, since customs posts on the Irish border will be necessary if the UK leaves the EU customs union. Technological approaches to this question, or non-border identity cards, will not solve it. The best way to control goods traffic for diversionary trade, while keeping the Irish border open, may be to impose controls on the Irish Sea at British points on entry; but that poses identity problems for unionists.

Ireland will stay in the EU, Kenny said, echoing widespread popular agreement (Eurobarometer, 2017). But he knows well that the case for doing so must be made repeatedly as Irish interests North and South are defended in the Brexit negotiations. He wants agreement that Northern Ireland (like East Germany in 1989–90) can enter the EU automatically in the event of concurrent referendum votes for Irish unity in Northern Ireland and the Republic. The unity issue arises directly from Brexit because the UK's dual sovereignty crisis threatens its ability to hold together. In Ireland this structural shift opens up a potentially non-nationalist case for reunification based on changing interests as well as political affinities.

If Brexit goes badly, significant elements of unionism may look more and more to Dublin to give the North voice and offer it a better (and probably federal) deal than London. In a period of accelerating change we should be ready to anticipate such shifts and debate how best they can be accommodated. One set of options then would look to new relationships between Ireland and Scotland, conceivably including a Dal Riada option bringing us into a confederal union within the EU (O'Leary, 2016; 2017). That would also be desirable if the EU disintegrates under pressure from the kind of sovereigntist populism exemplified by Brexit.

References

Eurobarometer 86 (2016), *Public Opinion in the European Union.* file:///C:/Documents%20and%20Settings/pgillespie/My%20Documents/Brexit/eb86_first_en.pdf

Gillespie, P. (2014a), 'The Complexity of British-Irish Interdependence', *Irish Political Studies,* 29 (1), pp. 37-57.

Gillespie, P. (2014b), *Scotland's Vote on Independence, The Implications for Ireland,* Dublin: Institute of International and European Affairs.

Gillespie, P. (2015), 'The Future of the United Kingdom', O'Ceallaigh, D. and Gillespie, P. (eds), pp. 69-93.

Gillespie, P. (2017), 'Issues facing the UK', in O' Ceallaigh, Daithi (ed.), pp. 23-26.

Hayward, K. (2017), 'The Irish Border and Brexit: An Explainer, Parts I & II', *Queen's University Belfast Brexit Resource Guide.* http://www.qub.ac.uk/home/EUReferendum/Brexitfilestore/Filetoupload,737794,en.pdf

Kenny, E. (2017), 'Ireland at the heart of a changing European Union', speech
    to IIEA, Dublin, 15 February.
http://www.iiea.com/ftp/Address%20by%20the%20Taoiseach%20to%20
    the%20Institute%20of%20International%20and%20 european%20
    Affairs%20on.pdf
O'Ceallaigh, D. and Gillespie, P. (2015), *Britain and Ireland: The Endgame, An
    Irish Perspective*, Dublin: Institute of International and European Affairs.
O'Ceallaigh, D. (ed.) (2017), *Brexit: a status report*, Dublin: Institute of Inter-
    national and European Affairs.
http://www.iiea.com/ftp/Publications/2017/StatusReport_V19.pdf
O'Leary, B. (2016), 'The Dalriada Document: Towards a Multinational
    Compromise that Respects Democratic Diversity in the United Kingdom',
    Political Quarterly, 87 (4), pp. 518-533.
O'Leary, B. (2017), 'Foreword' in O Dochartaigh, N., Hayward, K. and
    Meehan, E. (eds), *Dynamics of Political Change in Ireland, Making and
    Breaking a Divided Island*, London: Routledge, pp. xi-xxv.
Oppenheimer, M. F. (2015), *Pivotal Countries, Alternate Futures: Using Sce-
    narios to Mange American Strategy*, New York: Oxford University Press.

CHAPTER TWENTY-FIVE

The importance of border: Britain in flux

Madeleine Bunting

NATIONS DEFINE THEMSELVES by the stories they tell about themselves. That much we know, but what is less remarked upon is that particular weight is put on the stories nations tell about their edges – the borders and coastlines – and how they choose to define and mark them. Some of this is so familiar it's banal: think of the enduring significance of the white cliffs of Dover to English identity for example. The enduring popularity of the television series *Coast* speaks to that British fascination with its island identity. There is a powerful psychogeography to the edge; the recurrent stories of coastal erosion along the East Coast get extensive media coverage precisely because they unsettle, they challenge Britain's cherished island identity as singular, and steadfast. Or, as Shakespeare phrased it of England, in Richard II: 'this fortress built by Nature' with the sea serving 'in the office of a wall, Or as a moat defensive to a house.'

Despite Britain's intense affection for its coastal geography, the confusions have been legion as to how that maps onto its national identity. The historian Norman Davies in the introduction to his history, *The Isles*, takes the reader on an entertaining tour of how often England is mistaken for an island, and how often England and Britain are conflated even in the prestigious library catalogue systems (Davies, 1999).

Our Island Story: A History of England for Boys and Girls was published in 1905 and has been confusing generations of children ever since (Marshall, 2007). Of course, England shares an island with two other nations, Scotland and Wales, and is part of a political entity that straddles two islands, Britain and Ireland. In 2013 David Cameron, the former Prime Minister, offered an entertaining example of a senior politician getting himself horribly tangled in this stubborn geographical confusion. (Needless to say he once cited *Our Island Story* as one of his most formative childhood books.) A coastline is the one form of border that might offer clarity as well as continuity, but it seems not.

Less familiar than the white cliffs is the striking history over half a century of how the new nation of Britain used the North West coastline of Scotland to fashion a new set of stories for itself. During a few weeks in 1832 Mendelssohn's Hebrides Overture was premiered and JMW Turner's painting, *Staffa*, was unveiled in London. In the preceding few years both Sir Walter Scott and John Keats had joined the long queue of visitors, and penned poems extolling the wonders of Fingal's Cave. An uninhabited windswept island off the West Coast of Scotland had become central to the cultural life of Britain.

Fingal's Cave provided the still young nation with an iconic image: it represented a marvel of geology, a lost mythology and a subjugated people. All three were grist to a nation-building oriented to projecting the expansive vigour of empire and its greed to appropriate. The proximity to the ancient ruins of Iona underlined the point of an ancient, glorious past that confirmed a sense of historic destiny. Queen Victoria and Prince Albert duly paid their respects and the Victorian tourists balanced precariously on the basalt columns as they made their way to peer into the cave.

The intriguing point about Turner's treatment of this iconography was that the artist (raised on the shifting mud flats of the Thames) was not interested in the geology. His painting of Staffa puts a steamship centre, with its long plume of smoke pointing to the blurred headland of the cave. A third of the painting is a murky brown, and tiny pinpricks of red on the ship accentuate the loneliness of the imperial adventure. He has inverted the myth to describe the loneliness of empire, exile and immigration.

The North West edge of Britain is where the great projects of the British state petered out: many islands of the Western Isles remained Catholic in a country defined itself as Protestant. Many continued to speak Gaelic despite compulsory English in schools until the policy finally shifted in the late twentieth century. It's part of the appeal of borders and edges that they are liminal places of uncertainty where identity can frequently be contested.

Fascinated by these borderland uncertainties, on a holiday in eastern Finland, I once insisted that we drove our hired campervan to the Finnish-Russian border. This was once one of the most dangerous borders in Cold War Europe, but in 2008 the road approaching the frontier was lined with lorries in lay-bys. A long traffic jam of vehicles waited at the border crossing. We turned off and headed down a dirt track. It was a curiously idyllic stretch of countryside where fields were interspersed with birch woods and the verges were full of wild flowers. Finally, we arrived at a barrier with a sign warning us not to go any further. There was an empty guard post. The bees hummed in a gentle breeze.

A sign in English informed us of a three kilometre exclusion zone before the border which was patrolled by armed guards daily. A similar exclusion zone lies on the other side. It was eerie to stand there amongst the butterflies, and suspect that our every move was being relayed by satellite to some Russian surveillance centre. A strip of this silent countryside, six kilometres wide, runs along this eastern Finnish border; it's a land which the Finns fiercely defended in the Second World War. They still mourn the loss of the Karelia region (which included Finland's second city and its main industrial heartland – with an eighth of the population having to be resettled) in the post-war peace agreements.

Britain struggles to imagine this often traumatic European psychogeography of borders. Apart from Northern Ireland, it has had no land border for three centuries. This is what sets it apart from its Continental partners. It alone has been able to develop an identity around inviolability, while most Continental nations have experienced traumatic loss of territory, and mass displacement at some point in the last one and a half centuries. Countries shape-shift in Europe and borders have always proved provisional.

The travel writer Philip Marsden provides a vivid portrayal of this violent shape-shifting in his book, *The Bronski House* (Marsden, 1995). He traces the story of a Polish émigré who fled to Britain in the Second World War. Her family home was on territory contested by four nations: Lithuania, Belorussia, Russia and Poland. The house was in Russia at the beginning of the twentieth century, then Poland, finally Belorussia, but the nearest city was Vilnius, capital of Lithuania. The German and Russian armies swept back and forth while the surrounding forests in the Second World War became the haunt of a myriad of different 'partisan' movements. A land of anarchy. Such histories charge the politics of many countries in Europe with an intense insecurity.

The late eighties was a brief moment of unexpected hope that this historical burden of contested European borders might be no longer relevant. Those 'hard' borders of dogs, checkpoints, barbed wire and alarms 'softened' and the European Union pressed ahead on the Schengen agreement. Globalisation held out the promise of conquering space with new technologies and ease of movement. Air travel and hyperconnectivity seemed to make the geography of land, river, mountain range and sea, a matter only for tourism. Borders become purely bureaucratic and technological as queues stood in airports.

The illusion faded swiftly in the Bosnian war. But it was the extraordinary mass movements of Syrian refugees through south east Europe in the summer of 2015 which demonstrated that the crucial significance of geography had re-emerged. The images drove it home: refugees camped in fields in Slovenia or trudging down motorways to Austria. Borders which had been sleepy nondescript places only a few weeks before, became the flashpoints for political crises. We reached out for maps: we needed to learn geography again.

To feed this new appetite comes the wonderful timely book by Kapka Kassabova, *Border: A Journey to the Edge of Europe* (Kassabova, 2017). A Bulgarian who lives in the Scottish Highlands, Kassabova has plenty to tell the UK about borders. She takes the reader on a journey along the southern Bulgarian border with Turkey and Greece. Like the east Finnish border, this was a tense Cold War frontier where 'the sandals' as they called the young East Germans, were murdered as they attempted to flee to the west.

But long before, its soil was drenched in the blood of the Balkan Wars leading up to the First World War when the Ottoman Empire was dismembered. The new nations forced Bulgarians and Turks from their homes 'under pain of death' writes Kassabova, 'then for half a century, they were prohibited from crossing it under pain of death.' There were further extraordinary and under-reported mass movements of populations (300,000 Bulgarian Turks were deported in the last days of Communism). Now these densely wooded hills are criss-crossed with paths used by smugglers, refugees and all manner of secret traffic between Asia and Europe.

Such history no doubt confirms the British fear of borders and their delight in those coastlines and the 'silver sea' that serves as Shakespeare puts it, 'Against infection and the hand of war'. But Kassabova's writing depicts how borders are one of the most explicit expressions of the central state's power. This is where the character of that power is starkly revealed. At its most basic, does the power of the state reach its peripheries? Is the state apparatus – the crossings and checkpoints – competent and humane or violent and corrupt? The edges are where things fray and unravel. Borders and how they are kept in place, reveal nations to themselves.

References

Davies, N. (1999), *The Isles: A History*, London: Macmillan.

Kassabova, K. (2017), *Border, A Journey to the Edge of Europe*, London: Granta Books.

Marsden, P. (1995), *The Bronski House: A Return to the Borderlands*, London: Harper Collins.

Marshall, H. E. [1905] (2007), *Our Island Story: A History of England for Boys and Girls*, London: Civitas.

CHAPTER TWENTY-SIX

Soft power in hard times

John Edward

You come of a race of men the very wind of whose name has swept to the ultimate seas. (Barrie, 1922)

SCOTLAND IS WELL-STOCKED with quotations that speak to its uniqueness or ability to make a big noise for a small country. The Scottish parliament's Canongate wall offers a hit parade of them in carved permanence. Almost all speak to personality, character, impact or landscape; rather than might, weight or strength; and the country will need to employ all those assets in the months and years to come.

Scotland's own profile, its ability to make friends and influence people, has not, in modern times, been projected through military might or political occupation except via the United Kingdom. Recent history has shown a greater use of intangible assets such as education, sport and culture, which political administrations can support and defend but not appropriate or define. The relationship, in whatever form, with European neighbours and institutions, will need to be based on these.

The most recent 'As Others See Us' survey (British Council, 2016) of young people across several major European countries showed a decline in positive perceptions of the UK. The simple act of declaring an intention to leave the European Union appears to have suggested a lack of interest or engagement with our closest neighbours. It is likely to be through personal and cultural links, rather than political institutions, that relationships are repaired and maintained.

23 June 2016

One of the most referenced measures of soft power in recent years has been the 'Soft Power 30' index compiled by the Portland consultancy. Their 2016 edition was uncompromising in its pre-23 June prediction: 'A move for the exit door would definitely set British global influence back by forfeiting its voice in European affairs... a post-Brexit Britain would certainly see a decline in its soft power stores' (Portland, 2016). The report saw Brexit, the rise of UKIP, and 'increasingly incendiary rhetoric on immigration' as sending an unwelcoming message to the outside world, not least to its students. While the UK, including Scotland, is currently a member of what is seen as a unique and diverse range of the world's 'most influential organisations', that is about to change.

The nuanced view on such membership, that Scotland promoted both before and after the Brexit vote, is not a matter of political positioning alone. Recent history put the EU vote in a context discrete from the rest of the UK. The 2014 referendum rendered public platforms across political parties off-limits. The leave campaign language of excessive immigration and insufficient political and legal control was less resonant north of the border, where migration is an economic necessity and the previous 20 – since the 1997 referendum – had reminded the electorate that legal authority or political sovereignty had never really rested in one institution or city.

As a result, what lies ahead for Scotland will be built on past actions that demonstrated where Scotland might act distinctively without immediately triggering a party political fight, or without being distracted by one. The relationship in and with the European Union is a case in point – the developments of the past giving a substantial guide to what the future will require.

1 January 1973

The passage of Scottish political life since devolution has somewhat overshadowed the formal and informal ways in which Scottish interests had been represented almost since the UK finally acceded to the EEC in 1973. Despite the UK being one of the most centralised Member States of the Community, the importance of structural funding to certain regions soon began to create a sense of divergence. It is, perhaps, easy to forget in a world without an Iron Curtain, how far behind some parts of Europe the economies of the Highlands and Islands or West Central Scotland were.

Strathclyde was one of the first UK local authorities to take an active and distinctive role in European matters in the 1980's. They were joined in due course in Brussels by a consortium from the Highlands and Islands, the Convention of Scottish Local Authorities (COSLA), the Enterprise agencies and other companies and public bodies. The multiplier effect of a wide membership base was clear – any information passed down the chain reached several hundred organisations and any interest that the information generated could be conveyed back to the centre of Brussels, to within metres of the major institutions. It is a sign of how much has come to pass since that it was a Conservative Secretary of State for Scotland, Ian Lang MP, who established Scotland Europa in 1992, calling it 'a very significant milestone in the development of our links with our partners in the European Community' (Scotland Europa, 2013).

That development, at the dawn of the Single Market, was in the days when the EU was a Community of 12, the Economic and Monetary Union of the EU (EMU) was a work in progress, the Schengen agreement had still to take effect and Jacques Delors' Commission was in its pomp. The membership of the Union overall has grown first north, then east and south to more than double what it was in 1992. If, for Scotland, the main priority in Europe 25 years ago was access to, and effective use of, structural funds, ambitions developed beyond tracking down money. The enormous amount at stake for member states, businesses and related interest groups, has increasingly meant that close attention to the workings of the EU was necessary to avoid unpleasant surprises emerging from the legislative pipeline several years downstream. Outcry over EU legislation in the UK media, and some political circles, that helped feed the result in June 2016, traditionally ignores that timeline and focuses on the kitchen tap rather than the rainfall or the reservoir.

Small states and nations can, and do, influence opinion and decision-making in the European Union and beyond if they are adept and skilful at establishing a clear identity; identifying those few areas of key concern; and accumulating support from the range of other national, regional and sectoral interests represented in Brussels. Support on fisheries issues, for example, may not come from other states that produce, but states that consume.

The presence of Scotland in the EU has moved over time from a coalition of interested parties and partners, through the more formal role post-devolution of a 'legislative region', to the point where Scotland is watched carefully by other devolved entities – and by Member States – as it grapples with the existential issue of its constitutional and institutional status. By any standards, and compared with Flanders, Catalonia, Bavaria etc., it has been the international equivalent of rapid league promotion.

The affectionate remembrances of Donald MacInnes, Chief Executive of Scotland Europa over the period of devolution (Scotland Europa, 2013) demonstrate just how much of the projection of that new political muscle was done through traditional, or eccentric, soft power methods – Harris Tweed fashion shows, Burns suppers, cultural exhibitions or 'Schots Weekend' in Flanders. In all of this, Scotland in Europe has kept well away from the often tiresome politics around membership of the European Union itself, until 2014 made such debate unavoidable.

Now what?

The first 'As Other See Us' report (British Council, 2014) – the title itself a reference to the global reach of Scottish poets – highlighted the characteristics seen as making the UK most attractive:

1. Cultural and historic attractions
2. Cities
3. = Arts
4. = Countryside and landscape
5. History

These ought to give even the most jaded promoter of Scotland's image some reassurance, but therein lies the challenge. For all that leave voters stand by the decision they took in 2016, it does not alter the fact that the 27 other countries of the EU form (most of) the UK closest neighbours – in geography, legal recognition, professional compatibility, ease of association, artistic heritage, tourism, sport, and so on.

The 2014 British Council research highlighted the UK's perceived weaknesses in the eyes of the world. The top two might be met with a wry smile or even perverse sense of pride, being 'drinking too much' (27 per cent) followed by 'bad eating habits' (23 per cent). The following three traits ought now to give more cause for concern (beyond the public health community), being 'ignorance of other cultures' (22 per cent), 'too nationalistic' (22 per cent) and 'intolerance towards people from other countries' (20 per cent). Those within Scotland who discern a distinct and outgoing national sentiment, that differs from that found elsewhere in these islands, may wish to consider whether other nationalities will make such a generous and detailed distinction post-Brexit.

National power grid

In terms of how Scotland might seek to confound these expectations, there is no shortage of avenues to pursue, from the ceremonial to the mundane. For Scotland to maintain the distinctive identities and networks that future cooperation requires will take all the initiative of national institutions, and a substantial degree of non-partisan inventiveness. At the most symbolic level, there are ways in which Scotland has never ceased to project itself as formally or constitutionally discrete. Scandinavian Royal families have often visited Scotland as part of, or as the whole of, formal visits to the UK, in recognition of historic links of territory and dynasty. The same is true of recent Papal visits to the UK, where the independent 'filia specialis' status of Scotland in the Roman Catholic Church since 1218, has ensured Scotland featured on the itinerary for both John Paul II and Benedict XIV; Moderators of the General Assembly have traditionally made Vatican visits, as well as visits to the EU institutions, in return.

Scotland's oft-quoted focus on education will be a key part of future engagement with Europe, irrespective of the future of programmes such as Erasmus. That Scotland has four ancient universities, amongst nineteen higher education institutions, is a key part of the country's image and its international draw, in a world where 25 per cent already speak, or learn, English. Uncertainties over the future of research cooperation alone indicate the importance of Scotland's voice to the UK's eventual deal with its former EU partners, but education will have to work fast and hard to stay competitive in the context of Brexit in an increasingly competitive global knowledge economy.

There are other networks that have an equal impact, often with less domestic recognition or formal political intervention. Humanitarian NGOS, such as the Scottish Catholic International Aid Fund and the European HQ of Mercy Corps, have a substantial footprint in the world of development, and are at times forgotten as part of Scotland's soft diplomacy presence globally disbursing, at present at least, substantial portions of EU humanitarian and development funding. As small countries such as Ireland, Finland or Portugal have demonstrated, modest size can be a positive advantage, whether providing personalities considered impartial in larger geopolitical arenas, or chairing the EU Presidency.

The most underestimated profile of the country in popular culture comes through sport. Many 'regions' in Europe would sacrifice much for the distinctive reach, heritage and profile of Scottish sport and the cultural diplomacy it creates. Scotland's sporting reach is bolstered by unique characteristics, having been integral but distinct from the other parts of the UK in the early development and regulation of many, now global, sports. Just as no public information campaign could create the brand familiarity that Scottish golf does, no amount of legislative devolution or political divergence has given Catalonia, the Basque Country or Bavaria the 'national' profile in football that Scotland (even to this day) commands. The constituent parts of the British Isles work hard to preserve their premier position in rugby's Six Nations, a seemingly parochial contest that has the highest average attendance of any global sports event (UEFA, 2017).

European future

Looked at in the round, the network at Scotland's disposal, whether as an autonomous, independent or federated entity, is enviable. As early as 1957, the Treaty of Rome made explicit reference to 'progressive abolition of restrictions on international trade'. If Scotland wishes to remain some part of that progression, in whatever capacity, it will need smart thinking and manifest commitment to keep the attention of the capitals, economies and institutions of our European hinterland.

They are – after everything – useful neighbours to have, whether for a 'smart successful Scotland' or a 'wealthier, fairer and greener' one. The framework that now exists within the EU – financial, legislative and judicial – is in many ways the basic law for companies and individuals in Scotland. As that structure starts to shift, Scotland will need all of its available resources to hand to remain visible.

References

Barrie, J. (1922), *Courage: The Rectorial Address delivered at St. Andrews University.*
https://archive.org/stream/couragejamesoobarruoft/couragejamesoobarruoft_djvu.txt

British Council (2016), *As Others See Us, Perceptions of the* UK *among young people in* G20 *countries.*
https://www.britishcouncil.org/organisation/policy-insight-research/research/others-see-us-2016

Portland (2016), *The Soft Power 30, A Ranking of Global Soft Power.*
http://softpower30.portland-communications.com/

Scotland Europa (2013), *20th Anniversary Reflections.*
https://www.scotlandeuropa.com/paper-36-2013-20th-anniversary-reflections/

Culligan, K., Dubber J., Lotten, M. (2014), *As Others See Us Culture, attraction and soft power.*
https://www.britishcouncil.org/sites/default/files/as-others-see-us-report-v3.pdf

UEFA (2017), *The European Club Footballing Landscape - Club Licensing Benchmarking Report, Financial Year 2015.*
http://www.uefa.org/protecting-the-game/club-licensing-and-financial-fair-play/news/newsid=2435355.html

CHAPTER TWENTY-SEVEN

Somebody has to do it: Spain prepares for Brexit with an eye on Scotland and Gibraltar

Ana Romero Galán

THERE IS A sense of sadness in one of the top floors of the modern building that houses the Spanish Ministry of Foreign Affairs in Madrid known as Las Torres (The Towers). From here, overlooking the city across the main M30, officials work on the nitty gritty of Brexit, 30 years after Spain joined the European Union. The feeling is so different from the excitement felt in 1986 when everything was being built. 'Somebody has to do it' says one of the officials who has been keeping an eye on all things related to the referendum.

Just days after the vote last year, a so called Interministerial Commission started meeting every week at the Moncloa palace, the Spanish version of Downing Street, to prepare for Brexit. Led by Deputy Prime Minister Soraya Sáenz de Santamaría, they work on two new European treaties: an exit one that will be implemented after 2019, and then a Canadian-style commercial treaty that would take several years to negotiate, as explained to me by this official.

The whole process could be finished by 2023: 'With the UK, negotiations will be faster than they were with Canada. We know each other very well'. This official uses the word divorce many times when he refers to the negotiation process: 'The question is whether to make the main decisions – the house, the children – right at the beginning or when things have calmed down'.

Spanish sadness

I perceive the importance – and again the sadness – of what Spain is doing: 'For the British, the survival of the United Kingdom depends on a good negotiation. For us, it is about the survival of the European Union itself. All 27 members agree on this basic idea: the continuation of the European Union'.

At the start of this year, Spaniards received icily Theresa May's January speech setting out her plan for Brexit negotiations – often putting her words alongside those of Donald Trump. You might not like the coupling; but many Spaniards tend to put both leaders in the same bag, especially since May's main Brexit speech. 'Antipática' – something between unsympathetic and simply not nice – is the general feeling among ordinary people here when they try to describe Mrs May.

As I gathered thoughts, from those in government to citizens I'd run across in my daily business, and from across the political spectrum, one dominant view prevailed: how can May's proposals not be bad for Britain and perhaps for others, too?

The Spanish media were certainly unimpressed by the UK Prime Minister's words. *El País*, Spain's leading newspaper, was particularly hard, underlining 'delirium and haughtiness' in her speech. The staunchly pro-European Madrid daily accused her in its editorial of supporting a 'shameless and xenophobic nationalism'. It added that 'Nothing in May's speech sounds right. The promise to reach a "positive deal" is misguided. It is not positive to show contempt towards European citizens nor to discriminate against its residents. Neither does it make sense to threaten the Europeans Britain will have to negotiate with...' (*El País*, 2017).

The tone in almost all of the media was similar. Mrs May's words were described as challenging, hostile, hard, threatening, without concessions, illogical, extreme and fierce. According to Miguel Otero-Iglesias, a member of the main foreign affairs think-tank the Real Instituto Elcano: 'The time when the British empire used to decide the rules of the game was back in the 19th century' (Otero-Iglesias, 2017)

Some commentators, on both left and right, accused Mrs May of wanting to mistreat the 3.3 million EU citizens living in Britain, or of simply working to transform the country into a tax haven. Neatly pointing out the contradictions in the British position, writer José María Carrascal suggested that Britain would not get away with a 'hard Brexit for the Europeans and soft for them' (Carrascal, 2017).

How Britain is seen from Spain: May, Gibraltar and Scotland

The new Minister of Foreign Affairs, Alfonso Dastis, who took the job last November, is soft spoken and gentle compared with his predecessor, José Manuel García-Margallo. But even he was pretty clear: 'The European Union was born without the United Kingdom and it can continue perfectly well without it. In fact, besides being a challenge, Brexit can be an opportunity to renew the European project' (Dastis, 2017).

But he tried to calm the waters by underlining that Mrs May's words were meant 'for inside consumers and expected to create an exit narrative through forceful messages'. So there is also a recognition of UK domestic realities, and Dastis emphasised that Spain's attitude should be wait and see until Article 50 has been activated.

After a year of political turmoil, and a caretaker government, there is now a view in Madrid that Spain can play a leading role in the relaunch of the European project. Dastis insisted that the UK should formally report its will to leave the European Union as soon as possible; and that Spain is ready to start the separation process. Indeed, the stakes are so high that there are no divisions on this amongst the Spanish political class, normally very divided.

The Prime Minister, Mariano Rajoy, his powerful number two, Sáenz de Santamaría, and all of the top Spanish representatives, have echoed Dastis' insistence that all four European liberties (people, goods, services and capital) go together, and the UK will not get away with keeping only the commercial right.

While working on the process of saying farewell to the UK, Spaniards keep a close eye on Scotland and Gibraltar, on top of the eight public sectors identified as being affected by Brexit (Informe Deloitte, 2016). In both cases, European politics becomes domestic policy. Take Scotland, whose situation could compare dangerously to Catalonia, the northeast territory that is threatening to hold an independence referendum this summer. If Scotland were allowed to stay within the EU after Brexit, why not an independent Catalonia?

Spain feels deep sympathy for the Scottish people, a clear majority of whom have voted to stay in the European Union. But when it comes to the negotiation, the Spanish line is clear – 'The European Union is an international organization of States. There is no such thing as autonomous European citizenship. One has European citizenship because one belongs to a State. This is a question of pure international law. Nothing to do with regional problems, which we all have' (Interview, 2017a).

'With Brexit, the UK leaves the EU with its four nations and its four overseas territories – the Isle of Man, the Channel Islands, Gibraltar (a British Overseas Territory) and its bases in Cyprus (the two Sovereign Base Areas). Everything goes. About this question there is no doubt. All 27 members agree'. This is incorrect; in that British Overseas Territories and Crown Dependencies (the latter being the Isle of Man and Channel Isles) are not part of the UK: they constitutionally sit outside the UK and the EU (the exception being Gibraltar).

This takes us into Gibraltar, where Spain finds the silver lining to a sombre Brexit. Dastis is the opposite of his rambunctious predecessor Margallo, but he too has been very direct about the tiny peninsula perched on the tip of southern Spain and belonging to the UK since 1714, saying that 'Any decision on Gibraltar's relations with the post-Brexit EU will need Spain's approval' (Dastis, 2017). This attitude is what Picardo calls 'rain without thunder'; after Margallo's threats, the official policy remains unchanged (Picardo, 2017).

Spain has offered Gibraltar a joint sovereignty plan and is awaiting London's proposal. Picardo has flatly refused the offer. If Gibraltarians were forced to choose between British sovereignty and a special relationship with the European Union, they would certainly decide to stay British. Even if that means giving up both freedom of movement and their access to the common market.

'We are waiting for the UK to make either a joint proposal or four different ones' in respect of each Dependent Territory. 'What relationship will Gibraltar have with the European Union? Gibraltar is not Leeds, so it will have to factor in the need to secure Spain's agreement. Madrid is not going to accept Gibraltar being a satellite of the UK outside the EU, but retaining all the privileges of membership, in particular freedom of movement and the common market' (Interview, 2017b).

Spain's main concern is the 6,000 Spanish nationals who cross the frontier every day from the impoverished Spanish border town of La Linea into wealthy Gibraltar, to work as waiters, cleaning ladies and other service professions. The other 3,000, who daily cross from Spain to Gibraltar, are less of a concern to the Spanish government, namely the British nationals and other expats who live in the province of Cádiz but work in the financial area on the Rock.

Madrid's red lines – smuggling, mainly of tobacco, and Gibraltar's advantageous tax regime. 'On its own entry in 1973 to the EU, the UK negotiated very special conditions for Gibraltar. On its entry in 1986, Spain accepted them all. But now things have changed. If Gibraltarians want to deal commercially with us, they will have to pay the same taxes as we all do', said one diplomat.

Under Spain's proposal for joint sovereignty, the frontier that remained closed between 1969 and 1983 would disappear. Gibraltarians would remain British, but could also have a Spanish passport if they wanted to – 'it is time for them to stop just saying No, and to start making proposals. We are waiting'.

It is not only when it comes to Gibraltar that Spain feels the UK is on the losing side. As one top Spanish official put it to me: 'the British government is trying to make us think that we have a problem. They are the ones who have a problem. And it is a very big one'.

In the street, I hear similar sentiments. 'If they want to go and think only about themselves, then adiós' said Juan, who looks after the maintenance of a building in Madrid.

'May's speech wasn't that important – we are already feeling the consequences of Brexit in my office: the British have less money to spend' said Leticia, on her way from Madrid to Jerez de la Frontera in Andalucia where she works in the tourism sector, adding that 25 per cent of the tourists in Spain come from the UK. As it happened, Mrs May's speech coincided with Spain's yearly tourism fair in Madrid, where the negative effect of Brexit was a popular line of conversation.

Amid this turmoil, at least one Spaniard, 26-year-old Miguel Bescós, chose to be pragmatic: last week he joined the at least 200,000 Spaniards already living in the UK; and travelled to Liverpool to learn English and maybe work as a waiter. He can't find a job in Spain and thinks that soon it will be more difficult for him to go to the UK – 'Now you just buy a plane ticket and go. In a few months' time, who knows?'

Ironically, the newly appointed Spanish ambassador to the UK, Carlos Bastarreche, belongs to the so-called 'trinitarios', the group of top diplomats who, in the mid-eighties, worked from the Palacio de Trinidad, the then headquarters of Spain's Ministry of Foreign Affairs, negotiating Spain's entry into the European Union. They were considered the best and the brightest in the Foreign Service. There was no feeling of sadness then, just of hope and a new beginning.

Just before leaving for London, Bastarreche received a priority instruction from the government in Madrid; from the Spanish Consulate in Belgrave Square, to find a way of helping those whom Madrid feel now have the most to lose from Brexit. Namely, Miguel and the other Spaniards living, like him, in the UK. Them, and 65 million British people.

References

Carrascal, J.M. (2017), 'Brexit, ¿ por qué no?', ABC, 21 January.

Dastis, A. (2017), *Foro Nueva Economía*, 18 January.

El País (2017), 'Un Brexit extremista', 18 January.

Informe Deloitte (2016), 'El impacto del Brexit en el sector público', July.

Interview (2017a; 2017b), Spanish officials at the Ministry of Foreign Affairs.

Otero-Iglesias, Miguel (2017), "El incongruente Brexit de May", El País, 18 January.

Picardo, F. (2017), *El Mundo*, 25 January.

CHAPTER TWENTY-EIGHT

Brexit and the future of Europe: a German perspective

Michael Wohlgemuth

THE RESULT ON 23 June 2016 sent shock waves all over Europe, including Germany. Not only the government in Berlin but the German population also wanted the UK to stay in the EU. And for two good reasons. First, economically, the UK is an important trading partner (Germany exported 120 billion euros of goods and services to the UK, importing 63 billion euros in 2015) and an important location for direct investment of German companies (German direct investment in the UK worth 7 billion, about the same as direct UK investment in Germany). With a 'hard Brexit' – meaning reduced access to the single market – these trade relations could face new tariff and non-tariff barriers, and the German economy could shrink by around one percentage point by the year 2030 (Bertelsmann Stiftung, 2015).

Second, politically, the UK has been an important ally for Germany when it came to reforming the EU budget and fostering free trade. The southern EU member states in 'Club Med' will keep asking for 'more Europe', understood as more transfers, higher social standards, common European unemployment and deposit insurance, more interventionist industrial policies, less free trade – and less fiscal restraint. Without the UK votes in the European Council, Germany, the Netherlands, and Scandinavian member states could be systematically outgunned by states more interested in the EU as a transfer union than in a Europe of open markets and competitive entrepreneurship.

A poll commissioned by Open Europe Berlin and the British Chamber of Commerce in Germany (BCCG, 2015) before the referendum found that not only would 55 per cent of Germans regret the UK leaving the EU. It also showed wide support for David Cameron's reform proposals that led to the EU Council's decision on a 'new settlement for the United Kingdom within the European Union' in February 2016 (EUCO 4/16). It is important to note that we did not ask whether respondents supported the demands of David Cameron on behalf of the UK, but whether they generally agree e.g. with the view that 'more rights and competences should be returned from the EU to the member states' (54 per cent in favour), that 'national parliaments of EU member states should have the right to stop laws and directives of the EU if a certain number of member state parliaments reject them' (64 per cent in favour) or that 'EU member states should have a right to make welfare payments dependent on whether an EU-for-eigner has already payed contributions for a few years' (69 per cent in favour). If David Cameron had made it more clear that his reform proposals were indeed 'in the wider interests of the European Union as a whole' (Cameron, 2015) and not just another exceptionalist settlement for the UK, he could have found more support from other EU member states, especially from Germany.

The impossibility of British cherry-picking in Europe

One word constantly used in comments by both German government and German media before and after the Brexit referendum was 'Rosinenpickerei' – cherry-picking. If there is one model of European integration that most Germans favour least, it is Europe à la carte. Even our innocuous question: 'should all issues within the EU be decided by all member states or should it be possible within the EU that some states, with regard to some issues like fighting crime or migration policies, work closer together than other countries that do not wish to do so?' revealed this – 51 per cent answered that 'all decisions should be taken by all member states'.

Paul Krugman is not the first to have observed this Kantian element in German politics – and to deride it. In 1999 he argued: 'it's not Karl Marx vs. Adam Smith, it's Immanuel Kant's categorical imperative vs. William James' pragmatism. What the Germans really want is a clear set of principles; rules that specify the nature of truth, the basis of morality, when shops will be open, and what a Deutsche mark is worth. Americans, by contrast, are philosophically and personally sloppy; they go with whatever seems more or less to work' (Krugman 1999). Krugman has a point, this attitude is quite foreign to Germans, especially when it comes to European integration (See Wohlgemuth, 2011).

What Germans mainly hoped to get from joining an 'ever closer union of peoples' in the 1950s was an international 'Rechtsgemeinschaft' – a community built on the values and principles of the rule of law and the certainty of the law; and of laws applicable equally to all. This is why the glaring disregard for rules, like the Maastricht debt criteria or the no-bail-out-clause that should have made the Euro as stable as the *Deutschmark* and the ECB behave like the *Bundesbank*, has been such a shocking experience in Germany – but nowhere else. At the end, however, Germany grudgingly accepted some state of emergency pragmatism in dealing with the acute Euro-crisis – for the sake of European unity.

Germany and European integration

European unity and stability has been a priority of German politics since the beginning of post-war European integration. Back then, it was the major goal (and achievement) of Germany to be allowed back into a community of civilised nations. And still today, with some allowance for depreciation, this historical motive plays a role in German European politics. Nowhere else can one find evidence for a sort of 'sacralisation' of the European project, making it almost taboo to question European integration even where criticism is due or a healthy dose of 'sloppiness' could have helped (Graf Kielmansegg, 2015).

The German position during the Brexit-negotiations will be shaped by the same two 'typically German' attitudes: stickling for principles and prioritising European unity. In terms of principles, Angela Merkel, and politicians across the German party spectrum, made very clear early on that the 'four freedoms' of the European single market were 'inseparable', meaning that if the UK wanted to remain a *member* of the single market for goods, services and capital, it would have to also accept free movement of EU citizens (in addition to EU budget contributions, and EU legislation, as well as European Court of Justice jurisdiction on matters relating to the single market).

This Kantian insistence on legal principles applicable to all was not only a German obsession, but shared widely amongst EU member states and, of course, EU institutions. This categorical consent of the EU27 may have driven Theresa May to drop the 'Norwegian' option of leaving the EU, but remaining in the single market, although in Berlin this was long held to be the best option for Germany, the EU, and the UK as well.

So meanwhile Angela and Theresa, both daughters of pastors (and thus perhaps influenced by protestant ethics), have made their points. Now it remains to be seen how they (and many other players) can reach pragmatic solutions. On purely economic grounds, it would be reasonable for Germany and the EU to seek as much free trade as possible with the UK – which, after all, has a sizeable current account deficit with the rest of the EU and Germany in particular. In terms of political strategy, however, the second 'typically German', but in this case widely shared, attitude is likely to counter economic pragmatism: the fear of instability and of possible contagious effects from too amicable a divorce, that may prompt other EU leaders to play hardball using exit threats. Quite a few governments, officials in Berlin and Brussels fear, might be tempted to use Mr Cameron's strategy to win special treatment, opt-outs, rebates, or toleration of noncompliance with EU rules (such as fiscal debt restraints).

Brexit complications

This is why in Berlin many (including business leaders, even of the automobile industry) prioritise European unity and are inclined to use Brexit as an example (*Economist*, 2016). More exit-referenda used in order to achieve a special status in the EU in the form of opt-outs, concessions or rebates would undermine the EU's political, legal and economic unity, they argue. Hence, if the UK's former position of being a member of the EU, but with many opt-outs, has been only reluctantly accepted, the same would hold for the UK leaving the club, but with many opt-ins to attractive fields of cooperation.

Sure, the UK government will have many things to offer, such as its foreign policy expertise, military power and intelligence capacity exactly in areas where the EU is now facing new challenges. And provided that European leaders overcome the fallacy of trade as a zero-sum game, a 'wide reaching, bold and ambitious free trade agreement' should indeed be in the mutual interest of all parties (HM Government, 2017). On purely economic grounds, this also holds for financial services. It would be mutually damaging if the EU were to cut itself off from London as Europe's largest and most attractive financial centre and cause an artificial and costly fragmentation of financial services in Europe. But this issue is heavily politicised. Voters would not appreciate the EU giving post-Brexit 'privileges' (passports) to London's City bankers; even if time local politicians and media celebrate news of any number of the same London bankers relocating to Frankfurt, or Paris.

If all this were not enough, there are further complications from the territorial differences of the UK and Brexit – with Scotland and Northern Ireland's pro-EU majorities in the referendum vote. This is not of major concern to the German government and EU at the moment, but if the pro-independence Scottish government plays a calculated waiting game, it can maximise its friends and allies in the EU.

In the end – but not likely at the end of the two-year negotiation period – I expect a free-trade agreement to emerge that would entail some compromise between the 'four freedoms', notwithstanding the UK's decision to leave the single market. The EU single market is regarded an almost holy unity of individual freedoms, but at the same time it is a messy, uncompleted project. The freedom of every EU citizen to deliver services across the EU is still severely hampered, especially in Germany. And one does not have to be a *member* of the single market in order to have *access* to it. It would be bizarre to deny the closest, and one of the largest, trading partners that complies with EU market regulations since 1973 more market access than, say, Canada or South Korea.

Still, the mantra of the 'indivisibility of the four freedoms' is likely to re-emerge during the negotiations as a result of the political mantra that no leaver should be 'better off out'. Expect not only Poland or Romania to demand some freedom of movement into the UK. Also the German government is likely to stress that issue; not just as sticking to principles, but out of self-interest. If the UK decided to drastically limit the access of unskilled EU-citizens, many of them would turn to another attractive labour market and even more attractive welfare state: Germany.

Germany decides

Will the September 2017 general elections have an impact on the Brexit negotiations? Traditionally, foreign policy and European issues do not figure prominently in German election campaigns: centre-right and centre-left basically agree on Germany's constructive role in the EU. Still, in the run-up to the elections, the UK should not expect much goodwill from the German government. Most likely, there will be no pragmatic German position before the end of September, or rather a few weeks later when a new government is formed. Meanwhile, the German government is likely to take a tough stance as a principled defender of European unity and opponent of British 'cherry picking'. This effectively reduces the timeframe for pragmatic Article 50 negotiations by half a year.

But the election outcome could also make a difference this time. For years it has seemed clear that Ms. Merkel's centre-right Christian Democrats (CDU/CSU) will reap most of the votes. However (as of March 2017), with the appointment of former European parliament President Martin Schulz, it has become conceivable that Angela Merkel will not add another four years to her 12 years as German Chancellor. In the context of a likely six party parliament, a continuation of the present grand coalition, led either by Merkel or Schulz, seems the most likely outcome. But if numbers add up, as they did in the last election, a left majority could also lead to a SPD-Green-Left government this time.

Merkel or Schulz: this alternative matters when we enter the phase of serious Brexit negotiations. If there is one thing known about where Martin Schulz stands, it is his position as a 'great European', or die-hard EU federalist, who had a fair amount of unpleasant encounters with proponents of UK independence in the European parliament. Not even the UK Labour Party supported him as socialist 'Spitzenkandidat' during the elections for the European parliament. Schulz might even take some pleasure in punishing the Brits for their decision to leave, in order to demonstrate that the 'European social (democrat) model' is superior to what he dislikes as British 'neo-liberalism'. Compared to Schulz, Angela Merkel would take a more sober pragmatic approach and try to secure the mutual gains from trade and joint commitment in as many policy projects as possible.

But again, both would be ready to sacrifice some economic gains for the political priority of keeping the EU together and avert other member states' attempts to make leaving the Union a success. And both see 'Europe à la carte' as the worst possible model of integration. It would take a most extraordinary German to find full sympathy with the UK, both before and after Brexit. I found only one: Ralf Dahrendorf (1929-2009), Member of the German parliament, Parliamentary Secretary of State at the Foreign Office of Germany, European Commissioner, Director of the London School of Economics and Member of the House of Lords. In his Jean Monnet-Lecture (Dahrendorf 1979: 20) he said:

> I have often been struck by the prevailing view in Community circles that the worst that can happen is any movement towards what is called a Europe à la carte. This is not only somewhat odd for someone who likes to make his own choices, but also illustrates that strange puritanism, not to say masochism which underlies much of Community action: Europe has to hurt in order to be good... The European interest (it is said) is either general or it does not exist... I believe that... such a view is not only wrong, but in fact an obstacle to further European integration.

References

Bertelsmann Stiftung (2015), *Brexit – potential economic consequences if the UK exits the EU.*
https://www.bertelsmann-stiftung.de/fileadmin/files/BSt/Publikationen/Graue-Publikationen/Policy-Brief-Brexit-en_NW_05_2015.pdf
British Chamber of Commerce on Germany (BCCG) (2015), *Opinions on the development of the European Union and the potential exit of the United Kingdom from the EU.*
http://www.bccg.de/bild/webseite/news_313_2.pdf
Cameron, D. (2015), *A New Settlement for the United Kingdom in a Reformed European Union, letter to Donald Tusk.*
https://www.gov.uk/government/uploads/system/uploads/attachment_data/file/475679/Donald_Tusk_letter.pdf

Dahrendorf, R. (1979), *A Third Europe?*, European University Institute, Third
    Jean Monnet Lecture, 26 November.
http://aei.pitt.edu/11346/2/11346.pdf
Economist (2016), 'The quest for Brexit allies: German business lobbyists will
    not stop tariffs against Britain', 15 October.
http://www.economist.com/news/europe/21708720-unfortunately-brexi-
    teers-bmw-cannot-tell-angela-merkel-what-do-german-business-lobbyists
Graf Kielmansegg, P. (2015), *Wohin des Wegs, Europa? Beiträge zu einer über-
    fälligen Debatte*, Baden-Baden: Nomos.
HM Government (2017), *The United Kingdom's exit from and new partnership
    with the European Union.*
https://www.gov.uk/government/uploads/system/uploads/attachment_data/
    file/589191/The_United_Kingdoms_exit_from_and_partnership_with_the_
    EU_Web.pdf
Krugman, P. (1999), 'Why Germany Kant Kompete'.
http://web.mit.edu/krugman/www/kompete.html 1999
Wohlgemuth, M. (2011), Kant was no stickler for principles', in Ulrike Guérot
    and Jacqueline Hénard (eds), *What does Germany think about Europe?*,
    Berlin 2011, pp. 13-18.

CHAPTER TWENTY-NINE

The European Union's multiple crises

Fabian Zuleeg and Janis A. Emmanouilidis

State of play: Europe's poly-crisis

DESPITE ALL THE turmoil since 2008, the EU has been remarkably resilient in the face of the forces of disintegration. Over the last 60 years, European integration has become part of Europe's collective DNA. The many benefits of European integration and the ever-growing interdependence between member states, especially within the euro area, have made it extremely difficult and risky to abandon the European project. In addition, the EU has done much to address the number of highly-complex, multi-rooted and deeply interlinked crises ('poly-crisis'), which have hit the EU over the last decade. There have been some remarkable policy responses that would have been unthinkable before these storms struck.

Notwithstanding this resilience and the progress made, the EU remains in the grip of the fundamental poly-crisis that has undermined, and might even threaten the historic achievements of, European integration. None of the complex and interlinked crises that have buffeted the Union have been structurally resolved and the potential for a resurgence of crisis exists across a number of policy areas, including for Economic and Monetary Union (EMU) and with respect to the migration/refugee crisis.

The range of challenges the EU continues to face in 2017 include:

a. The 'euro area crisis', which stands for a much broader set of challenges, including a debt crisis, a banking crisis, a growth and employment (divergence) crisis and, in the end, also a political crisis undermining democratic structures at European and national level;

b. A migration and refugee crisis of unprecedented magnitude with millions of people knocking on Europe's doors, which has not been overcome despite the substantial reduction of numbers since March 2016;

c. The geopolitical crisis involving the political stand-off between the 'West' and Russia over Ukraine, as well as the many other instabilities in Europe's immediate neighbourhood, including the war in Syria and other major sources of uncertainty, for example, in Northern Africa or Turkey;

d. (Islamist) terrorism – as the number of terrorist attacks in Europe has been on the rise since 2013, which has dramatically heightened the sense of vulnerability among Europeans;

e. The Brexit vote in the United Kingdom, which will absorb much political energy in the coming years. For the first time, the European integration process is reversing and many questions remain on the future of the UK-EU relationship; and

f. Additional sources of geopolitical insecurity and potential threats to the global economic order deriving from the election of Donald Trump, given his unilateral and 'America-first' focus. Even though the exact impact of the new US administration cannot be evaluated at this point time, one can expect that it will increase the pressure on the EU and its members to assume more responsibility and defend their interests, but it is unclear whether Europeans will be ready to live up to this new challenge.

In addition, the poly-crisis has already eroded some of the foundations of European cooperation. Collateral damage caused by the interlinked crises include: (i) fragmentation and high levels of distrust between member states and national societies, which affect not only governments and decision-makers but also societies; (ii) European cooperation is no longer seen as a 'win-win' exercise from which all member states and their citizens profit, more or less; (iii) a growing perception that the EU's governance structures are unable to fairly balance national interests to further the collective European interest; (iv) increasing divergence in real terms and in terms of thinking, which has widened the gap and makes it much harder to strike compromises at EU level; (v) widespread frustration with the EU's inability to tackle the poly-crisis affecting not only 'ordinary citizens' but also political, economic and intellectual elites; (vi) social cleavages and political constraints within member states fostering a growing sense of social injustice which has fuelled indignation, despair and even anger in many parts of society; and (vii) external reputational damage evident both in the EU's immediate neighbourhood and at global level.

This collateral damage is reducing the ability of the EU and its members to act and thus to manage, let alone overcome, the poly-crisis, which raises essential questions about the Union's future. Even when the EU manages to act, there is increasingly non-implementation of collective decisions, undermining the credibility of the integration process.

The underlying causes of the challenge to European integration

'Zukunftsangst' (fear of the future) of citizens and the 'politics of fear' at domestic level make it increasingly difficult for member states to act cooperatively at EU level. This results in a growing spirit of 'anti-cooperation'; a spirit which, at all levels of political life, makes it more and more difficult to forge compromises. The key trend that is driving this development is the increasing polarisation of our societies. Divided societies are the fertile ground on which extremists and populists on all sides of the political and societal spectrum thrive. The main dividing line is between the (potential and perceived) 'winners and losers of change', which includes, but also goes further, than the challenges arising from globalisation.

This polarisation is fuelled by multiple insecurities in an age of massive transformation; not 'only' socio-economic, but also societal and cultural, generational, technological and security insecurities. Growing numbers of people (including the middle classes) feel overwhelmed by the pace of change, fearing future marginalisation. An increasing number of citizens no longer see the benefits of cooperation, but are increasingly inclined to either withdraw from traditional political processes or to 'stand up' and protest against the establishment.

What is at stake is much more than the EU itself: it is the danger of a regressive, closed and illiberal Europe – a Europe in which key values, orientations, norms and principles are being undermined. A Europe that is backward- and inward-looking, more inclined to oppose globalisation, trade and exchange, migration, heterogeneity, cultural diversity, self-determination and the principles of an open society. A 'closed Europe' in which the influence of those advocating simplistic solutions to complex challenges is increasing, with their political rhetoric and ideology framing or even dominating the public discourse.

The mainstream has struggled to present a credible counter-narrative, especially in the face of post-factual discourse and post-truth politics. Simplistic rhetoric and radicalism are infiltrating, guiding or even dominating debates. Many arguments previously considered unthinkable and unsayable have become socially and politically acceptable, publicly expressed and multiplied by traditional and new social media, which are increasingly manipulated.

This is not just a European phenomenon. A glance across the Atlantic shows that. However, the EU is much more vulnerable to the populist onslaught. It has become an easy target and prey, being less rooted than national institutions and generally enjoying less trust than traditional nation-states.

What (not) to expect?

The commemoration of the 60th anniversary of the Treaty of Rome, as well as the Brexit process, provides a good opportunity to ask a basic question: given the current state of the Union and the populist challenge, what can the EU realistically achieve in 2017 and beyond?

More European federalism or the start of a substantive treaty change process is unlikely in the current climate. There are strong arguments as to why a higher level of cooperation and integration, and more discretionary powers at EU level, would be a more effective response to the challenges facing Europe. But at this juncture the mood in the member states does not allow for major further steps in integration. In fact, at this point in time, any attempt to fundamentally reform the EU by substantially amending the Union's Treaties might well backfire, given the major differences between member states and the collateral damage caused by the poly-crisis.

In light of this mood and the challenges to the European integration process, as well as the inevitable impact of upcoming elections, European leaders should be cautious about overpromising but underdelivering. Ambitious cooperation in the field of external and internal security might well be desirable and some incremental progress seems possible, but there are doubts as to whether the member states will be able and willing to live up to some of the high expectations already raised in the current debate.

Despite the lack of forward momentum, an attempt to scale back European integration is also unlikely. While there will be a tendency to aim for 'subsidiarity max', (i.e. only providing the EU with the powers it strictly needs to deal with the current unavoidable challenges), the benefits of European cooperation and integration would make it extremely costly to abandon or radically renationalise the European project. 'Less Europe' would not help tackle the many current and future challenges in an increasingly interdependent European and global environment. Renationalisation would reverse the European integration process without any clear guarantee of where this might end, which would create even more uncertainties inside and outside Europe.

The above analysis implies that 'muddling through' remains the most likely path for the foreseeable future. This does not mean a standstill, but rather implies an incremental step-by-step process driven by immediate pressures, but based on lowest common denominator approaches and without a clear, proactive vision of the future. But is muddling through going to be enough? Probably not. However, in the short term, there are few other options. There is a need to rebuild trust in the European integration project by focusing on concrete steps, aiming to build the basis for more substantial reforms in the future.

However, there is the disruptive effect of a number of key elections in 2017, although it is far too early to predict the outcome of elections in the Netherlands, France and Germany, and maybe even Italy. Radical populist forces are unlikely to gain decisive victories and absolute majorities, but populism will heavily affect the public discourse at national and EU level.

But in this era of great volatility, there might also be positive surprises: in both the French and German elections a more positive vision of Europe might emerge, potentially leading to a window of opportunity. Post-elections, there might well be a chance to prepare a long term deal on the future of Europe, which is supported by both France and Germany, combining solidarity and responsibility, as well as security and protection.

Brexit starts in earnest

While the beginning of negotiations of the UK's withdrawal are an important item on the 2017 agenda, it should not be allowed to dominate European decision-making. Progress is needed in a number of policy fields, regardless of the trajectory of the UK-EU relationship. Given the uncertainty of the Brexit process, including timing, transition and in what areas the UK might continue to cooperate, there is a need to make forward-looking decisions between the EU27 only.

Regarding the negotiations with the UK, these can only start when Article 50 has been triggered. The EU should assess the likely end-point of the negotiations in light of the content of the Article 50 notification and adjust its negotiation stance accordingly. However, in any scenario it should be very clear that the full range of opportunities and protection provided by European integration can only be enjoyed if you are a full member; the UK deal has to be inferior to full membership.

Given the UK's decision to not be part of the single market or the customs union post Brexit will most likely start to have significant negative economic impact once Article 50 is triggered. In addition, the decision of going for a 'hard Brexit' is almost certain to trigger a second independence referendum in Scotland.

The short and long-term nature of the UK-EU relationship has become highly uncertain. It is far from clear how long it would take to negotiate a free trade agreement and whether such an agreement would pass ratification in all 27 member states and the European parliament. This uncertain long-term trajectory makes transition arrangements hard to envisage, as these would need to involve major concessions of the UK to maintain the current *status quo*.

But a low prospect of a long-term settlement will also complicate the Article 50 negotiations, which will inevitably include difficult issues, including the divorce bill (in the tens of billions) and the rights of EU citizens in the UK (for example, with regard to benefit payments). There is a chance that domestic UK politics will lead to a breakdown in talks, with the potential outcome of a fast and chaotic Brexit process.

On the agenda for 2017

For the EU27, there should be a focus on delivering a 'Europe of real results'. However, given the limits to the powers, competences and instruments allocated to the European level, the EU must be careful to avoid creating false expectations. It should concentrate on projects and initiatives where it can deliver results that are likely to make a tangible difference. Frantic measures launched simply to show that the 'Union' is doing 'something' should be avoided.

This should also be the guiding thought when it comes to the start of the negotiations of the next Multiannual Financial Framework (MFF): the demands on what the EU should do must correspond to the means member states are willing to allocate to EU policies. With additional pressures (the increasing need to find resources for issues such as migration and security) and a likely reduction in the overall size of the budget (given the loss of the UK as a net payer), the crucial question will be what the EU is either not going to do anymore, or going to do very differently, in a way which requires far less resource.

There are many concrete issues on the table for the EU, including increasing border protection capacities, delivering on the digital and energy Single Market agendas, further completing the banking union, encouraging public and social investment by using economic governance provisions and the next MFF, developing a new logic and process for the EU's role in trade, including driving forward trade deals with countries like Japan, developing a strategic approach to Europe's industrial transformation, defining a social pillar of real substance, further cooperation on taxation, combatting the abuse of free movement, enhancing anti-terrorism cooperation and agreeing, and consistently implementing, a joint strategy in Europe's neighbourhood. None of these on their own address the poly-crisis. But taken together, they could demonstrate that the EU continues to effectively move forward together on concrete issues.

The period after the 2017 elections might be the right moment in time to define a more ambitious European agenda. In the medium term, the EU will have to engage in the fundamental political battle which is looming in the coming years: no longer between left and right, but between those who favour openness, cooperation, and European integration, and those trying to close borders and minds. The outcome of this confrontation will decide the long-term future and direction of the European project and the nature of our democracies.

CHAPTER THIRTY

Brexit and the political economy of Tory Britain

Jim Buller

Introduction

HOW IS BREXIT likely to impact on the political fortunes of the May government? What opportunities or indeed pitfalls face the Conservative Party as it attempts to negotiate Britain's exit from the European Union? Bearing in mind the current travails of the Labour Party, such a question might appear almost redundant. It could be asserted (only half-jokingly) that it does not matter what the May government does in office post-2017 general election such are the dynamics of the British political landscape and arithmetic of a bigger parliamentary majority. Be that as it may, this chapter argues that Brexit poses challenges to the future of Conservative Party statecraft. Because of constraints of space, the focus here is on political economy. The party is in danger of forgetting the significance of the EU (especially the Single Market programme) for helping to manage a range of difficult governing problems in the area of economic policy. This chapter begins by describing these governing advantages, before suggesting that some of these problems may already be returning to the political agenda as Theresa May prepares to begin negotiations with the EU following the triggering of Article 50.

The Conservatives and the single market project: external solutions to domestic problems

Despite Britain's growing semi-detachment from its continental European partners, membership of the EU has always conferred certain governing advantages on Conservative leaders. In the 1980s in particular, the project to complete the single market helped to legitimate the Thatcher government's free market supply-side strategy that had generated so much controversy. As negotiations began to implement what would become known as the '1992' programme, the British economy had just gone through a sustained recession, had witnessed the closure of a number of businesses, experienced mass unemployment, not to mention industrial unrest and inner-city riots. In this context, ministers began to claim that completion of the single market would eliminate non-tariff barriers to trade, help to reduce costs and prices, and trigger a competitive shock to the economy. Greater competition would encourage technical innovation, increases in productivity, growth and employment (HMG, 1984). Research by the European Commission estimated this initiative would boost EU GDP by 4.5 per cent, plus help to create 1.8 million new jobs in the medium term (Emmerson et al, 1988). It is true that the precise details of this argument probably eluded much of the electorate at this time. But it did provide the Conservatives with a more positive narrative to deploy in the party political arena. In doing so, a direct link was made between the fortunes of British exporters in European markets and the performance of the British economy (Howe, 1988; 1994: 445).

However, membership of the single market offered an additional, less articulated governing benefit after 1979. Faced with widespread criticism of its neo-liberal ideas, it helped Conservative leaders to resist calls for a return to the discretionary and interventionist policies of the 1960s and 1970s. According to such arguments, the best way to reverse deindustrialisation and reduce large-scale joblessness in Britain was through public ownership of key strategic industries, trade barriers, economic planning and prices and incomes agreements. The problem for the Conservatives was that this governing style necessitated direct and continual contact between ministers, business groups and trade unions if it was to be successfully implemented. Thatcher and her advisers worried that such an approach would politicise economic policy, especially after the experience of the Heath government in the 1970s. As a stakeholder in this interventionist and discretionary strategy, the Conservative Party would be held responsible for the outcomes and would be blamed if results were not forthcoming (Lawson, 1992; Thatcher, 1993: 93; 1995: 223-30). The beauty of the single market programme was that it placed the burden of culpability on businesses and workers to improve the British economy by taking the opportunities at the EU-level created for them by Conservative politicians. At the same time, as the single market became a part of the EU law, policies like import controls, restrictions on capital movements or state aid to declining industries would be illegal, thus further entrenching this market supply-side strategy.

Another reason why the single market project legitimised the neo-liberal economic policy of the Thatcher government was because it helped ministers to rebuild relations with the business community. As bankruptcies and factory closures accelerated in the first half of the 1980s, many industrialists protested at what they saw as the Conservative's wilful neglect of manufacturing industry. The president of the Confederation of British Industry threatened a bare-knuckled fight with the government, while 364 economists organised a letter to *The Times* calling for a Keynesian reflation of the economy, as well as specific measures to aid the high number of jobless. Promises to push for the completion of the Single Market struck a chord with business, who had been lobbying for similar action for years (Buller, 2000: 82-83). Never mind that it was the City of London that was most likely to gain from this policy development because Britain's financial services sector was the most competitive in Europe.

Finally, the single market project helped to sooth nerves within the Conservative parliamentary party at this time. During the first Thatcher government, it was widely acknowledged that the majority of Conservative MPS were ambivalent, if not genuinely concerned, about the wisdom of monetarism as an economic doctrine. As the adverse effects of monetarism on British industry became more visible, many on the left of the party also began to argue for a return to the Keynesian ideas associated with the post-war period. However, it needs to be remembered that those on the left of the party tended to be the most pro-European. Promotion of the single market was something that not only appealed to the neo-liberal instincts of Thatcherites, it chimed with the communautaire sympathies of the 'wets'. The single market initiative had the further benefit of easing tensions between Number Ten and the Foreign Office. The latter in particular had become uncomfortable with the aggressive diplomatic approach that Thatcher had employed throughout the negotiations leading to resolution of the British budgetary question (ibid. 80-86).

Brexit and the challenge to Conservative statecraft

If EU membership helped to legitimise the neo-liberal economic policies of successive Conservative (and Labour?) governments since the 1980s, might Brexit pose a challenge to this statecraft? Such an assertion appears incredible, especially when neo-liberal ideals have remained dominant despite the global financial crisis (2007–8). The May government has constantly stressed that Brexit does not mean the UK is turning inward; Britain's future economic prosperity remains heavily dependent on exporters being able to take advantage of new trading opportunities (May, 2017). May herself is hoping to negotiate a 'bespoke' deal with the EU 27, allowing certain sectors of the British economy to retain tariff free access to the customs union, perhaps in return for continued payments into the EU budget. However, there are no guarantees that this diplomatic strategy will be successful. Ivan Rodgers (former British ambassador to the EU) believes Angela Merkel will rule out such a sector-by-sector approach (Mance, 2017). If such a rejection takes place and Britain falls back on World Trade Organisation (WTO) rules, it could take years before Whitehall is in a position to conclude bi-lateral trade agreements. Even when this happens, a 'hard Brexit' is likely to reduce the UK's attractiveness as a trading partner, as it no longer provides a 'backdoor' into the single market.

If ministers struggle to secure favourable trade deals over the next few years, they may start to come under pressure to adopt a more intervention-ist and discretionary approach to domestic economic management. Fore-casts continue to predict that Brexit will eventually result in a slow-down in economic growth. In this event, the impulse to step in and support certain industries (viewed as 'special cases') may prove difficult to resist, especially if such a downturn is accompanied by capital flight. Indeed, it could be argued that such pressure is already in evidence. Nissan's decision to build the new Qashqai SUV at its Sunderland plant was only taken after private assurances from Number Ten that Brexit would not affect its current trading conditions with the EU (Campbell and Mance, 2016). Recent reports suggest that the PSA Group, which is in talks to buy Vauxhall, has received similar promises after concerns that the factory at Ellesmere Port might be vulnerable to cut-backs and redundancies (Campbell, 2017). Of course, such promises set a precedent and observers have already started to ask why car manufacturers should get special treatment (Mance, 2016). Membership of the single market (and neo-liberal policies more generally) were introduced in the 1980s pre-cisely to avoid Conservative politicians getting sucked into such discretionary behaviour.

Avoiding such a discretionary and interventionist governing style is important for Conservative leaders because it may negatively impact on their credibility and reputation for competence. Put simply, the danger surrounding discretionary decision-making is it will lead the party to make promises that it cannot keep, resulting in the politicisation of policy as ministers are held accountable for their misjudgement. The more specific question in this context is: what assurances did the May government give Nissan and the PSA Group and can they deliver them? If (as Number Ten maintains) the promise was simply to get the best deal possible from the Article 50 process, the risk is that any agreement will fall short of expectations, particularly if the EU 27 want to play hardball. If (in the event of a 'hard Brexit') the government has promised compensation for EU tariffs, then the potential financial liability could be enormous, especially if other sectors of the economy prove successful at gaining the assurances that Nissan and the PSA Group have received. And this is assuming such compensation is legal under World Trade Organisation (WTO) rules, a judgment that may turn out to be mistaken.

If the completion of the single market was something that the Conservatives and business could unite behind in the 1980s, Brexit risks increasing divisions between the two. May has already signalled a more sceptical stance towards the corporate sector, championing workers representatives on company boards and binding shareholder votes on executive pay (May, 2016). For their part, business groups have urged ministers to provide reassurance that EU staff hired since the referendum will not be required to leave when Britain ceases to be a member. Such tensions are likely to continue as British negotiators try to balance the promise of stricter controls on EU migrants, with the desire to secure the best trade agreement possible. EU migrants help to counteract skills shortages in a range of sectors of the UK economy. If the May government places significant restrictions on EU migrants (or they simply emigrate as a result of Brexit) businesses have warned such developments will make it more difficult for them to operate (Parker, 2017).

Finally, Brexit is likely to complicate Conservative party management, despite the hope that the referendum would resolve the European question once and for all. Not surprisingly (because it is an issue that resonates with business) we have already seen evidence of such divisions over the future of Britain's immigration policy, as the May government appears set to institute a new work permit regime for EU citizens coming into Britain. Former remain campaigners want what has been termed a 'free movement minus' approach.

For example, William Hague has argued for a system whereby any EU citizen with a UK job offer should get a work permit. Such a scheme would avoid ministers having to second guess the needs of the market through the sector-by-sector allocation of permits. Pro-Brexit Conservatives fear such a 'free movement minus' approach would fail to significantly reduce EU migration and risk the wrath of the 52 per cent of the public who voted to leave. Instead, the government should have the power to decide the total number of work permits issued to EU-citizens each year: a policy that mirrors the current regime for non-EU migrants (Parker and Warrell, 2017). It could be argued that such splits are a proxy for future arguments within the party concerning whether the May government should pursue a 'hard' or 'soft' Brexit.

References

Buller, J. (2000), *National Statecraft and European Integration: The Conservative Government and the European Union, 1979-1997*. London: Pinter.

Campbell, P. (2017), 'Peugeot Offered Nissan-style Brexit Promises to Save Vauxhall', *Financial Times*, 17 February.

https://www.ft.com/content/3137c028-f517-11e6-8758-6876151821a6#my-ft:list:page [accessed 28 February 2017]

Campbell, P. and Mance, H. (2016), 'Nissan Warned Government on Fate of Sunderland Without Deal', *Financial Times*, 28 October.

https://www.ft.com/content/21346414-9d25-11e6-a6e4-8b8e77dd083a [accessed 28 February 2017]

Emerson, M. et. al (1988), *The Economics of 1992: the EC Commission's Assessment of the Economic Effects of Completing the Internal Market.* Oxford: Oxford University Press.

HMG (1984) Europe – the Future. *Journal of Common Market Studies*, 23 (1), pp. 269-82.

Howe, G. (1988), *The Conservative Revival of Britain*, London: Conservative Political Centre.

Howe, G. (1994), *Conflict of Loyalty*, Basingstoke: Macmillan.

Lawson, N. (1992), *The View From Number Eleven*, London: Bantam.

Mance, H. (2016), May Change of Tone Raises Prospect of Sector by Sector Deals. *Financial Times*, 28th October.

Mance, H. (2017), 'Former UK Top Diplomat Warns EU Will Oppose Sectoral Brexit Deals', *Financial Times*, 22 February.

https://www.ft.com/content/25656e1a-f8ed-11e6-9516-2d969eod3b65#my-ft:list:page [accessed 28 February 2017]

May, T. (2016), *Speech to the Conservative Party Conference.*

http://blogs.spectator.co.uk/2016/10/full-text-theresa-mays-conference-speech/ [accessed 28 February 2017]

May, T. (2017) *Speech to the World Economic Forum, Davos, 19 January.*

https://www.weforum.org/agenda/2017/01/theresa-may-at-davos-2017-her-speech-in-full/ [accessed 28 February 2017]

Parker, G. (2017), 'Entrepreneurs Urge May to Avoid Collapse in Migration', *Financial Times*, 5 January.

https://www.ft.com/content/22b1b972-d367-11e6-b06b-680c49b4b4c0
     [accessed 28 February, 2017]
Parker, G. and Warrell, H. (2017), 'UK Work Permits at the Heart of Brexit
     Immigration Plan', *Financial Times*, 16 January.
https://www.ft.com/content/031d6ae6-dbf2-11e6-9d7c-be108f1c1dce
     [accessed 28 February, 2017]
Thatcher, M. (1993), *The Downing Street Years*, London: Harper Collins.
Thatcher, M. (1995), *The Path to Power*, London: Harper Collins.

CHAPTER THIRTY-ONE

What becomes of British Labour?

Stephen Bush

THROUGHOUT THE 20TH century, Labour has been the natural home for people who are either in poverty, or who are concerned about poverty. The first group include those in minimum wage jobs or on zero hours' contracts, and in social housing or the private rented sector. On the other hand, it has spoken for what Michael Frayn dubbed 'the Herbivores': 'the radical middle-classes, the do-gooders; the readers of the News Chronicle, the Guardian, and the Observer; the signers of petitions; the backbone of the BBC' (Frayn, 1963).

That coalition has been enough to guarantee at least a silver medal at every election since 1922. Although the phrase 'aspirational' grew farcical from overuse in the 2015 election, the governments of 1945, 1964 and 1997 were all built upon adding the votes of that group to the Labour bedrock of the socially-concerned and the economically-straitened.

What it means to be 'aspirational' changes, of course. In the 1950s, when Labour lost three elections in succession, it meant to enjoy ITV, which Labour opposed as an act of gross privatisation, and to buy things on hire-purchase. In the 1980s, when Labour lost four elections on the bounce, it meant buying your own council house and the fruits of financial deregulation. What it means in the 2010s and 2020s is up for debate, but it may be that it takes Labour five defeats to work it out.

21st Century Labour problems

To the party's recurring 20th century problem, the 21st century has added another: Labour's two core groups cannot agree about immigration. The Herbivores regard it as a good-in-of-itself, a positive both economically and socially. The remainder of Labour's vote is much like the country: it would prefer immigration to go down, provided that reduction comes at no personal cost.

That hairline fracture is the one every Labour leader since 2007 has struggled to navigate, mostly taking different routes to reach the same position. Robotics researchers spend much of their time trying to stay out of the 'uncanny valley': the point where robots become lifelike enough to unnerve people but not human enough to reassure them. On immigration, Labour under Gordon Brown, Ed Miliband and Jeremy Corbyn has managed to locate its own version of the uncanny valley: hostile to immigrants as far as the Herbivores are concerned, while seeming overly welcoming to Labour's other core and much of the country besides.

It was that divide that played itself out in Britain's referendum on the European Union, which was dominated by arguments over the single market and border control. On the one hand, the leave campaign argued that only an out vote would secure the ability to manage the flow of people to the United Kingdom, on the other, the remain campaign warned that control would come at the price of recession and a permanent reduction in living standards and growth.

The result? Labour's Herbivores voted to stay; the rest of the Labour vote split 50/50 based on whether or not they thought they would have to get poorer to reduce immigration. Labour voters in Newcastle and Manchester may have shared much demographically and economically with Labour voters in Sunderland and Salford: they differed only on if they thought an Out vote came without a bill, or at least, not a bill that would change their lives one way or the other.

The Brexit vote has turbocharged the party's immigration problems, not least because it has deprived its politicians of the ability to shrug and blame immigration on the European Union. And although a majority of Labour votes backed a remain vote in 2016, the overwhelming majority of Labour seats went for Brexit. Labour remainers are a majority only in England's great cities and university towns: London, Manchester, Liverpool, Bristol, and Newcastle (Hanratty, 2016). John Curtice analysed this further showing that Labour's 2015 vote in constituencies it held was 63 per cent pro-remain: the same figure as nationally; but this important caveat isn't the end of the psephological argument or Labour's predicament (Curtice, 2017).

Thanks to first-past-the-post, that might not necessarily be electorally fatal. There are very few constituencies in which under a third of people voted to remain in the European Union, and in a multi-party election, a party that can secure the votes of a third of the vote can win, and sometimes at a canter. The support of remainers is, arguably, more electorally valuable as the remain coalition – affluent, well-educated and liberal – is more likely to vote than the leave one.

That prospect, comforting as it is to remainers and superficially attractive on paper, has two major hurdles. The first is that although there may be a theoretical path to victory for Labour that runs through the 48 per cent, it is not one without trade-offs. A remain voter who trusted David Cameron and worries about her house price is an electoral prize for somebody, but certainly not for Jeremy Corbyn. Nor is it one that any of his possible successors can grasp without a substantially different message to that offered by Labour in 2015 or any of the challengers to Corbyn in 2015 or 2016.

And as Ian Warren's analysis shows, while Labour's 2015 vote is largely remain, the voters that backed it in 2005, when it last won an election, largely opted to leave. 65 per cent of Labour voters in the North who backed the party in 2005 but went elsewhere in 2015 voted to leave. 67 per cent of their cohort in the Midlands did the same, as did 57 per cent in the South and 56 per cent in Wales. Even in London, the remain citadel, 54 per cent of the voters Labour has lost since 2005 voted to leave. Only in Scotland did a majority vote to remain, and even there, 43 per cent opted to leave (Warren, 2016).

But Labour's referendum headache is not simply a question of what box people ticked on 23 June, or even one of whether or not immigration to Britain is too low or too high. The vituperative tone struck by the leave campaign, whether that be Nigel Farage's poster warning that Britain was at 'Breaking Point' thanks to immigration or Vote leave's threat that a remain vote would open Britain's borders to 75 million Turks is, for some remainers, the opening shot in a culture war that has to be resisted.

Support for remaining in the European Union has become, for the modern Herbivore, what a subscription to the *Guardian* or the *News Chronicle* was to those of 1963: a signal about the politics in which you believe and the country you aspire to create. For other remainers, the vote of 23 June was a unique event for a different reason. They might have watched in horror or elation as Blair triumphed in 1997 or Cameron prevailed in 2010, but regardless of which party has been in power, their houses have increased in value and their salaries have increased despite the recession. Now they are not just observers but participants in political change, and they are desperate to reverse the tide.

These two groups are the motor behind the Liberal Democrats' close-run thing in the Witney by-election and their victory in Richmond Park. They make up about 22 per cent of the electorate: not enough to win power, but without them Labour not only cannot win the 2017 election, but the election after that, and may not even survive as a serious force in parliament.

For the Liberal Democrats, 22 per cent is not power but is a striking improvement on the eight per cent they secured in 2015. Their challenge is easier: they have nothing to lose so they might as well set themselves out as the natural home for angry pro-Europeans.

The calculation for Britain's third centre-left force, the SNP, is harder than it looks. The great post-referendum mystery is the robustness of the pro-unionist side in polls on Scottish independence. In 2014, Better Together campaigned, both implicitly and explicitly, on the promise that the Conservative government in Westminster was an interregnum between Labour administrations rather than a reversion to the mean. A Yes vote was attacked as a vote to lose Scotland's membership of the European Union. Now, Labour looks to be decades away from power and the only way to save Scotland's membership of the European Union is a vote for independence. Yet support for the status quo remains practically unchanged. Whether, like Wile E. Coyote, support for the union is simply running on thoughtlessly and will plummet the second that Nicola Sturgeon's Road Runner asks voters to look down at the ground is an open question. But it comes with not one, but two downside risks. The first is the effect on SNP morale and unity of a second successive referendum defeat. The second is the prospect that a second referendum campaign does for the Scottish Conservatives what the first did for the SNP, and unites the bulk of the unionist vote behind their party at Westminster.

The SNP's problem is one of principle – having committed to a second referendum should the nature of the union change, does the prospect of Brexit mean that they are honour-bound to hold another? Or can they, should they, wait until their path to victory looks clearer than it did in 2014 and it does today?

But the SNP's dilemma holds within it the beginnings of Labour's solution. The party has a clear goal – independence – and its challenge is how best to achieve that goal at the ballot box. Outside of Scotland, the centre-left's difficulty emerges from seeing Brexit and its strains on the Labour coalition as an obstacle on the road to its mission – redistribution – rather than an essential element.

Although ritual defences of the party's last stay in office still attract cheers at party conference, much of the party's upper levels have wholly accepted, whether subconsciously or consciously, that New Labour's electoral success was built on using the party's principles for electoral ballast. Now, whether they were critics or supporters of New Labour, the modern Labour party believes that its Brexit problem can be solved by burning a few ideals for fuel. An anti-immigration mug here. A whipped vote to trigger Article 50 there. A series of speeches setting out the road to Brexit, perhaps. Or the search for a series of positions that can be finessed or bartered away in order to keep the party's two cores on speaking terms and to reach out to the great number of people who didn't vote for Labour in 2015.

But New Labour *wasn't* based on the sacrifice of principles in return for votes. It was, as John Prescott put it, about putting 'traditional values in a modern setting', the repackaging and reimagining of Labour ideals to make them relevant and successful once more.

That insight matters, because Labour's biggest Brexit problem is not the question of who finishes ahead of who in a constituency election. It is whether or not a programme of a centre-left government can be achieved if Britain is outside of the single European market and outside the political structures of the European Union. If the answer to that is yes, then the problem becomes: what can Labour say to depressed and angry remain voters to keep them onside? If the answer is no, the problem becomes: how can Labour win support for the closest possible relationship with the nations of the European Union in the short term and re-entry to the European Union in the long term?

The victory of the outside in the referendum was not based on watering down or retreating from the ideals of Euroscepticism. It was based on selling Brexit as the way to achieve the twin desires of Britain's leave voters: a reduction in the number of immigrants and an increase in spending on the National Health Service.

That isn't to say that finding an electoral majority either for centre-left politics outside the European Union or for centre-left politics and re-entry to the bloc is easy. But it is a reminder that the centre-left's problem is winning consent for its programme, not finding a programme that has already received consent.

References

Curtice, J. (2017), 'Is Labour's Brexit Dilemma Being Misunderstood?', *The UK in a Changing Europe*, 17 February.
http://ukandeu.ac.uk/is-labours-brexit-dilemma-being-misunderstood/
Frayn, M. (1963), 'The Herbivores', in Michael Sissons and Philip French (eds), *Age of Austerity 1945-1951*, London: Hodder and Stoughton.
Hanretty, C. (2016), 'The EU Referendum: How did Westminster Constituencies Vote?', June 29.
https://medium.com/@chrishanretty/the-eu-referendum-how-did-westminster-constituencies-vote-283c85cd20e1#.6rwf8fwzb
Warren, I. (2017), 'Brief Response to John Curtice', March 2.
https://election-data.co.uk/brief-response-to-john-curtice

CHAPTER THIRTY-TWO

A global UK? The UK after Brexit

Andrew Gamble

BREXIT WAS A long time in the making. It had been spoken about and predicted for years. Almost as soon as Britain joined the European Community in 1973 the UK government showed reluctance to support projects of deeper integration, such as the Economic and Monetary Union of the EU (EMU), and it was not long before it was demanding special treatment, first on the budget, and later on opt-outs in respect of membership of the Schengen area and the Eurozone. Those who were on the losing side of the referendum in 1975 never gave up trying to reverse the decision. Eight years after the referendum Labour fought a general election in 1983 with a manifesto commitment to take Britain out of the European Community. The long campaign waged by some Conservative newspapers and MPs, and the strength of popular feeling against Europe, made Britain appear at best a semi-detached member of the European Union, half-in and half out (George, 1998). Jacques Delors, sometime before the 2016 referendum, suggested that the British might be happier to exchange full membership for an associate status (BBC *News*, 2012). The British government rejected the idea.

Although widely anticipated, the vote was still a shock when it occurred. The winning margin was narrow, but decisive. The disorientation in Whitehall and British embassies as well as British companies has been intense. They have been cast adrift on an uncertain sea. Referendums rarely reject the status quo, especially when this was backed by such an impressive array of establishment opinion, both from inside and outside the UK. The argument 'why risk it?' is normally decisive. What was surprising was not the high votes for Brexit in northern working class English constituencies, which voted largely as they had done in 1975. The referendum was lost because 58 per cent of Conservative voters who had given David Cameron his election victory only a year before now rejected his advice and voted to leave. The main task of the new government formed by Theresa May has been beginning the huge task of sorting out the implications of that decision.

Brexit and Britain's three historic circles

One of the most important of these is what Brexit means in geopolitical terms. Like most aspects of Brexit this is far from obvious. Britain's place in the world is uncertain following Brexit because one of the key anchors of UK geopolitical strategy for the past 60 years has just been cast aside. In 1946 Churchill claimed that Britain stood at the centre of three overlapping circles, Empire, Europe and Anglo-America (Dumbrell, 2006). But it was out of date almost immediately. Britain no longer had the will or capacity to sustain its Empire. Indian independence in 1947 initiated an unstoppable process of imperial withdrawal. Britain was forced, reluctantly, to give much greater priority to the circles of Europe and Anglo-America. Britain stood aloof from the negotiations that led to the Treaty of Rome in 1956 but it quickly became apparent, especially after the debacle of the Suez invasion later in 1956, that Britain could no longer act independently of the United States and neither could it ignore the dynamic new common market emerging in Europe.

Harold Macmillan reset UK policy to take account of these two geopolitical realities, repairing relations with the United States and consolidating the military alliance by signing the Polaris deal, while at the same time preparing the ground for Britain's first application to join the EEC. Britain's new role was to be the chief ally to the United States, leading a United West. Membership of a prosperous and expanding EEC went hand in hand with membership of NATO. Europe needed to set aside its conflicts and unite so that it could partner the United States in the defence of the West. Macmillan's grand project was held up by General De Gaulle, who perceived, entirely accurately, that the British were never likely to make Europe their priority, but would always act as a Trojan horse for the United States. It fell to Edward Heath to finish what Macmillan had begun and Britain finally succeeded in entering the EEC in 1973 (Young, 1998).

This grand project is now shattered, and not just because of Brexit. Over the last two decades the new rising powers, led by China, India and Brazil, have begun to shift the balance of power in the international economy. In 2000 the richest and most powerful states were almost the same as in 1900. But by 2050 that will no longer be true. The West is shrinking in weight and importance. A second major change has been the changing fortunes of the United States. After the collapse of the Soviet Union in 1991 the power of the United States was for a time unchallenged. It was a unipolar moment.

A new extended era of peace and prosperity seemed to be within reach. But this phase proved relatively short-lived, and by the end of the 1990s, even before 9/11, had given way to a new period of intervention and war to combat terrorism and promote western political institutions. But these interventions had mixed success, and after the financial crash in 2008 the Obama administration sought to scale back US operations and disengage from foreign conflicts. The world was taking on a more multipolar character. A new group of potential great powers had emerged, each with its own sphere of interest.

Trump in context: watershed for the US, UK and world?

Under Obama this relative disengagement of the US was combined with still-strong US support for rules-based international market order with its networks of multilateral institutions and military alliances that the US had designed and helped sustain. The election of Donald Trump has put this commitment into question. It may take time for a settled policy to emerge from the Trump administration, and it may prove less radical than some of the campaign rhetoric and early moves of the Trump administration suggest.

But at the very least it is likely to strengthen the move to a more disengaged, isolationist United States, much more concerned with its own interests, and with a transactional rather than strategic view of the international order it created over the last seven decades. Trump's long-standing view is that the US has been ripped off by the rest of the world, and needs to bring back jobs and money to the US and make other countries pay for their own security (Simms and Laderman, 2017). If these views of Trump are even partly translated into policy his administration could mark a watershed in the role of the United States in the international order. Multilateral institutions will decline in importance and there will be a new emphasis on bilateral relationships between the great powers, and a preference for striking deals based on respecting spheres of influence. The world will become increasingly multipolar, or even possibly bipolar if China maintains its current trajectory.

The policy of the UK after Brexit will have to take account of these new geopolitical realities. The election of Donald Trump came after the decision to leave the EU but considerably complicates it. Theresa May's government and many of the leading campaigners for Brexit have been adamant that they want a global and more open Britain, not an economic nationalist and relatively closed Britain, even though it was the latter that many leave voters thought they were voting for. They may yet get it, because the project of a global Britain assumes that the rules based multilateral trading order continue to function.

If instead we are entering an era of competing great powers and rival military and economic blocs, Britain's decision to leave the protection of the European Union may come to seem foolhardy. It is certainly risky. The EU has much greater power in trade negotiations than Britain will have on its own, so the benefits for Britain of being, in the words of Foreign Secretary Boris Johnson 'liberated' (Boffey, 2017) to conclude its own trade deals may prove illusory. If new trade deals are struck, Britain may have to make major concessions, allowing US companies access in sensitive areas like GM food, health services and education, or easing restrictions on the movement of Indian nationals to the UK.

Many supporters of Brexit argue that the central plank of Britain's new geopolitical doctrine should be a reaffirmation of the special relationship. Trump, and some of his team, have encouraged such talk. But if the US administration is intent on disengaging further from Europe, allowing Russia to rebuild its sphere of interest, and instead focusing US attention on Asia, and to lesser extent on the Middle East, then the practical advantages of a close alliance between the US and the UK will be much diminished from the US viewpoint. The UK was important in the Cold War both because of the influence it could still exert in its former empire, and also because it was a lynchpin of the Western alliance in Europe, resisting Soviet expansion (Dumbrell, 2006). But if Russia is no longer perceived as a direct threat to US interests, the US no longer needs to support NATO or the EU, or at least not give them the same priority they had in the past.

It is important to emphasise that this profound shift did not begin with Trump. It has been the logic of events since 1991, but the Trump presidency has given it a new focus. The US is a continental sized economy that can afford protectionism. So can the EU. Smaller economies outside one of the big blocs will find it much harder. This is why Theresa May and Boris Johnson are so keen to insist that Britain after Brexit has to be a global Britain. A group of pro-Brexit economists has gone further, arguing that the UK has nothing to fear from Brexit. The government should not seek to negotiate a trade deal with the EU, or even fall back on WTO rules. It should simply declare a policy of unilateral free trade with the rest of the world. Britain would impose no tariff on imports from anywhere in the world, even if other countries imposed tariffs against Britain (Minford et al, 2016). Such a policy would seek to make Britain Great again by restoring the free trade policy of the nineteenth century (Trentmann, 2009), but Britain at that time was not only the leading naval and industrial power in the world, it also had control of the world's largest empire. Things are different today.

A further complication is that while England and Wales voted to leave the EU, Scotland and Northern Ireland did not. The Republic of Ireland also has no intention of giving up its EU membership and becoming dependent again on the UK. But this means that some way of imposing a hard border in Ireland will have to be found. The problem becomes even more serious if Scotland holds another referendum and votes to leave the UK. The United Kingdom is anything but united and faces an uncertain future in a world retreating from the rules-based multilateral order. Much will depend on what happens to the EU.

The EU may fall apart over the next few years, either because of a further crisis in the Eurozone or the victory of a populist party in one of the leading member states. But if the EU survives it is likely to become more integrated and a more powerful player in defence and security as well as trade. In that case future British governments having gone to the trouble and expense of disentangling the UK from the EU will be obliged to seek a new associate status with it. In the new geopolitics that is emerging they will have little choice.

References

Boffey, D. (2017), 'Boris Johnson accused of bad taste for calling Brexit "liberation"', *The Guardian*, 22 February.
https://www.theguardian.com/politics/2017/feb/22/boris-johnson-accused-of-bad-taste-for-calling-brexit-liberation

BBC *News* (2012), 'EU Federalists: UK could be "associate member"', 12 December.
http://www.bbc.co.uk/news/world-europe-20875755

Dumbrell, J. (2006), *A Special Relationship: Anglo-American Relations from the Cold War to Iraq*, Basingstoke: Palgrave-Macmillan.

George, S. (1998), *An Awkward Partner*, Oxford: Oxford University Press.

Minford, Patrick et al (2016).
www.economistsforBrexit.co.uk

Simms, B. and Laderman, C. (2017), *Donald Trump: The Making of a World View*, London: Endeavour Press.

Trentmann, F. (2009), *Free Trade Nation: Commerce, Consumption and Civil Society in Modern Britain*, Oxford: Oxford University Press.

Young, H. (1998), *This Blessed Plot: Britain and Europe from Churchill to Blair*, London: Macmillan.

Contributors

RT. HON. DOUGLAS ALEXANDER is Senior Fellow, Harvard University's Kennedy School and Visiting Professor at King's College, London. He served in numerous senior UK Ministerial positions (2001–2010), including as Minister for Europe, Minister for Trade and Investment and Foreign Affairs, and as Secretary of State for Scotland and the UK's Governor of the World Bank.

GRANT ALLAN is Lecturer in the Department of Economics and Deputy Director of the Fraser of Allander Institute, in the Strathclyde Business School. Grant's research interests are in empirical economic analysis and energy-economy-environmental modelling, and he has been involved in a number of interdisciplinary research projects, including for UK Research Councils, DEFRA, the European Union and the Scottish Government.

MARCO G. BIAGI is a former Minister of the Scottish Government and now consultant to Edinburgh strategic communications company Message Matters. Also a PhD student in Comparative Politics at Yale University, he divides his time between Scotland and the United States.

JIM BULLER is a Senior Lecturer in Politics at the University of York. He has written widely on the subject of Britain and the European Union, including recent articles in the *New Political Economy*, *British Journal of Politics and International Relations*, *West European Politics*, *Contemporary European Politics and British Politics*. His latest book, *The Dynamics of Depoliticisation in Comparative Perspective* (with Pinar Donmez, Adam Standring and Matthew Wood) will be published by Palgrave in 2017.

MADELEINE BUNTING was for many years a columnist for *The Guardian* and is the author of *The Model Occupation: The Channel Isles under German Rule, 1940-45*, *Willing Slaves: How the Overwork Culture is Ruling Our Lives*, *The Plot: A Biography of an English Acre* and her latest book, *Love of Country: A Hebridean Journey*.

STEPHEN BUSH is Special Correspondent at the *New Statesman*.

JONNY BYRNE is currently a Lecturer in Criminology in the School of Criminology, Social Policy and Politics at Ulster University. He teaches on issues relating to policing and security, countering violent extremism and psychology within the criminal justice system.

GRIFFIN CARPENTER is an economist at the New Economics Foundation. He has written extensively on the socio-economics of fisheries with recent publications comparing quota limits to scientific advice and a report on how countries allocate their fishing opportunities.

DAVID COMERFORD is Research Associate in Economics and Environmental Modelling in the Fraser of Allander Institute working across environmental and energy economics. He currently leads the Fraser of Allander/ Scottish Government work linking agricultural and ecosystems models with economy-wide models, which seek to understand the contribution of agriculture and related ecosystem services to the wider Scottish economy.

LAURA CRAM is Professor of European Politics and Director of NRlabs Neuropolitics Research at Edinburgh University. She acted as Special Advisor to the Scottish parliament, European and External Relations Committee, on the Inquiry into the Impact of the Treaty of Lisbon on Scotland. She has published widely on the governance of the European Union and held a Senior Fellowship on the ESRC's 'UK in a Changing Europe' programme during the EU referendum.

ANDREW CUMBERS is Professor of Regional Political Economy at the University of Glasgow and managing editor of the journal *Urban Studies*. He has researched and written extensively on questions of urban and regional economic development for over 25 years. His recent book *Reclaiming Public Ownership: Making Space for Economic Democracy* (Zed) won the 2015 Myrdal Prize for Political Economy.

JOHN CURTICE is Professor of Politics at Strathclyde University and Senior Research Fellow at ScotCen Social Research. He is chief commentator at whatscotlandthinks.org and a regular media commentator on Scottish politics.

JOHN EDWARD currently works in education, is a Trustee of the Scottish European Educational Trust and Scotland advisor for Open Britain. Previously, he was Head of the European parliament's Office in Scotland; EU Policy Manager in Scotland Europa; and personal assistant to Max Kohnstamm.

JANIS A. EMMANOUILIDIS is the Director of Studies at the European Policy Centre. He has published widely on the EU's overall political and institutional development and the perspectives of differentiated integration in the EU. He has been an advisor to various governments, EU institutions, European parties, think tanks and NGOS on a broad range of issues related to European integration.

MARIA FLETCHER is Senior Lecturer in European Law at the University of Glasgow. She researches in the field of EU Criminal Justice and EU Citizenship and Immigration and has recently co-edited a book on *The European Union as an Area of Freedom, Security and Justice* (2017, Routledge). She is an Associate

Editor of *European Papers* (Europeanpapers.eu) and she is co-founder and on the management board of the Scottish Universities Legal Network on Europe (sulne.ac.uk).

ANDREW GAMBLE is Professor of Politics at the University of Sheffield and Emeritus Professor of Politics at the University of Cambridge. His most recent books are *Crisis without end? The unravelling of western prosperity* (2014) and *Can the welfare state survive?* (2016). In 2005 he received the Isaiah Berlin Prize from the UK Political Studies Association for lifetime contribution to political studies.

PAUL GILLESPIE is a columnist and leader writer for *The Irish Times* (from which he retired as foreign policy editor in 2009 after 39 years of service) and a Senior Research Fellow adjunct in the School of Politics and International Relations, University College Dublin. His main research areas, journalism and publications are in European integration and political identities, Irish-British relations, comparative regionalism, media and foreign policy, and the EuroMed region.

RUSSELL GUNSON is Director of IPPR Scotland, IPPR's dedicated, cross-party thinktank for Scotland. He was previously Director of the National Union of Students (NUS) Scotland and has been head of IPPR Scotland since its inception in 2015. Significant work has included research on Scotland's new tax and benefit powers, skills, Scotland's economy, school education and the attainment gap, and fiscal analysis of UK and Scottish Government budgets.

GERRY HASSAN is a writer, commentator, academic and Research Fellow with IPPR Scotland. He is the author and editor of numerous books of which the latest is *Scotland the Bold: How Our Nation Has Changed and Why There is No Going Back* (Freight Books, 2016) examining Scotland post-indyref and post-Brexit and the prospective political terrain of a second referendum. Other books include *The Strange Death of Labour Scotland* (Edinburgh University Press, 2012), *Caledonian Dreaming: The Quest for a Different Scotland* (Luath Press, 2014) and *Independence of the Scottish Mind: Elite Narratives, Public Spaces and the Making of a Modern Nation* (Palgrave Macmillan, 2014).

KEVIN HANNAM is Head of Tourism and Languages and Professor of Tourism Mobilities in the Business School at Edinburgh Napier University. He is a founding co-editor of the journals *Mobilities* and *Applied Mobilities*. He has a PhD in geography and is a Fellow of the Royal Geographical Society (FRGS), Vice-Chair of the Association for Tourism and Leisure Education and Research (ATLAS) and a research affiliate at the University of Johannesburg, South Africa.

KIRSTY HUGHES is director of the Scottish Centre on European Relations. She has written extensively on EU politics and policy, and has worked for a number of leading EU think tanks including Chatham House, Friends of Europe and the Centre for European Policy Studies, as well as at senior level in the European Commission.

OWEN KELLY was Chief Executive of Scottish Financial Enterprise from 2008 to 2016. He now works as an academic at Edinburgh University and Edinburgh Napier University.

RICHARD KERLEY is Emeritus Professor of Management at Queen Margaret University, Edinburgh and Co-Chair of the Centre for Scottish Public Policy.

TOBIAS LOCK is a Senior Lecturer in EU Law and co-director of the Europa Institute at the University of Edinburgh. His main research interests concern the multilevel relationships of EU law with other legal orders. In recent months the focus of this research has turned to all things 'Brexit'.

AILEEN MCHARG is Professor of Public Law at the University of Strathclyde. She has written extensively on energy regulation at EU, UK and Scottish levels. She is a member and former chair of the Academic Advisory Group to the International Bar Association's Section on Energy, Environment, Resources and Infrastructure Law.

RICHARD MARSH is an analyst and economist with 4-consulting, elected fellow of the Royal Statistical Society and member of a Scottish Government expert group advising on economic modelling and statistics.

SVEA MIESCH is Research and Policy Manager at ScotlandIS, the trade body for Scotland's digital technologies industry. She joined ScotlandIS in April 2016 to develop an in-house research and policy unit and worked previously in policy research and public affairs role in Edinburgh and Brussels.

DUNCAN MORROW is Director of Community Engagement at the University of Ulster, responsible for developing the University's partnerships with groups and organisations across the community. He is also a lecturer in Politics.

ANDREA M. NOLAN is Professor of Veterinary Pharmacology and Principal and Vice Chancellor of Edinburgh Napier University.

ANGELA O'HAGAN is a researcher and lecturer at Glasgow Caledonian University with long experience in equalities and public policy in Scotland and Europe, with a particular interest in equality analysis and scrutiny of public policy, particularly budget processes. She is Convenor of the Scottish Women's Budget Group and Co-Convenor of the European Gender Budgeting Network.

ED G. POOLE is a lecturer in at the Wales Governance Centre at Cardiff University. His work focuses on territorial politics and decentralised public finance, including *Government Expenditure and Revenue Wales*, a multi-year analysis of Wales' public spending, revenues and fiscal balance. Ed previously worked in a number of positions in budget and finance in the United States.

MATTHEW QVORTRUP, DPhil (Oxon) is a lawyer and a political scientist. The winner of the Oxford University Law Prize, he is currently Professor of Political Science at Coventry University and a Fellow of Kings College, London. His books include *Referendums and Ethnic Conflict* (University of Pennsylvania Press, 2014) and *Referendums Around the World* (Palgrave, 2017).

PETE RITCHIE is Executive Director of Nourish Scotland and has a background in community development and social policy. As well as working at Nourish, Pete runs Whitmuir Organics with his partner Heather Anderson.

ANA ROMERO Galán is a writer and political analyst who lives in Madrid and Cádiz.

ADAM TOMKINS MSP is a Conservative MSP for Glasgow. Before his election to the Scottish Parliament he spent 25 years as a legal academic, specialising in constitutional and EU law.

MICHAEL WOHLGEMUTH is Founding Director of Open Europe Berlin.

REBECCA ZAHN is Senior Lecturer in Law at the University of Strathclyde. She researches in the field of labour law (national, European and comparative) and is the author of *New Labour Laws in Old Member States* (Cambridge University Press, 2017). She serves as the elected Secretary of the University Association for Contemporary European Studies (UACES) and is on the management board of the Scottish Universities Legal Network on Europe (sulne.ac.uk).

FABIAN ZULEEG is Chief Executive and Chief Economist of the European Policy Centre. He was appointed to the Standing Council on Europe, established by Scotland's First Minister after the Brexit vote in June 2016.

About IPPR Scotland

IPPR Scotland is Scotland's leading progressive think tank. It is cross-party, independent and dedicated to Scottish issues and is an autonomous part of IPPR. In its first two years of existence IPPR Scotland has led the public policy debate on a range of issues in Scotland, securing influence and profile, and it stands ready to support decision makers with new ideas and public policy solutions relevant to the opportunities and challenges facing Scotland.

IPPR Scotland was formed in 2015 and, since its creation, has produced a number of high profile reports on Scotland's new tax and benefit powers, Scotland's economy, the skills system, and school education and the attainment gap. It has also undertaken a fiscal analysis of UK and Scotland government budgets. Its report *New Powers, New Scotland?*, on the potential use of tax and benefit powers in the Scottish parliament, was crucial in setting the agenda during the 2016 Scottish parliamentary election.

In relation to Scotland and Europe, and the fallout from the June 2017 EU referendum, IPPR Scotland was quick to respond, successfully organising and hosting a series of respected events in the days and months following the result, which included Nicola Sturgeon MSP, Scotland's First Minister, Gordon Brown, former UK Prime Minister, David Mundell MP, Secretary of State for Scotland, and Kezia Dugdale MSP, leader of Scottish Labour.

Across the UK, IPPR has an impressive track record of over 30 years of influential public policy work, with expertise across public policy. As well as IPPR Scotland, IPPR established IPPR North ten years ago, based in Manchester and Newcastle. This makes IPPR the only UK-wide think tank, with a footprint and expertise in policy fields across the UK and with an understanding of the increasing differentiation across the nations and regions which make up the UK. Further details of IPPR Scotland can be found at: http://www.ippr.org/scotland

Luath Press Limited

committed to publishing well written books worth reading

LUATH PRESS takes its name from Robert Burns, whose little collie Luath (*Gael.*, swift or nimble) tripped up Jean Armour at a wedding and gave him the chance to speak to the woman who was to be his wife and the abiding love of his life. Burns called one of the 'Twa Dogs' Luath after Cuchullin's hunting dog in Ossian's *Fingal*. Luath Press was established in 1981 in the heart of Burns country, and is now based a few steps up the road from Burns' first lodgings on Edinburgh's Royal Mile. Luath offers you distinctive writing with a hint of unexpected pleasures.

Most bookshops in the UK, the US, Canada, Australia, New Zealand and parts of Europe, either carry our books in stock or can order them for you. To order direct from us, please send a £sterling cheque, postal order, international money order or your credit card details (number, address of cardholder and expiry date) to us at the address below. Please add post and packing as follows: UK – £1.00 per delivery address; overseas surface mail – £2.50 per delivery address; overseas airmail – £3.50 for the first book to each delivery address, plus £1.00 for each additional book by airmail to the same address. If your order is a gift, we will happily enclose your card or message at no extra charge.

Luath Press Limited
543/2 Castlehill
The Royal Mile
Edinburgh EH1 2ND
Scotland
Telephone: +44 (0)131 225 4326 (24 hours)
email: sales@luath. co.uk
Website: www. luath.co.uk